AQA GCSE (9–1)
Physics
for Combined Science: Trilogy
Student Book

Sandra Mitchell
Charles Golabek
Series editor: Ed Walsh

William Collins' dream of knowledge for all began with the publication of his first book in 1819.

A self-educated mill worker, he not only enriched millions of lives, but also founded a flourishing publishing house. Today, staying true to this spirit, Collins books are packed with inspiration, innovation and practical expertise. They place you at the centre of a world of possibility and give you exactly what you need to explore it.

Collins. Freedom to teach

HarperCollins Publishers
1 London Bridge Street
London SE1 9GF

Browse the complete Collins catalogue at
www.collins.co.uk

First edition 2016

10 9 8

© HarperCollins*Publishers* 2016

ISBN 978-0-00-817506-1

www.collins.co.uk

A catalogue record for this book is available from the British Library

Commissioned by Lucy Rowland and Lizzie Catford
Edited by Hamish Baxter
Project managed by Elektra Media Ltd
Copy edited by Jim Newall
Development edited by Aidan Gill
Proofread by Jan Schubert, Jo Kemp and Laurice Suess
Typeset by Jouve India and Ken Vail Graphic Design
With thanks to contributing author Crispin Myerscough
Cover design by We are Laura
Printed by CPI Group (UK) Ltd, Croydon, CR0 4YY
Cover images © Shutterstock/Jurik Peter, Emilio Segre Visual Archives/American Institute Of Physics/Science Photo Library

MIX
Paper from responsible sources

FSC™ C007454

FSC™ is a non-profit international organisation established to promote the responsible management of the world's forests. Products carrying the FSC label are independently certified to assure consumers that they come from forests that are managed to meet the social, economic and ecological needs of present and future generations, and other controlled sources.

Find out more about HarperCollins and the environment at
www.harpercollins.co.uk/green

Approval message from AQA

This textbook has been approved by AQA for use with our qualification. This means that we have checked that it broadly covers the specification and we are satisfied with the overall quality. Full details of our approval process can be found on our website.

We approve textbooks because we know how important it is for teachers and students to have the right resources to support their teaching and learning. However, the publisher is ultimately responsible for the editorial control and quality of this book.

Please note that when teaching the GCSE Combined Physics course, you must refer to AQA's specification as your definitive source of information. While this book has been written to match the specification, it cannot provide complete coverage of every aspect of the course.

A wide range of other useful resources can be found on the relevant subject pages of our website: aqa.org.uk

ACKNOWLEDGEMENTS

Every effort has been made to trace copyright holders and to obtain their permission for the use of copyright material. The publishers will gladly receive any information enabling them to rectify any error or omission at the first opportunity.

Chapter 1

p12 Alex Staroseltsev/Shutterstock, Christos Siatos/Shutterstock, Kzenon/ Shutterstock, Neil Mitchell/Shutterstock; p13 You can more/Shutterstock, Ivan Smuk/Shutterstock, Filip Fuxa/Shutterstock; p14 bunnyphoto/Shutterstock, oknoart/Shutterstock, john michael evan potter/Shutterstock; p16 Digital Storm/Shutterstock; p17 WICHAI WONGJONGJAIHAN/Shutterstock; p18 Maria Masich/Shutterstock, bikeriderlondon/Shutterstock; p19 Chris Jenner/Shutterstock; p21 Izf/Shutterstock, Vlacheslav Lopatin/Shutterstock; p23 sasipixel/Shutterstock; p26 rdonar/Shutterstock, alterfather/Shutterstock; p27 Image Point Fr/Shutterstock; p28 Valeriy Lebedev/Shutterstock; p30 gravitylight.org; p31 zhu difeng/Shutterstock; p33 Michael Wick/Shutterstock; p34 Steve Collender/Shutterstock; p35 Parinyabinsuk/Shutterstock, Harri Aho/Shutterstock; p43 Ivan Smuk/Shutterstock

Chapter 2

p44 asadykov/Shutterstock, Gearstd/Shutterstock, StudioFI/Shutterstock; p45 Timothy Hodgkinson/Shutterstock, a_v_d/Shutterstock; p53 Chones/Shutterstock; p58 ANDREW LAMBERT PHOTOGRAPHY/SCIENCE PHOTO LIBRARY; p62 Lukasz Pajor/Shutterstock; p63 michaeljung/Shutterstock, Markus Gebauer/Shutterstock; p64 cristi180884/Shutterstock, _LeS_/Shutterstock; p66 Lilyana Vynogradova/Shutterstock; p67 imagedb.com/Shutterstock, You can more/Shutterstock; p68 Kotkot32/Shutterstock; p69 CPM PHOTO/Shutterstock, SvedOliver/Shutterstock, Monkey Business Images/Shutterstock

Chapter 3

p76 Freer/Shutterstock, Zmaj88/Shutterstock, Bplanet/Shutterstock; p77 Kekyalyaynen/Shutterstock, Petr Malyshev/Shutterstock; p79 SpaceKris/Shutterstock; p80 bilha Golan/Shutterstock; p81 Hurst Photo/Shutterstock; p82 Waraphorn Aphai/Shutterstock; p83 practicalaction.org; p87 Kekyalyaynen/Shutterstock; p89 Tyler Olson/Shutterstock;
p90 Everett Historical/Shutterstock

Chapter 5

p122 Digital Storm/Shutterstock, Marius Pirvu/Shutterstock; p123 popvartem.com/Shutterstock, thieury/Shutterstock, Danshutter/Shutterstock; p128 Fedor Selivanov/Shutterstock; p129 Mariusz Szczygiel/Shutterstock; p141 Oleksandr Kalinichenko/Shutterstock; p142 VOLKER STEGER/SCIENCE PHOTO LIBRARY; p144 mandritoiu/Shutterstock; p154 Georgios Kollidas/Shutterstock, ChameleonsEye/Shutterstock, Vorm in Beeld/Shutterstock; p155 Graeme Dawes/Shutterstock

Chapter 6

p162 SirinS/Shutterstock, Tom Tom/Shutterstock, CristinaMuraca/Shutterstock; p163 isarescheewin/Shutterstock; p164 Paul J Martin/Shutterstock; p168 Joshua Rainey Photography/Shutterstock; p169 asharkyu/Shutterstock, Ryan Jorgensen – Jorgo/Shutterstock; p175 Tumarkin Igor – ITPS/Shutterstock; p176 Serg64/Shutterstock; p180 Denise Lett/Shutterstock, Suttha Burawonk/Shutterstock; p181 ZEPHYR/SCIENCE PHOTO LIBRARY; p182 Anna Kaminska/Shutterstock; p183 JIANG HONGYAN/Shutterstock, Ivan Smuk/Shutterstock

Chapter 7

p196 shooarts/Shutterstock; p197 zhengzaishuru/Shutterstock; p198 ChameleonsEye/Shutterstock; p199 revers/Shutterstock; p206 Chatchai-Rombix/Shutterstock; p209 goldenjack/Shutterstock

Contents

How to use this book

Remember! To cover all the content of the AQA Physics Specification you should study the text and attempt the End of chapter questions.

These tell you what you will be learning about in the lesson and are linked to the AQA specification.

This introduces the topic and puts the science into an interesting context.

Each topic is divided into three sections. The level of challenge gets harder with each section.

Each section has level-appropriate questions, so you can check and apply your knowledge.

Physics

Radioactive half-life

KEY WORDS

half-life

Learning objectives:

- explain what is meant by radioactive half-life
- calculate half-life
- calculate the decline in activity after a number of half-lives.

Radioisotopes are often used to monitor a biological process in the body or in the environment. We need to know the half-lives of different radioisotopes so that we can minimise contamination or irradiation.

Half-life

We cannot predict when the nucleus of one particular atom will decay. It could be next week or not for a million years. Radioactive decay is a random process. If there is a very large number of atoms, some of them will decay each second. We plot a graph of activity against time and draw a curve of best fit. We can then use this curve to find when the activity has halved (Figure 4.11). The **half-life** of a radioisotope is the average time it takes for half the nuclei present to decay, or the time it takes for the activity to fall to half its initial level. We use half-life because we cannot predict the time it will take for all the atoms to decay.

The activity of a radioactive substance gets less and less as time goes on. The graph line in Figure 4.11 gets closer and closer to the time axis but never reaches it because the activity halves each half-life.

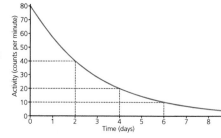

Figure 4.11 The time it takes for the activity to halve is constant

1. Explain why you can't predict when a particular atom will decay.

2. Explain what is meant by 'half-life'.

3. What will the activity in Figure 4.11 be after:
   a 2 days? **b** 4 days? **c** 6 days? **d** 8 days?

Calculating half-life

To calculate the half-life of a radioisotope, plot a graph of count rate detected (which is proportional to the total activity) against time, as shown in Figure 4.12. The background count should be subtracted from each reading before the graph is plotted. Plot the points and then draw a smooth curve of best fit through the points. Then find several values for the half-life from the graph by finding the time for the activity in counts per minute to fall from 80 to 40, 40 to 20, 20 to 10 and so on. You should calculate the average of the values you have found. The time for the activity to halve may not be exactly the same each time. Any differences will be due to the random nature of radioactive decay.

KEY INFORMATION

When you draw a curve of best fit on a graph of activity against time for a radioisotope, not all of the points will be on the curve. Some will be above the curve and some will be below the curve because of the random nature of radioactive decay.

110　AQA GCSE Physics for Combined Science: Trilogy: Student Book

4.5

④ Calculate the half-life of the radioisotope shown in Figure 4.12.

Figure 4.12

⑤ The table shows the activity of a radioactive sample over time.

a Draw a graph of activity against time.

b Draw a best-fit curve through the points.

c Calculate the half-life by looking at time for the activity to halve at three different points on your curve. Calculate the average.

⑥ The activity of a radioactive sample took 4 hours to decrease from 100 Bq to 25 Bq. Calculate its half-life.

Time in minutes	Activity in Bq
0	100
0.5	76
1.0	51
1.5	40
2.0	26
2.5	18
3.0	12
3.5	10
4.0	8

HIGHER TIER ONLY

Calculating decline in activity

For some applications such as a smoke alarm, a radioisotope with a long half-life is most suitable so that the rate of decay does not decrease significantly. Some radioisotopes are used as tracers, using the radiation they emit to trace the path of a substance the radioisope is attached to.

Radioisotopes can be used as environmental tracers (such as detecting a leak in a pipe) or medical tracers. For these applications, a short half-life is best. This means that the activity will decrease to a level similar to the background count fairly quickly because the time taken for half the radioactive nuclei to decay is very short.

⑦ Technetium-99m is widely used in medicine. It has a half-life of 6 hours. How much of it remains after 1 day?

⑧ What fraction of the original sample remains after 80 minutes in Figure 4.12?

⑨ Caesium-134 has a half-life of 2 years. If its activity was monitored for 6 years, what fraction of the original activity level would it have dropped to after 6 years?

DID YOU KNOW?

The half-lives of different radioactive isotopes vary from a fraction of a second to millions of years.

Google search: 'half-life' 111

The first page of a chapter has links to ideas you have met before, which you can now build on.

This page gives a summary of the exciting new ideas you will be learning about in the chapter.

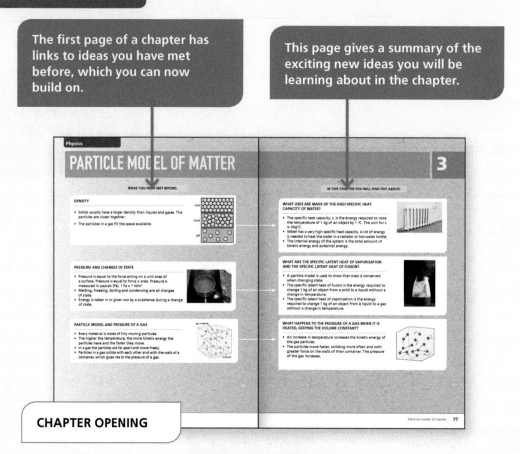

CHAPTER OPENING

The Key Concept pages focus on core ideas. Once you have understood the key concept in a chapter, it should develop your understanding of the whole topic.

KEY CONCEPT

There is a dedicated page for every Required Practical in the AQA specification. They help you to analyse the practical and to answer questions about it.

The tasks – which get a bit more difficult as you go through – challenge you to apply your science skills and knowledge to the new context.

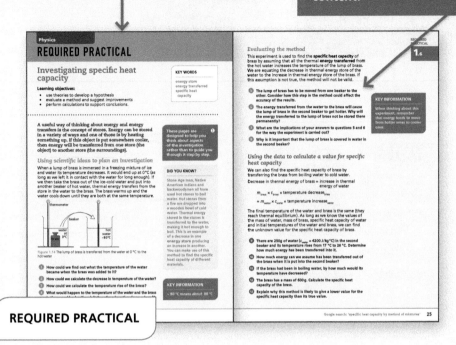

REQUIRED PRACTICAL

The Maths Skills pages focus on the maths requirements in the AQA specification, explaining concepts and providing opportunities to practise.

MATHS SKILLS

These lists at the end of a chapter act as a checklist of the key ideas of the chapter. In each row, the green box gives the ideas or skills that you should master first. Then you can aim to master the ideas and skills in the blue box. Once you have achieved those you can move on to those in the red box.

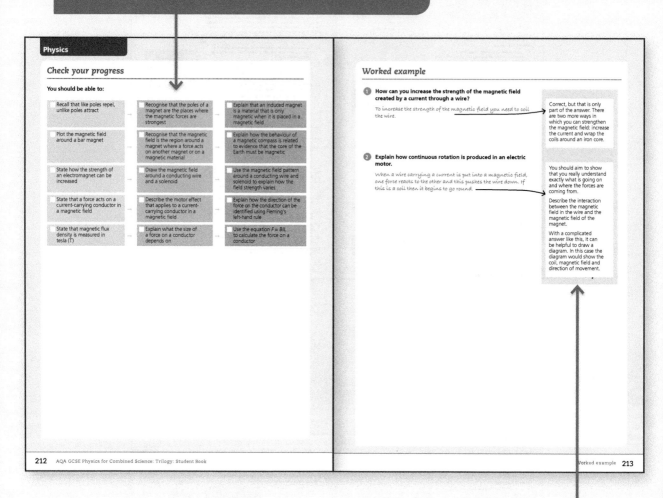

Use the comments to help you understand how to answer questions. Read each question and answer. Try to decide if, and how, the answer can be improved. Finally, read the comments and try to answer the questions yourself.

END OF CHAPTER

The End of chapter questions allow you and your teacher to check that you have understood the ideas in the chapter, can apply these to new situations, and can explain new science using the skills and knowledge you have gained. The questions start off easier and get harder. If you are taking Foundation tier, try to answer all the questions in the Getting started and Going further sections. If you are taking Higher tier, try to answer all the questions in the Going further, More challenging and Most demanding sections.

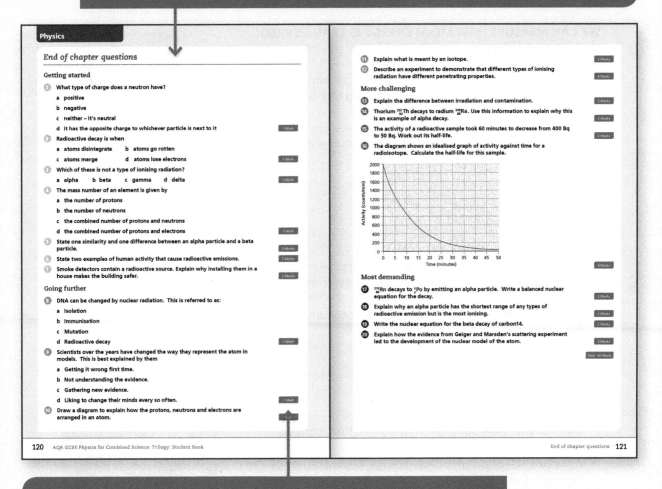

End of chapter questions

Getting started

1. What type of charge does a neutron have?
   a positive
   b negative
   c neither – it's neutral
   d it has the opposite charge to whichever particle is next to it
   1 Mark

2. Radioactive decay is when
   a atoms disintegrate   b atoms go rotten
   c atoms merge   d atoms lose electrons
   1 Mark

3. Which of these is not a type of ionising radiation?
   a alpha   b beta   c gamma   d delta
   1 Mark

4. The mass number of an element is given by
   a the number of protons
   b the number of neutrons
   c the combined number of protons and neutrons
   d the combined number of protons and electrons
   1 Mark

5. State one similarity and one difference between an alpha particle and a beta particle.
   2 Marks

6. State two examples of human activity that cause radioactive emissions.
   2 Marks

7. Smoke detectors contain a radioactive source. Explain why installing them in a house makes the building safer.
   2 Marks

Going further

8. DNA can be changed by nuclear radiation. This is referred to as:
   a Isolation
   b Immunisation
   c Mutation
   d Radioactive decay
   1 Mark

9. Scientists over the years have changed the way they represent the atom in models. This is best explained by them
   a Getting it wrong first time.
   b Not understanding the evidence.
   c Gathering new evidence.
   d Liking to change their minds every so often.
   1 Mark

10. Draw a diagram to explain how the protons, neutrons and electrons are arranged in an atom.
    4 Marks

11. Explain what is meant by an isotope.
    2 Marks

12. Describe an experiment to demonstrate that different types of ionising radiation have different penetrating properties.
    4 Marks

More challenging

13. Explain the difference between irradiation and contamination.
    2 Marks

14. Thorium $^{232}_{90}$Th decays to radium $^{228}_{88}$Ra. Use this information to explain why this is an example of alpha decay.
    2 Marks

15. The activity of a radioactive sample took 60 minutes to decrease from 400 Bq to 50 Bq. Work out its half-life.
    2 Marks

16. The diagram shows an idealised graph of activity against time for a radioisotope. Calculate the half-life for this sample.

    4 Marks

Most demanding

17. $^{219}_{86}$Rn decays to $^4_2$Po by emitting an alpha particle. Write a balanced nuclear equation for the decay.
    2 Marks

18. Explain why an alpha particle has the shortest range of any types of radioactive emission but is the most ionising.
    2 Marks

19. Write the nuclear equation for the beta decay of carbon14.
    2 Marks

20. Explain how the evidence from Geiger and Marsden's scattering experiment led to the development of the nuclear model of the atom.
    4 Marks

    Total: 40 Marks

There are questions for each assessment object (AO) from the final exams. This will help you develop the thinking skills you need to answer each type of question:

AO1 – to answer these questions you should aim to **demonstrate** your knowledge and understanding of scientific ideas, techniques and procedures.

AO2 – to answer these questions you should aim to **apply** your knowledge and understanding of scientific ideas and scientific enquiry, techniques and procedures.

AO3 – to answer these questions you should aim to **analyse** information and ideas to: interpret and evaluate, make judgements and draw conclusions and develop and improve experimental procedures.

ENERGY

IDEAS YOU HAVE MET BEFORE:

WE CAN MEASURE HOW MUCH ENERGY IS TRANSFERRED AND HOW QUICKLY

- Energy can be stored and also transferred from one store to another. Energy changes are measured in joules (J) or kilojoules (kJ).
- The energy values of different foods can be compared.
- The power ratings of appliances are measured in watts (W) or kilowatts (kW).

TEMPERATURE AND ENERGY

- Temperature tells us how hot something is.
- When there is a difference in temperature between two objects, energy is transferred from the hotter object to the colder one.
- Energy transfer tends to reduce the temperature difference.

TRANSFER OF THERMAL ENERGY

- Thermal energy is transferred by conduction, convection and radiation.
- In conduction and convection, energy is transferred by the movement of particles.
- Radiation is the only way energy can be transferred in a vacuum.

FOSSIL FUELS AND ALTERNATIVE ENERGY RESOURCES

- Fossil fuels are burnt to release the energy stored in them.
- Fossil fuels were formed over millions of years and supplies are running out.
- There are alternative energy resources which have advantages and disadvantages.

IN THIS CHAPTER YOU WILL FIND OUT ABOUT:

WHAT IS THE CONNECTION BETWEEN ENERGY TRANSFER AND POWER?

- Energy is transferred by heating, by an electric current in a circuit, and when work is done by a force.
- We can measure the rate at which energy is being transferred or the rate at which work is done – this is called power.

WHAT IS THE CONNECTION BETWEEN ENERGY CHANGES AND TEMPERATURE CHANGE?

- We can calculate the energy stored in or released from a system when its temperature changes.
- The rate of cooling of a building is affected by the thickness and the thermal conductivity of its walls. Insulation can be used to reduce the transfer of energy by conduction and convection.

HOW CAN WE MONITOR AND CONTROL THE TRANSFER OF ENERGY?

- Energy can be transferred usefully, stored or dissipated. The total amount of energy does not change. We can calculate the energy efficiency for any energy transfer. Some energy transfers are wasteful; we can try to reduce them.

WHAT IS THE ENVIRONMENTAL IMPACT OF DIFFERENT ENERGY RESOURCES?

- Fuels such as coal, oil, gas and nuclear fuel are not renewable. Supplies will run out.
- The use of fossil fuels is changing as more renewable energy resources are used for transport, electricity generation and heating.
- Most renewable resources do not generate a predictable (reliable) amount of electrical power.
- There are different environmental issues for each different energy resource.

Potential energy

Learning objectives:

- consider what happens when a spring is stretched
- describe what is meant by gravitational potential energy
- calculate the energy stored by an object raised above ground level.

KEY WORDS

elastic potential
  energy
gravitational
  field strength
gravitational
  potential energy

On Jupiter, gravity is three times stronger than on Earth. If the same mass was lifted to the same height on Earth and Jupiter, on Jupiter it would store three times the gravitational potential energy.

Stored energy

When a spring is stretched it stores energy. We call this **potential energy**. The stretched spring stores **elastic potential energy**. It stretches more if a greater force is applied, and returns to its original length when the force is removed.

Compressed springs are also used to store elastic potential energy; for example, in a wind-up clockwork toy.

Figure 1.1 A stretched catapult stores elastic potential energy

1. **Imagine slowly stretching a rubber band. Describe what you would feel as you stretch it more.**

2. **Suggest what happens to the amount of energy stored in the spring inside a the toy in Figure 1.2 as the key is turned.**

Water stored behind a dam also stores potential energy. It is called **gravitational potential energy (GPE)**. The gravitational potential energy stored by an object can be increased by moving it upwards. For example, you gain gravitational potential energy by going up stairs.

Figure 1.2 Turning the key twists a spring inside the toy. This stores elastic potential energy which can be transferred to kinetic energy.

3. **An aircraft is flying horizontally at a height of 10 000 m. Explain whether its gravitational potential energy is increasing, decreasing or remaining constant.**

Calculating changes in gravitational potential energy

Tom lifts a box. The amount of gravitational potential energy gained by the box depends on:

- the mass of the box, m, in kilograms, kg
- the height Tom raises the box, h, in metres, m.

We can calculate the amount of gravitational potential energy gained (E_p) using the equation:

$E_p = mgh$

Figure 1.3 The stored gravitational potential energy of water held behind a dam can be transferred to kinetic energy if the water is released

where m is measured in kg, g is the **gravitational field strength** in N/kg and h is measured in m.

The pull of gravity on the box (its weight) is calculated from the equation:

weight = mass × gravitational field strength, W = m × g

The gravitational field strength is the pull of gravity on each kilogram. The value of g is 9.8 N/kg at the Earth's surface. Changes in E_p are measured in joules (J).

Zack gains gravitational potential energy when he walks up some stairs (Figure 1.4). The E_p Zack gains can be calculated using $E_p = mgh$ where h is the vertical height he raises his body.

Zack then walks on a level floor. He does not gain or lose any gravitational potential energy now because his height above the floor does not change.

4. **Lars is a weightlifter. He lifts a mass of 300 kg through a height of 2 m. Calculate the gravitational potential energy gained by the mass.**

5. **Sian picks up a ball from the floor and holds it 2 m above the ground. The ball has a mass of 60 g. Calculate the gravitational potential energy gained by the ball.**

Calculating elastic potential energy

The amount of elastic potential energy stored in a spring can be increased by:

- increasing the extension of the spring, e, in metres, m
- increasing the spring constant, k, in newtons per metre, N/m.

We can calculate the elastic potential energy, E_e, stored in a spring using the equation:

$$E_e = \frac{1}{2} ke^2$$

Example: Calculate the energy stored in a spring when it is extended by 6 cm. The spring constant is 150 N/m.

Answer:

6 cm = 0.06 m

$E_e = 0.5 \times 150 \text{ N/m} \times (0.06 \text{ m})^2$

$\quad = 0.27 \text{ J}$

6. **Calculate the energy stored in a spring which has a spring constant of 300 N/m and is extended by 0.1 m.**

7. **A spring has a spring constant of 500 N/m. The original length of the spring is 20 cm. It is stretched to a length of 25 cm. Calculate the energy stored in the spring.**

8. **A spring stores 12 J when it is stretched by 16 cm. Calculate the spring constant.**

9. **A stretched spring has a total length of 20 cm and a spring constant of 200 N/m. It is storing 0.25 J in its elastic potential energy store. Determine the unstretched length of the spring.**

Figure 1.4 Vertical height, h

DID YOU KNOW?

A new pumped storage hydropower project in Chile will use solar power to pump water from the Pacific Ocean 600 metres above sea level to the top of a cliff. The total reservoir capacity of about 55 million cubic metres gives a maximum total energy stored of about 3.3×10^{14} J. However, the amount of water that can be pumped by solar power is only 4.5 million cubic metres per day.

Figure 1.5 Extension of a spring

MATHS

Always put values into an equation using SI units (time in seconds, distance in metres etc). If the values in the question are not in SI units, you have to change the values to SI units before starting the calculation.

REMEMBER!

Use the **vertical** height when finding the change in an object's height.

Investigating kinetic energy

KEY WORDS

energy store
gravitational
 potential energy
kinetic energy

Learning objectives:

- describe how the kinetic energy store of an object changes as its speed changes
- calculate kinetic energy
- consider how energy is transferred.

Formula One racing cars reach speeds of 300 km/h or more. This means the kinetic energy store is very large. If the car is involved in a collision, this energy store may be reduced to zero very rapidly, causing lots of damage.

Kinetic energy

Energy must be transferred to make things move. A car uses energy from petrol or diesel to move. The greater its mass and the faster it goes, the more energy is transferred to the car's **kinetic energy** store and the higher the rate at which fuel is used.

1. Why does an adult have more kinetic energy than a child when running at the same speed?

2. What is the 'fuel' for a child running around a playground?

Figure 1.6 The engine applies a force that transfers energy from a store in the fuel to a store of kinetic energy

Calculating kinetic energy

The kinetic energy store of a moving object can be increased by:

- increasing the mass of the object, *m* in kg
- increasing its speed, *v* in m/s.

We can calculate the kinetic energy (E_k) of an object by using this equation:

$$E_k = \frac{1}{2} mv^2$$

Example: A car of mass 1600 kg is travelling at a steady speed of 10 m/s.

a Calculate the car's kinetic energy.

b The car's speed increases to 20 m/s. Calculate how much its kinetic energy store increases.

a E_k at 10 m/s $= \frac{1}{2} mv^2 = \frac{1}{2} \times 1600$ kg $\times 10$ (m/s)²

$= \frac{1}{2} \times 1600 \times 100 = 80\,000$ J

b E_k at 20 m/s $= \frac{1}{2} mv^2 = \frac{1}{2} \times 1600$ kg $\times 20$ (m/s)²

$= \frac{1}{2} \times 1600 \times 400 = 320\,000$ J

The increase in the car's E_k = 320 000 − 80 000 = 240 000 J.

Doubling the speed has increased the car's E_k by a factor of 4. Note that speed is squared in the equation for E_k.

DID YOU KNOW?

Hollywood star Idris Elba smashed an 88-year-old record by driving at an average speed of 180.361 mph over a measured mile across the Pendine Sands in Wales in May 2015. The award-winning star beat the 1927 record set by Sir Malcolm Campbell.

3   **a**   **Meena is riding her bicycle at 2 m/s. She has a mass of 50 kg. Calculate her kinetic energy.**

      b   **Meena doubles her speed. What happens to her kinetic energy?**

We can convert from km/h to m/s by:

- multiplying by 1000 (there are 1000 m in a km)
- dividing by 3600 (there are 3600 seconds in an hour).

For example, 300 km/h = $\dfrac{(300 \times 1000 \text{ m})}{3600 \text{ s}}$ = 83.3 m/s

4   **A car of mass 1200 kg increases its speed from 10 m/s to 30 m/s. By how much has its E_k increased?**

5   **Change a speed of 240 km/h to m/s.**

> **REMEMBER!**
>
> Take care when calculating kinetic energy using $\frac{1}{2}mv^2$. Only the speed is squared. Start by squaring the speed.

Dropping a ball

If a ball is held 2 m above the ground, it has **gravitational potential energy** relative to a ball on the ground. Allowing it to fall transfers energy from a gravitational potential **energy store** to a kinetic energy store as it drops. The ball hits the ground and bounces. As it moves upwards, the kinetic energy store decreases as energy is transferred back to the gravitational potential energy store. The ball does not return to its original height though, because some of the energy is transferred to the surroundings by heating.

> **KEY INFORMATION**
>
> Energy is transferred from one **energy store** to another. Before the ball is dropped it has a store of gravitational potential energy. As the ball falls, energy is transferred to a store of kinetic energy.

Figure 1.7 Time-lapse photo showing the path of a ball

6   **At what point does the ball in the photo:**

    a   have most gravitational potential energy?

    b   have most kinetic energy?

7   **Describe the changes to energy stores that take place when a ball is thrown upwards.**

8   **A ball with a mass of 2 kg is dropped from a height of 20 m. Assuming all of the GPE transfers to E_k, calculate the speed of the ball as it hits the ground (g = 9.8 N/kg).**

Work done and energy transfer

Learning objectives:

- understand what is meant by work done
- explain the relationship between work done and force applied
- identify the transfers between energy stores when work is done against friction.

People on a roller coaster experience rapid energy changes and G-forces similar to those experienced by astronauts.

Work done by a force

In science, **work** is only done by a **force** when an object moves.

More work is done when:

- the force is bigger
- the object moves further – its displacement is bigger.

Sam's car has broken down. He tries to push it but the car does not move. He is not doing any work though. Work is only done when a force *moves*. Sam gets some friends to help. Together, they can push with a larger force and the car moves. They are all doing work.

1. What affects the amount of work done by a force?

2. What force moves when someone jumps off a wall?

REMEMBER!

Work is only done when a force causes a displacement of the object (that is, movement along the line of action of the force).

Figure 1.8 These men are doing work because the car is moving

Calculating work done

The equation that links work, force and distance is:

work done = force × distance moved along the line of action of the force

$W = F\,s$

where work done (W) is in joules, force (F) is in newtons and distance (s) is in metres.

When a person climbs stairs or jumps in the air the force moved is their weight.

Example: Dev climbs a flight of stairs rising a vertical height of 5 m. He weighs 600 N. Calculate the work Dev does by lifting his weight up the stairs.

Work done = force × distance moved along the line of action of the force

Work done = 600 N × 5 m = 3000 J

3. A gymnast (Figure 1.9) weighs 400 N. How much work does she do when she jumps from the ground onto a beam 1.5 m above the ground?

ADVICE

1 joule of work is done when a force of 1 newton causes a displacement of one metre.

Figure 1.9 The gymnast does work when she jumps up onto the beam from the floor

4 Mia is holding a 20 N weight without moving. How much work is she doing?

5 Amrita does 300 J of work in lifting a box with a force of 200 N. How high does she lift it?

Energy calculations

When work is done on an object there can also be a change in its **kinetic energy**. We can use this to calculate the force needed to stop a car when the distance it travels while coming to rest is known.

Example: A car of mass 1000 kg does an emergency stop when travelling at 15 m/s. It stops in a distance of 20 m. Calculate the braking force.

$$E_k \text{ of car} = \frac{1}{2}mv^2$$

$$= \frac{1}{2} \times 1000 \text{ kg} \times (15 \text{ m/s})^2$$

$$= 112\,500 \text{ J}.$$

Work has to be done to reduce the kinetic energy of the car and bring it to a stop. The force that does the work is the friction force between the brakes and the wheel. The work done by the braking force is 112 500 J.

$W = F\,s$, where F is the braking force and s is the distance moved during braking. We can rearrange this to make F the subject of the equation.

$$F = W/s$$

$$= \frac{112\,500 \text{ J}}{20 \text{ m}}$$

$$= 5625 \text{ N}.$$

Work done against the frictional forces acting on an object causes a rise in the temperature of the object. The temperature of the brakes increases.

6 Tom does 3000 J of work against friction in pushing a small van a distance of 12 m. How big is the friction force he has to push against?

7 A car of mass 800 kg is travelling at 12 m/s.

  a Calculate its kinetic energy.

  b The brakes are applied. What force from the brakes is needed if the car stops after travelling 8 m?

8 A pole vaulter has a weight of 500 N.

  a She vaults to a height of 4 m. How much work does she do?

  b How much kinetic energy does she have just before she lands?

  c When she lands, her trainers compress by 1 cm. Calculate the average force acting on her trainers as she is landing.

DID YOU KNOW?

A water-powered inclined railway has no engine. The top car has a full water tank which makes it slightly heavier than the car at the bottom. The two cars are attached by a cable going over a pulley. The extra weight of the top car does work to lift the lower car up the slope. Work is also done to overcome the force of friction.

Figure 1.10 Inclined railway

MAKING LINKS

You will need to link the information given here to the forces topic 5.13, where you will look at the factors that affect stopping distance.

Understanding power

KEY WORDS

energy transfer
power

Learning objectives:

- define power
- compare the rate of energy transfer by various machines and electrical appliances
- calculate power.

A human being can be considered an energy transfer device. Our energy comes from our food, about 10 MJ (10 million joules) every day.

Power

Imagine a tall office block with two lifts of the same mass. One lift takes 40 s to go up to the tenth floor; the other, newer lift, takes 25 s. Both lifts do the same amount of work but the newer one does it more quickly. The transfer of energy is more rapid; the new lift has more **power.**

Power is the rate of doing work or transferring energy. A machine that is more powerful than another machine transfers more energy each second.

Power is measured in watts (W). If one joule of energy is transferred in one second, this is one watt of power: 1 W = 1 J/s.

The table shows the typical power of various electrical appliances.

	Power / W
Kettle	2500
Microwave oven	1100
Iron	1000
Hairdryer	2000
Vacuum cleaner	1600
Television	114
Food blender	150

1 Which appliance is the most powerful?

2 Explain why a television might do more work than a food blender.

Calculating power

$$\text{Power} = \frac{\text{work done in J}}{\text{time in s}} \text{ or } \frac{\text{energy transferred in J}}{\text{time in s}}$$

These formulae can be written as:

$$P = \frac{W}{t} \text{ and}$$

$$P = \frac{E}{t}$$

Example: A machine does 1000 J of work in 8 seconds. What power does it develop?

$$\text{Power} = \frac{\text{work done}}{\text{time}} = \frac{1000\,\text{J}}{8\,\text{s}} = 125\text{ W}$$

ADVICE

Energy is measured in joules (J) and power in watts (W). An energy transfer of 1 joule per second is equal to a power of 1 watt.

3 A toaster transferred 108 000 J of energy in 2 minutes. What is the power of the toaster?

4 An electric kettle is rated at 2 kW (2000 W). How much energy is transferred in 30 s?

5 A crane lifts a load weighing 4000 N through a height of 6 m in 20 s.

  a How much work does the crane do to lift the load, assuming there is no friction?

  b What is the power of the crane?

Personal power

Mel decides to work out her leg power. She runs up 16 stairs, each 20 cm high, in 10 s (Figure 1.11). Mel's mass is 50 kg.

Work done = force × distance moved in the direction of the force.

The force moved is Mel's weight. Assume g = 9.8 N/kg.

Weight = 50 × 9.8 = 490 N.

The **vertical** height of the stairs (in m) = 16 × 0.2 = 3.2 m.

Work done = 490 N × 3.2 m = 1568 J.

$$\text{Power} = \frac{\text{work done}}{\text{time taken}} = \frac{1568\,\text{J}}{10\,\text{s}} = 156.8\text{ W}$$

Figure 1.11 How can Mel measure the vertical height?

6 Al weighs 800 N. He climbs 5 m vertically in 10 s when he runs up the stairs of an office block.

  a How much work does he do?

  b Calculate his power.

7 The Eiffel Tower in Paris (Figure 1.12) is 300 m high. Louis took 15 minutes to climb its 1792 steps. He has a mass of 60 kg. What was his average power output during the climb?

8 Emma decides to measure her personal leg power doing step-ups. The step is 10 cm high. Emma does 20 step-ups in 30 s. Her mass is 60 kg. Calculate her leg power.

9 A car is moving at 108 km/h and the engine provides a constant force of 1000 N. Calculate:

  a the distance the car moves in 1 second

  b the power of the engine.

Figure 1.12 The Eiffel Tower

Specific heat capacity

Learning objectives:

- understand how things heat up
- find out about heating water
- find out about specific heat capacity.

KEY WORDS

specific heat capacity

If you eat a jam sponge pudding soon after taking it out of the oven, the jam seems to be hotter than the sponge, even though they have been cooked at the same temperature. This is because at the same temperature, the jam stores more thermal energy than the pudding around it.

Hot and cold

It takes more energy to get some things hot than others. Different materials need different amounts of energy to raise the temperature by a given amount. Imagine a 1 kg block of copper and a 1 kg block of steel. From experiments we can show that:

- it takes 380 J of energy to raise the temperature of 1 kg of copper by 1 °C
- it takes 450 J of energy to raise the temperature of 1 kg of steel by 1 °C.

The amount of energy needed to change the temperature of an object depends on:

- its mass
- what it is made of
- the temperature change.

COMMON MISCONCEPTION

Heating and temperature are not the same thing. When something is heated, thermal energy is being transferred to it. Temperature is a measure of how hot or cold something is.

1. **The same mass of two different substances is heated. The amount of thermal energy transferred is the same in each case. Why does one material have a bigger increase in temperature?**

Hot water

It takes a lot of energy to raise the temperature of 1 kg of water by a certain amount; more than for most other substances.

Specific heat capacity is a measure of how much energy is required to raise the temperature of 1 kg of a substance by 1 °C.

You can calculate the amount of energy stored in a system when it is heated by using the equation:

| change in thermal energy | = | mass | × | specific heat capacity | × | temperature change |

$\Delta E = mc\Delta\theta$

where ΔE is in J, m is in kg, c is in J/kg°C and $\Delta\theta$ is in °C.

Example: Calculate the change in thermal energy when 2 kg of water is heated from 20 °C to 80 °C.

Substance	c in J/kg°C
Water	4200
Copper	380
Steel	450
Concrete	800

MATHS

In maths, the symbol Δ means the difference or change in a quantity. ΔE means a change in energy; $\Delta\theta$ means a change in temperature.

$\Delta E = mc\Delta\theta$

$= 2 \text{ kg} \times 4200 \text{ J/kg}°C \times (80 °C - 20 °C)$

$= 504\,000 \text{ J}$

$= 504 \text{ kJ}$

2 How much energy is needed to heat 1 kg of copper by 20 °C?

3 How much energy is given out when the temperature of 2 kg of steel falls by 30 °C?

Water has a very high specific heat capacity. This means it can absorb a large amount of thermal energy from a hot object for a given temperature change of the water. Water is used to cool many car engines. The thermal energy store in the engine decreases and the thermal energy store in the water increases. Energy is then transferred from the thermal energy store in the water to the store in the air surrounding the radiator.

Figure 1.13 Water is used to cool many car engines

Water can also release a lot of energy without a large temperature decrease. This makes it a very useful way of transferring large amounts of thermal energy around a house in a central heating system.

4 Explain why a hot-water bottle is so effective at warming a bed.

5 What is meant by specific heat capacity?

6 How much energy is needed to raise the temperature of 3 kg of steel by 15 °C?

More about specific heat capacity

Example: 0.5 kg of copper at 90 °C is added to 2 kg of water at 10 °C. Calculate the final temperature of the copper and water (θ).

Assume that the decrease in thermal energy store of the copper = increase in thermal energy store of the water.

Change in thermal energy store of copper

$= 0.5 \text{ kg} \times 380 \text{ J/kg}°C \times (90 °C - T) = 17\,100 - 190\theta$

Change in thermal energy store of water

$= 2 \text{ kg} \times 4200 \text{ J/kg}°C \times (T - 10 °C) = 8400\theta - 84\,000$

So $8400\theta - 84\,000 = 17\,100 - 190\theta$

$8590\theta = 101\,100$

$\theta = 101\,400 \div 8590 = 11.8°C$

7 A 1 kg steel block at 80 °C is added to 0.5 kg of water at 10 °C. Calculate the final temperature of the block and the water.

8 A night storage heater contains 50 kg of concrete. The concrete is heated during the night when electricity is cheaper, gradually emitting stored energy during the day. How much thermal energy is required to warm the concrete from 10 °C to 30 °C? Suggest why concrete is chosen.

REQUIRED PRACTICAL

Investigating specific heat capacity

Learning objectives:

- use theories to develop a hypothesis
- evaluate a method and suggest improvements
- perform calculations to support conclusions.

A useful way of thinking about energy and energy transfers is the concept of stores. Energy can be stored in a variety of ways and one of those is by heating something up. If this object is put somewhere cooler, then energy will be transferred from one store (the object) to another store (the surroundings).

Using scientific ideas to plan an investigation

When a lump of brass is immersed in a freezing mixture of ice and water its temperature decreases. It would end up at 0 °C (as long as we left it in contact with the water for long enough). If we then take the brass out of the ice-cold water and put into another beaker of hot water, thermal energy transfers from the store in the water to the brass. The brass warms up and the water cools down until they are both at the same temperature.

Figure 1.14 The lump of brass is transferred from the water at 0 °C to the hot water

1 How could we find out what the temperature of the water became when the brass was added to it?

2 How could we calculate the decrease in temperature of the water?

3 How could we calculate the temperature rise of the brass?

4 What would happen to the temperature of the water and the brass in the second beaker if we left them for a long time (e.g. an hour)?

These pages are designed to help you think about aspects of the investigation rather than to guide you through it step by step.

DID YOU KNOW?

Stone Age man, Native American Indians and backwoodsmen all have used hot stones to boil water. Hot stones from a fire are dropped into a wooden bowl of cold water. Thermal energy stored in the stones is transferred to the water, making it hot enough to boil. This is an example of a decrease in one **energy store** producing an increase in another. You can make use of this method to find the specific heat capacity of different materials.

KEY INFORMATION

~ 80 °C means *about* 80 °C

Evaluating the method

This experiment is used to find the **specific heat capacity** of brass by assuming that all the thermal **energy transferred** from the hot water increases the temperature of the lump of brass. We are equating the decrease in thermal **energy store** of the water to the increase in thermal energy store of the brass. If this assumption is not true, the method will not be valid.

5 The lump of brass has to be moved from one beaker to the other. Consider how this step in the method could affect the accuracy of the results.

6 The energy transferred from the water to the brass will cause the lump of brass in the second beaker to get hotter. Why will the energy transferred to the lump of brass not be stored there permanently?

7 What are the implications of your answers to questions 5 and 6 for the way the experiment is carried out?

8 Why is it important that the lump of brass is covered in water in the second beaker?

KEY INFORMATION

When thinking about this experiment, remember that energy tends to move from hotter areas to cooler ones.

Using the data to calculate a value for specific heat capacity

We can also find the specific heat capacity of brass by transferring the brass from boiling water to cold water.

Decrease in thermal energy of brass = increase in thermal energy of water

$$m_{brass} \times c_{brass} \times \text{temperature decrease}_{brass}$$

$$= m_{water} \times c_{water} \times \text{temperature increase}_{water}$$

The final temperature of the water and brass is the same (they reach thermal equilibrium). As long as we know the values of the mass of water, mass of brass, specific heat capacity of water and initial temperatures of the water and brass, we can find the unknown value for the specific heat capacity of brass.

9 There are 250g of water (c_{water} = 4200 J/kg°C) in the second beaker and its temperature rises from 17 °C to 26 °C. Determine how much energy has been transferred into it.

10 How much energy can we assume has been transferred out of the brass when it is put into the second beaker?

11 If the brass had been in boiling water, by how much would its temperature have decreased?

12 The brass has a mass of 600g. Calculate the specific heat capacity of the brass.

13 Explain why this method is likely to give a lower value for the specific heat capacity than its true value.

Dissipation of energy

Learning objectives:

- explain ways of reducing unwanted energy transfer
- describe what affects the rate of cooling of a building
- understand that energy is dissipated.

Thermograms (Figure 1.15) are infrared photographs in which colour is used to represent temperature.

Reducing energy transfer

Sometimes the transfer of thermal energy is useful, such as in cooking, but on other occasions we might want to reduce it. For example, pushing a supermarket trolley with stiff wheels needs a lot of work to be done against frictional forces. This means the wheels transfer some energy to the surroundings as thermal energy. This energy is wasted and we would want to reduce this energy transfer.

> **Lubrication** – oiling the parts of a machine, or lubricating them, reduces the friction force. Less energy is wasted as thermal energy.

We might want to reduce thermal energy being transferred so that a parcel of fish and chips stays hot for longer or so that a block of ice cream stays frozen until we get it home.

> **Thermal insulation** – surrounding a hot object with insulating material, or thermal insulation, reduces the rate at which energy is transferred away from it so the hot object cools more slowly (Figure 1.16). Clothing made of wool is a good insulator. Air is trapped between the wool fibres. Wool and air are bad conductors of thermal energy.

1 The wheels of a scooter do not move freely. Describe how unwanted energy transfers in the wheels can be reduced.

2 Explain why a wrapping of newspaper is as good at keeping fish and chips hot as it is at keeping a block of ice cream cold.

Figure 1.15 White represents the hottest area and blue the coolest

Figure 1.16 Thermal insulation in a roof

Insulating a building

A building needs to be well insulated so that less energy is needed to keep the building warm. Loft and cavity wall insulation reduce the rate of energy transfer from inside a building to the colder outside.

Look at Figure 1.15. White, red and yellow represent the hottest areas. Black, dark blue and purple represent the coldest areas.

The diagram of thermal energy losses from a house (Figure 1.18) shows that it is important to insulate the walls and roof.

Insulation reduces the amount of energy transfer by **conduction**. The lower the **thermal conductivity** of the insulating material and the thicker the layer, the more the rate of energy transfer by conduction is reduced.

Figure 1.17 The wheels of the car are red because they are hot

3 Looking at Figure 1.18, where is most thermal energy lost? Explain how you could reduce this unwanted energy transfer.

4 Explain, using examples, how an eco home that has no heating system can stay warm.

Energy dissipation

A system is an object or group of objects. The total energy in a closed system is always constant. Energy is never created or destroyed.

Work done against the frictional forces acting on a moving object cause energy to be transferred from the object. This energy transfer raises the temperature of the surroundings by such a small amount that it is of no use. This is wasted energy – energy is transferred to a store where it cannot be used. Some energy is always **dissipated** when it is transferred.

5 Explain why we are unable to reclaim thermal energy arising from energy due to friction or air resistance.

6 A car engine is designed to transfer energy from fuel into kinetic energy, making the car move. Name the other energy transfers that are likely to take place.

7 Look at the thermal image in Figure 1.17. Describe some of the features you can see. Use technical terms such as *thermal energy*, *thermal conductivity* and *dissipated* in your description.

Figure 1.18 Thermal energy loss from a house

Energy efficiency

Learning objectives:

- explain what is meant by energy efficiency
- calculate the efficiency of energy transfers
- find out about conservation of energy.

> **KEY WORDS**
>
> conservation of energy
> energy efficiency

Electric cars have an efficiency of about 85% compared with about 15% for a petrol car. This means an electric car can transfer a greater portion of energy in the form of kinetic energy from the original energy store. But batteries have to be charged – and the fossil fuel plant supplying the electric current is only about 35% efficient.

Useful energy output of a system

It is not possible for the useful energy output of a system to be greater than the total input energy. The law of **conservation of energy** also says that when a system changes, there is no change to the total energy of the system.

Even so, not all of the total energy input to a system is stored or usefully transferred. Some energy is always dissipated. This reduces the amount of energy that is usefully transferred.

For example, as an electric car accelerates, the engine transfers energy from the chemical energy store of the battery to the kinetic energy store of the car. Some of the input energy is wasted by transfer of thermal energy by heating the wheels and the surrounding air.

Figure 1.19 The least efficient light bulbs are being replaced with more energy-efficient alternatives, including compact fluorescent and LED light bulbs

1. What effect does the waste energy from a light bulb have on the surroundings?

2. Suggest why an electric vehicle is more efficient than a petrol or diesel vehicle.

Calculating energy efficiency

Efficiency is an indication of how much of the energy supplied to a device is transferred as a useful output. If all of the energy supplied was transferred usefully, the transfer would be 100% efficient.

$$\text{efficiency} = \frac{\text{useful output energy transfer}}{\text{total input energy transfer}}$$

OR

$$\text{efficiency} = \frac{\text{useful power output}}{\text{total power input}}$$

> **MATHS**
>
> To convert from a decimal to a percentage, multiply the decimal by 100.

Quite a lot of energy transfers are not very efficient; a lot of energy is transferred in a way that isn't useful.

Example: Tina is an athlete. She applies a force of 75 N for a distance of 100 m using 44 000 J of chemical energy stored in food. What is her efficiency? Give your answer as a percentage.

Useful work done = force × distance = 75 N × 100 m = 7500 J

$$\text{Efficiency} = \frac{\text{useful energy output}}{\text{total energy input}}$$

$$= \frac{7500 \, \text{J} \times 100}{44 \, 000 \, \text{J}} = 17\%$$

When you exercise, you get hot – your body temperature increases. Most of the chemical energy stored in food is transferred to thermal energy of your body.

3 **For every 100 J of energy supplied to a motor, 80 J of useful work is done. Calculate the efficiency of the motor. Give your answer as a percentage.**

4 **For every 500 J of energy in coal, 135 J are transferred to a room as thermal energy from a coal fire.**

  a **Calculate its efficiency.**

  b **Suggest why coal fires are inefficient.**

5 **Suggest why a kettle is not 100% efficient.**

6 **The efficiency of a television is 0.65. Calculate the useful energy output if the total energy input = 200 J.**

Conservation of energy

Energy cannot be created or destroyed, only transferred from one store to another. In a closed system (one in which no energy can enter or leave) the *total* amount of energy put into the system equals the total amount of energy output. We say that energy is conserved. This is the law of conservation of energy. However, only some of the energy output is useful to us. The rest is dissipated as wasted energy. This affects the efficiency of a machine.

7 **What is meant by 'conservation of energy'?**

8 **Explain why some energy is often wasted as thermal energy or sound.**

9 **When sound transfers energy from the store in a vibrating cymbal to your eardrums, the decrease in the kinetic energy of your eardrums does not equal the increase in the kinetic energy store of your eardrums. Suggest how some of the energy is wasted.**

10 **An electric car is 85% efficient. The electricity for the car is supplied by a coal power station with an efficiency of 35%. Determine how much energy is needed from the chemical energy store of the coal for the car to provide 100 J of useful energy.**

DID YOU KNOW?

The efficiency of a filament bulb is less than 5% – over 95% of the energy supplied is transferred directly as thermal energy to the surroundings.

COMMON MISCONCEPTION

You often hear phrases like, *'Conserve energy*; turn off the lights.' However, to scientists, *conservation of energy* means that there is no net change to the total energy of a system.

Using energy resources

KEY WORDS

non-renewable resource
renewable resource

Learning objectives:

- describe the main energy sources available for use on Earth
- distinguish between renewable and non-renewable sources
- explain the ways in which the energy resources are used.

Across the world we use over five hundred million trillion joules of energy every year. This has to come from somewhere.

The need for energy

Industrial societies use huge amounts of energy. Much of it is used for the generation of electricity in power stations. Electricity is useful because appliances can use it to transfer energy to many different types of useful energy stores. For example, a kettle can use electricity to transfer energy to the thermal energy store of the water that it is heating up.

1 Identify an electrical device that transfers energy to:

   a a kinetic energy store

   b a gravitational potential energy store.

We can also use electricity for transport (such as trains and electric cars) and for heating. However, it is often cheaper and easier to use energy resources directly for these purposes.

2 Give an example of an energy resource being used to heat something.

3 State the energy resource you are using when you ride a bicycle.

4 Suggest why we mainly use electricity to power trains but fuel to power aeroplanes.

Figure 1.20 A gravity light has been developed that transfers the gravitational potential energy of a falling 12 kg weight into electrical energy to power a light

DID YOU KNOW?

Tidal energy comes from the gravitational potential energy store of the Moon. Nuclear fuels store energy that was originally produced by stars exploding in a supernova.

Energy resources

Most of the energy resources available to us store energy that has originally come from the Sun. These include fossil fuels (coal, oil and gas), biofuel, wind, wave, hydroelectric and solar energy. Other resources include geothermal energy (from hot, underground rocks), tidal energy and nuclear energy.

All of these resources have advantages and disadvantages. For example, in fossil fuels the energy is very concentrated – a small amount of fuel stores a large amount of chemical energy. Biofuels (such as wood pellets) are produced from plants and animals. They are not as concentrated as fossil fuels so you need a much larger mass to release the same amount of energy.

Reliability is another issue. Some energy resources are available all the time but others are not. It is difficult to capture solar energy during bad weather or at nighttime. Rain is needed for hydroelectric power, and wind and wave energy require it to be windy.

5 Give two ways of generating electricity in which no fuel is burnt.

6 Suggest why wave energy is only useful for a few countries.

7 Satellites orbiting the Earth use solar panels to provide them with their energy needs. Suggest why they also carry rechargeable batteries.

Figure 1.21 Wind turbines are usually placed on high hills or out at sea

Renewable and non-renewable energy resources

Renewable resources never run out (at least not for the foreseeable future). They can be replenished as soon as they are used.

- Solar, wind, wave and hydroelectric resources are intermittently available and the quantity varies according to location. The Sun always shines and it always creates wind and rain. However, there may be short periods of time when there is little wind or rain and no waves.

- Any thermal energy extracted from hot rocks from the geothermal resource is replenished by physical processes in the rocks.

- The Moon produces tides every day, whether we extract energy from them or not.

8 Wood is a form of biofuel. Explain why we can regard wood as a renewable resource.

Non-renewable resources will run out eventually. This is because they are not being replenished at the same rate that we are using them.

9 Identify a non-renewable resource that is not a fossil fuel.

10 Both biofuels and fossil fuels are formed from plants and animals. Explain why biofuels are renewable resources but fossil fuels are non-renewable.

11 a Describe the difference between *energy* and *energy resource*.

   b Explain why energy is conserved but an energy resource is not conserved.

Global energy supplies

KEY WORD

efficiency

Learning objectives:

- analyse global trends in energy use
- understand what the issues are when using energy resources.

The white clouds coming from a power station are not smoke but water vapour coming from the cooling towers. In a coal-fired power station about half the energy stored in coal is lost in this way. We need the electricity, but do we have to have the waste?

Global trends

Figure 1.22 shows how energy resources have been used in the past and how they are likely to be used in the future.

You can see that the amount of energy we need increases every year. This is partly because the population of the world is increasing. Also, more countries are developing technologically and need more energy for industry. China's energy use, for example, grew rapidly between 2000 and 2015.

Although there are environmental problems with fossil fuels, they are likely to provide the world with most of its energy for many years to come.

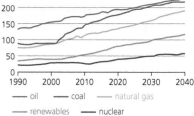

Figure 1.22 The world's use of energy resources

1 **Explain why some of the lines on the graph in Figure 1.22 will eventually stop rising.**

2 **Look at Figure 1.22. Which single type of fuel is used the most?**

3 **Suggest why fossil fuels are likely to provide most of the world's energy for the foreseeable future.**

Energy issues

Scientists have discovered that using some energy resources is having an environmental impact. For example, fuel-burning power stations cause pollution.

They release carbon dioxide into the atmosphere which traps the Sun's energy and contributes to global warming. They also emit sulfur dioxide which causes acid rain.

Nuclear power stations create waste, some of which remains dangerous for thousands of years. There is also the danger of a nuclear accident which could contaminate the area with radioactive materials.

Scientists do not always have the power to make the decisions about energy use – these decisions are made by governments.

DID YOU KNOW?

Mean sea level has risen by about 20 cm in the last 100 years. Most scientists think this is due to global warming. Levels are expected to rise as much as a further 240 cm in the next 100 years.

Governments have to weigh up ethical, social and economic considerations as well as the likely impact on the environment. They also need to make sure they represent the views of the population that elected them.

Ethical considerations are to do with whether something is morally right or wrong. An example is making sure that energy resources are plentiful for the future. Although it will not affect us, it would be wrong to cause problems for future generations.

Social considerations concern how they affect people. Fossil fuel power stations may need to be built to power factories and so provide people with jobs.

Economic considerations involve money. A particular technology might be less harmful to the environment but be far more expensive to construct or maintain.

Figure 1.23 A protest sign against plans to extract shale gas from the ground

4 **A local council has plans to extract shale gas from the ground and to burn it as fuel. Suggest some considerations that the council needs to make before they decide whether to go ahead.**

HIGHER TIER ONLY

Using energy resources efficiently

One way of preserving energy resources is to use them efficiently. This means you need to find ways to reduce the amount of wasted energy in any energy transfer.

The table shows the efficiencies of some typical engines and motors.

	Efficiency (%)
Petrol engine	25
Diesel engine	35
Electric motor	80

Fuel-burning engines have a low efficiency. It is impossible to transfer thermal energy into kinetic energy without wasting most of it.

You can use this formula to calculate **efficiency:**

$$\text{Efficiency} = \frac{\text{useful power output} \times 100}{\text{total power input}}$$

5 **Suggest why the electric motor is more efficient than the fuel-burning engines.**

6 **The output power of an electric motor is 3 kW. Calculate the input power it needs.**

7 **The power station that produced the electricity for the electric motor is 35% efficient. Use this value and your answer to question 6 to determine whether using an electric motor is more efficient than a diesel engine.**

8 **Besides increasing the efficiency of the engine, what else could you do to increase the efficiency of a car?**

KEY CONCEPT

Energy transfer

Learning objectives:

- understand why energy is a key concept in science
- use ideas about energy stores and transfers to explain what happens when a system is changed
- understand why accounting for energy transfers is a useful idea.

KEY WORDS

dissipate
energy
energy store
transfer

Young children often love to run around and play on swings. After a while they'll get tired. 'I've run out of energy!' they'll say, and flop down. A few minutes later they're up again, announcing 'I've got my energy back!' and running off.

What is energy?

The concept of **energy** is one of the most important ideas in science. We use it to explain what's happening when a torch is turned on – and when the batteries run flat. We talk about an energy crisis, and whether we have enough energy to keep our lamps lit and our cars on the road. It's important in chemistry because when reactions take place energy is transferred, and it's important in biology because cells need energy to carry out important processes.

However, we sometimes find it difficult to explain what we mean by energy. It's easier to understand what stores energy, rather than what energy is.

1. **Decide which of these is an energy store:**
   a a ball rolling down a hill
   b a stretched string
   c hot object
   d a mixture of oxygen and fuel.

2. **For each of a to d in question 1, suggest if and how energy might be transferred from one store to another and used for something useful.**

Transferring energy

Sometimes we use names for energy, such as electrical, kinetic or gravitational potential. Actually it's more useful to identify where the energy is. This tells us more. We can then work out how it's been transferred.

Think about a wind-up torch (Figure 1.24). When you turn the handle you **transfer** energy from your muscles to the energy store in the torch's battery. The **energy store** in

Figure 1.24 Energy is transferred into this torch when it is wound up and out of it when it used to project light

your body decreases while the energy store in the battery increases. When you turn the torch on, the energy store in the battery decreases and an electric current transfers energy in the bulb. The internal energy of the bulb increases (it increases in temperature), and the bulb transfers energy by light waves to the surroundings. The bulb **dissipates** energy to the surroundings, increasing the internal energy of the surroundings. When the battery is flat, its energy store is zero and all the energy has been transferred to the surroundings.

3 **Draw a flow diagram to represent where energy has been transferred from and to.**

4 **Identify which energy store increases and which decreases:**
   a **in a bicycle being ridden**
   b **in a match being struck.**

Accounting for energy

Energy does not disappear when it is transferred to other stores. It is still there but it is sometimes hard to see where it is being stored. For example, a charged battery is storing energy. When the battery is flat, the energy has been transferred to the surroundings.

Figure 1.25 Accounting for energy is rather like checking the number of bricks in a set

The physicist Richard Feynman suggested that one of the ways of understanding accounting for energy was to compare it to a set of child's building blocks. The parent knows how many blocks there are in the set. If there is a block missing when you put them away, you look for it. Energy is similar. When you start with a certain amount of energy in a system, it is all still there, but you may have to look for it.

Coal has a chemical energy store. When the coal is burnt, the chemical energy store of the coal decreases and the thermal energy store of the coal increases. In a steam engine, energy is transferred from the store in the coal to the water (as steam) in the boiler. The steam turns the wheels and makes the train move, so there is a kinetic energy store associated with the train. At the end of the journey the coal is burnt, the steam used and the train has come to rest, but the energy is still there – the thermal energy store of the surroundings has increased.

Figure 1.26 Energy is being transferred here – can it all be accounted for?

5 **How does the story of the child's bricks explain the concept of conservation of energy?**

6 **Energy is conserved within a system. In the case of the steam engine, what does the system include?**

Because scientists think this is an important idea, they go to a lot of trouble to measure the amounts of energy (look at the labels on prepared food), to account for the energy transfers and to calculate the efficiency from this (which can be given as a percentage).

MATHS SKILLS

Calculations using significant figures

KEY WORDS

rearrange an
  equation
significant figures
subject of an
  equation
substitute

Learning objectives:

- substitute numerical values into equations and use appropriate units
- change the subject of an equation
- give an answer to an appropriate number of significant figures.

People have been trying to invent a perpetual motion machine for centuries. Perpetual motion means moving forever. But where there are energy transfers, some energy is always dissipated. This is why the idea of perpetual motion is an impossible dream.

Calculating changes in energy

Example: A diver dives into water from a board 10.0 m above the water surface. The mass of the diver is 50.0 kg. The gravitational field strength is 9.8 N/kg.

a Calculate the change in gravitational potential energy of the diver as she falls from the board to the surface of the water.

b Calculate the diver's speed when she hits the water.

   a   Use $E_p = mgh$

           $E_p = 50.0 \text{ kg} \times 9.8 \text{ N/kg} \times 10.0 \text{ m}$

              $= 4900 \text{ J}$

   b   As the diver falls, energy is transferred from a gravitational potential energy store to a kinetic energy store.

       The energy transferred from the gravitational potential energy store to the kinetic energy store = 4900 J

       Use $E_k = \frac{1}{2} mv^2$

       You need to **rearrange the equation** to find v (make v the **subject of the equation**).

       Multiply both sides by 2: $2E_k = mv^2$

       Divide both sides by m: $\dfrac{2E_k}{m} = v^2$

       So: $v = \sqrt{\dfrac{2E_k}{m}}$

       Substituting the values for E_k and m:

       $v = \sqrt{\dfrac{2 \times 4900}{50}}$

       $v = \sqrt{196}$

       $v = 14 \text{ m/s}$

Figure 1.27 An idea for a perpetual motion machine. Such a machine could not work because it would violate the law of conservation of energy.

1 Calculate the change in gravitational potential energy of a diver of mass 70.0 kg who dives from a board 2.0 m above the water.

2 Calculate the gravitational potential energy gained by a ball of mass 50.0 g thrown to a height of 10.0 m.

Significant figures

The answer to a calculation can only have the same number of **significant figures** as the data provided.

Example: A diver stands on a board 5.0 m above water. The mass of the diver is 50.0 kg. The gravitational field strength is 9.8 N/kg. Calculate the diver's speed when he hits the water. Give your answer to two significant figures.

Increase in kinetic energy store = decrease in gravitational potential energy store

$= mgh$

$= 50.0$ kg $\times 9.8$ N/kg $\times 5.0$ m

$= 2450$ J (Do not round to two significant figures yet.)

Energy transferred to the kinetic energy store, $E_k = 0.5\ mv^2$

Rearranging as before, $\dfrac{2E_k}{m} = v^2$

$$v = \sqrt{\dfrac{2E_k}{m}}$$

$$= \sqrt{\dfrac{2 \times 2450}{50}}$$

$$= \sqrt{98}$$

$$= 9.899,\ \text{or } 9.9 \text{ m/s, to two significant figures}$$

3 A spring of spring constant $k = 350$ N/m is extended by 9.0 cm. Calculate the elastic potential energy, E_e, stored in the spring. Give your answer to two significant figures.

Two-step problems

Example: A lift raises four people with a combined weight of 3500 N to the third floor of a building in 25.0 seconds. The height gained is 15 m. Calculate the power required.

You need to use: power $= \dfrac{\text{work done}}{\text{time taken}}$, or $P = \dfrac{W}{t}$

You have the time taken, but not the work done. You must approach this problem in two steps. First, calculate the work done, then **substitute** that value into the equation for power.

Work done = force × distance along the line of action of the force

The force used (the weight that is lifted) is 3500 N.

Work done = 3500 N × 15 m

$\quad\quad\quad\quad = 52\,500$ J, or 52.5 kJ

Substituting this value for work done into the power equation:

Power $= \dfrac{52\,500\text{ J}}{25.0\text{ s}}$

$\quad\quad = 2100$ W, or 2.1 kW

KEY INFORMATION

You should keep at least one extra significant figure in your calculations to avoid rounding errors. Only round to the required number of significant figures when you have calculated the answer.

KEY INFORMATION

To round a number to two significant figures, look at the third digit. Round up if the digit is 5 or more, and round down if the digit is 4 or less.

MAKING LINKS

A set of readings taken with the same instrument should all have the same number of significant figures. So if the extension of a spring is measured with a ruler as 4.1, 4.2, 5.9 and 6 cm, the table of data should list 6 cm as 6.0 cm.

MATHS SKILLS

Handling data

Learning objectives:

- explain the use of tables and frequency tables
- explain when to use scatter diagrams, bar charts and histograms
- recognise the difference between mean, mode and median.

KEY WORDS

anomalous
bar chart
continuous data
correlation
dependent variable
frequency table
histogram

independent variable
line of best fit
mean
median
mode
scatter diagram

The purpose of an experiment is to find out the relationship, if there is any, between the variables you are investigating. You do this by looking for a pattern in the data that are collected. It is difficult to spot a pattern from a mass of numbers, but it is much easier from a picture – a graph or a chart.

Tables and frequency tables

Tables are used to capture the information from an experiment and from graphs. A simple table is used for **continuous data**, where information is measured on a continuous scale – for example, when loading a spring with different weights and measuring the extension produced (Table 1.1).

Force (N)	Extension of spring (mm)		
	1st reading	2nd reading	3rd reading
10	8	9	7
20	19	16	15
30	23	21	29
40	34	32	33
50	35	44	39

Table 1.1 Investigating the relationship between force and the extension of a spring

Another way of collecting data is to use tally marks and make a **frequency table**. This method is best where your data can only have certain values, such as shoe sizes, or the information can be categorised, such as the names of countries.

Using scatter diagrams, bar charts and histograms

The data in Table 1.1 are continuous and are best displayed by using a **scatter diagram** (Figure 1.28). The force is the **independent variable** so it goes on the horizontal axis. The extension is the **dependent variable** so it goes on the vertical

Figure 1.28 Data from Table 1.1. A scatter graph with a line of best fit.

Country	Tally marks	Number of new nuclear power stations being built
Russia	IIII II	7
UK	IIII	5
India	IIII I	6
USA	IIII	5
Pakistan	III	3

Table 1.2 Number of new nuclear power stations being built in selected countries

axis. Plotting the data points will give a clearer picture of the relationship between the two variables, to see if there is a **correlation**. If there is a correlation, you can draw a **line of best fit** (this may be a curve) and then use this to extrapolate further trends and information.

The data in Table 1.2 are not continuous. They are best represented by a **bar chart** (Figure 1.29).

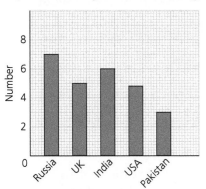

Figure 1.29 Data from Table 1.2. A bar chart.

Age	Tally	Frequency
11–20	IIIII IIII	9
21–30	IIIII IIIII IIIII I	16
31–40	IIIII IIIII II	12
41–50	IIII	4
51–60	IIIII I	6
61–70	I	1

Table 1.3 Frequency distribution of the ages of people on a street

Figure 1.30 Data from Table 1.3. A histogram.

The data in Table 1.3 are grouped. They are best represented by a **histogram**. Each bar represents a group of data, and the frequency of the data is shown by the area of each bar (Figure 1.30).

Mean, median and mode

To find the **mean**, add up all the values and divide by the number of values.

Example: The mean of four repeated measurements of temperature, 7 °C, 12 °C, 9 °C and 11 °C, is

$$\frac{7 \text{ °C} + 12 \text{ °C} + 9 \text{ °C} + 11 \text{ °C}}{4} = 9.75 \text{ °C}$$

or 10°C, rounded to the nearest whole number.

The **median** is the middle value when the values are rearranged in sequence. For example, from the data set above:

7 °C, 9 °C, 11 °C, 12 °C

When there are an odd number of data points, it is easy to spot the median. If there is an even number of data points, calculate the median as the midpoint of the two middle values. In this example, the median is halfway between 9 °C and 11 °C. So the median is 10 °C, even though that is not one of the data points.

The **mode** is the value, or item, that occurs most frequently in a set of data. It is easy to spot the mode in a frequency table. In Table 1.4 the mode is 'Biomass & renewable waste'.

When should you use which average? In the repeated measurements of temperature above, the mean and the median turn out to be the same value. But if one of the measurements was **anomalous**, for example, 22 °C instead of 12 °C, this would skew the mean.

Renewable energy resource with the greatest share of total renewable energy production	Frequency
Solar energy	2
Biomass & renewable waste	31
Geothermal energy	0
Hydropower	0
Wind energy	1

Table 1.4 Renewable energy sources in the EU for 2013

Example: The mean of 7 °C, 22 °C, 9 °C and 11 °C is

$$\frac{7 \text{ °C} + 22 \text{ °C} + 9 \text{ °C} + 11 \text{ °C}}{4}$$

= 12.25 °C

or 12 °C, rounded to the nearest whole number.

The median, 10 °C, is unchanged, so it is the more accurate representation of your data set when there are some anomalous results (or 'outliers').

Check Your Progress

You should be able to:

Describe how energy can be stored by raising an object up or by stretching or compressing it

→ Use the equations for gravitational potential energy and elastic potential energy

→ Apply the equations for gravitational potential energy and elastic potential energy in a variety of contexts, and change the subject of these equations

Describe how a moving object has kinetic energy

→ Know that kinetic energy is related to mass and velocity squared and use the formula to calculate it

→ Use the equation for kinetic energy to solve problems, including changing the subject of the equation

Recognise that when a force moves an object along the line of action of the force, work is being done

State that various devices do work and, in doing so, transfer energy

→ Calculate the work done by a force from the size of the force and the distance moved

→ Use the equation for work done to solve problems, including changing the subject of the equation

State that some materials require more energy than others to increase a certain mass by a certain temperature

→ Describe what is meant by the specific heat capacity of a material and use the equation for specific heat capacity

Plan an experiment to measure the specific heat capacity of a material

→ Calculate temperature changes, masses or specific heat capacities given the other values

Evaluate an experiment to measure the specific heat capacity of a material

Recognise that some energy transfers are unwanted

→ Describe how lubrication and insulation can be used to reduce unwanted energy transfers

Calculate energy efficiency

Describe how some energy transfers are more useful than others

→ Explain how thermal conductivity affects the rate of energy transfer across a material and affects the rate of cooling of a building

Recognise that in a closed system there may be energy transfers that change the way energy is stored, but there is no net change to the total energy

State that various resources are used as fuels and to generate electricity

→ Describe the advantages and disadvantages of fossil fuel, nuclear and renewable energy resources

→ Evaluate and justify the use of various energy resources for different applications

Worked example

Jo's group is investigating the energy changes that take place when a toy car runs down a ramp.

① The mass of the car is 500 g, *g* is 9.8 N/kg and the vertical height of the top of the ramp is 20 cm. Calculate the GPE of the car at the top of the ramp.

$GPE = mgh = 500 \times 9.8 \times 20 = 98\,000\,J$

> This answer correctly uses the formula to multiply the variables together but hasn't converted the mass or the height into standard units. It should be 0.5 kg × 9.8 N/kg × 0.2 m = 0.98 J

② The pupils use a speed detector to measure the speed of the car when it gets to the bottom of the ramp. They find out it is travelling at 0.8 m/s. Calculate its kinetic energy.

$KE = \frac{1}{2}mv^2 = \frac{1}{2} \times 0.5 \times 0.8 \times 0.8 = 0.16$

> This answer correctly uses the formula and has converted g to kg. The speed (only) is squared but there is no indication of the correct unit at the end.

③ a How could they calculate the percentage efficiency of the system at converting GPE into KE?

b Explain why it will be less than 100%.

Efficiency could be found by dividing output by input, so $\frac{KE}{GPE}$.

Nothing is perfect and efficiency is always less than 100%

> This is correct in that it is the output divided by the input but it is important to use the **useful** output. Furthermore, the question asked for the efficiency as a percentage, so the answer has to be multiplied by 100%.

> This is true but is not an explanation. The reason it is not 100% is because not all of the GPE store has been transferred to the kinetic energy store of the car. Some energy is dissipated to the surroundings, raising the temperature of the car body and the surrounding air.

④ Jo says that if the ramp was 100% efficient, then doubling the height of the top of the ramp would double the speed at the bottom. Referring to the relevant formulae, suggest whether she is correct.

$GPE = mgh$ and $KE = 1/2mv^2$. Increasing h will increase GPE and this will increase KE which will increase v so Jo is correct.

> This quotes the correct formulae and identifies that an increased *h* will mean an increased GPE. In fact, doubling *h* will double the GPE, which will double the KE (if it's 100% efficient). However, KE = ½ *mv²* and the squaring means that although the speed will increase, it won't double (it will actually go up by a factor of about 1.4). If the question includes a quantitative approach (it refers to doubling), it's not enough to give a qualitative response (say **how much** it increases).

End of chapter questions

Getting started

1 Sally is choosing a new electric kettle. One is rated at 1.5 kW and the other at 2 kW. What does this show?   `1 Mark`

 a The first one is smaller.

 b The second one is a newer design.

 c The first one will keep the water hot for longer.

 d The second one will transfer energy more quickly.

2 Write down the equation for efficiency.   `1 Mark`

3 What is meant by a **non-renewable** resource?   `1 Mark`

4 Two steel blocks, one with a mass of 100 g and the other with a mass of 200 g, are placed in boiling water for several minutes. Which of these statements is **not** true?   `1 Mark`

 a They are both at the same temperature.

 b They are made of the same material.

 c They have the same amount of stored thermal energy.

 d They remain solid.

5 Order these light bulbs from most to least powerful.   `2 Marks`

 15 W, 0.1 kW, 60 W, 0.08 kW, 150 W

6 Describe the difference between **elastic potential energy** and **gravitational potential energy**.   `2 Marks`

7 Elise has a weight of 400 N and can clear a high jump of 2 m. Calculate how much work she does in raising her body up 2 m.   `2 Marks`

Going further

8 When energy is being wasted we say it is   `1 Mark`

 a diffusing

 b propagating

 c dissipating

 d refracting

9 Which of these does **not** affect the amount of energy needed to heat up a material?   `1 Mark`

 a Its colour.

 b Its mass.

 c Its specific heat capacity.

 d The temperature rise.

10 Explain why bubble wrap is an effective insulator.   `2 Marks`

11 Look at the image of the house.

Use the image to name the part of the building that needs insulating the most. Explain your answer.

`2 Marks`

12 What has to be done for wood to be a renewable resource?

`2 Marks`

13 Using the idea of heat capacity, explain why a fairly small hot water bottle can warm a bed.

`2 Marks`

More challenging

14 The power of a kettle is 2000 W. Explain what **2000 W** means in terms of energy transfer.

`1 Mark`

15 Write down what each of the symbols stands for in $\Delta E = mc\Delta\theta$

`1 Mark`

16 Night storage heaters charge up during the night time and release energy during the day. Explain why they are made from a material with a high specific heat capacity.

`2 Marks`

17 A student was given some rods made from different materials. He was asked to arrange the rods in order of increasing thermal conductivity. Describe a procedure the student could follow to carry out the task safely by using a fair test.

`6 Marks`

Most demanding

18 Explain the difference between stored thermal energy and temperature.

`2 Marks`

19 Explain why energy is conserved within a closed system.

`2 Marks`

20 A student was investigating how the efficiency of a squash ball changed with temperature. The efficiency of a squash ball can be worked out by using the formula:

gravitational potential energy associated with the squash ball when it reaches its maximum height after it bounces / gravitational potential energy associated with the squash ball before it is dropped.

The student placed the ball in a beaker of water and heated the water to the desired temperature. She then removed the ball from the water and dropped it from a height of 1 m onto a hard surface. Once the ball had bounced, the student measured the height that the ball bounced up to by using a metre ruler.

Here are her results:

Mass of squash ball = 25 g

Gravitational field strength on Earth = 9.8 N/kg

Temperature (°C)	20	30	40	50	60
Bounce height 1 (cm)	6	28	39	43	45
Bounce height 2 (cm)	18	23	36	40	42

The student concluded that the higher the temperature of the squash ball, the more efficient it was.

Discuss whether the student came to a valid conclusion and evaluate the limitations of the experiment.

`6 Marks`

`Total: 40 Marks`

ELECTRICITY

IDEAS YOU HAVE MET BEFORE:

ELECTRIC CURRENT

- An electric current is due to a flow of charge.
- Resistors are used to control the current in circuits.
- Ohm's law is used to calculate resistance.

ELECTRICAL ENERGY

- Cells are sources of electricity.
- A battery is a number of cells joined together.
- Energy sources can be used to drive electrical generators to produce electricity.

ELECTRICITY IN THE HOME

- Electricity supplied to the home is alternating current (a.c.).
- Care must be taken when using mains electricity as it has a high potential difference (230 V).
- Fuses and circuit breakers switch off the current if a fault occurs.

IN THIS CHAPTER YOU WILL FIND OUT ABOUT:

WHAT ARE THE KEY CONCEPTS IN ELECTRICITY?

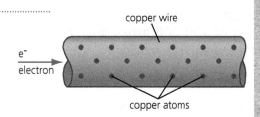

copper wire

e^-
electron

copper atoms

- Electric current is the rate of flow of charge through a conductor.
- Some electrical components resist the flow of electrons more than others so have greater resistance.
- Potential difference is a measure of the energy transferred per unit charge as charges move between two points in a circuit.

WHAT ARE THE CHARACTERISTICS OF SOME ELECTRICAL COMPONENTS?

- When electrical components are connected in parallel there is more current passing through each component than when they are connected in series.
- A fixed resistor at constant temperature obeys Ohm's law, so the current through it is directly proportional to the potential difference across it.
- Diodes, thermistors and light-dependent resistors do not obey Ohm's law.

HOW CAN ELECTRICITY BE USED SAFELY IN THE HOME?

- Connecting a live wire to earth is dangerous.
- The earth is connected to the Earth so it provides a path for the current if there is a short circuit.
- The higher the power (in W) of an electrical device, the more expensive it is to use it.

Electric current

Learning objectives:

- know circuit symbols
- recall that current is a rate of flow of electric charge
- recall that current (*I*) depends on resistance (*R*) and potential difference (*V*)
- explain how an electric current passes round a circuit.

KEY WORDS

coulomb
parallel
potential
  difference (pd)
resistance
voltmeter

Japanese scientists have managed to achieve an electric current of 100 000 amperes – by far the highest to be generated in the world.

Electric current and charge

Current is a rate of flow of electric charge. Electric charge is measured in **coulombs** (C). We now know that an electric current in a metal is actually a flow of electrons from negative to positive. Electric current is measured in amperes (A). This is often abbreviated to amps.

$$\text{charge flow, } Q = \text{current, } I \times \text{time, } t.$$
$$\text{(in C)} \qquad \text{(in A)} \qquad \text{(in s)}$$
$$Q = It$$

Example: A wire carries a current of 1.2 A for 30 s. How much charge flows?

$$Q = It = 1.2\,\text{A} \times 30\,\text{s} = 36\,\text{C}$$

1. **Calculate the current when 80 C of charge flows in 16 s.**

2. **A charge of 96 C flows in a wire carrying a current of 6 A. Calculate how long it takes for this amount of charge to flow.**

Potential difference

Potential difference (pd) is the energy transferred per unit charge as charges move between two points in a circuit. It is measured in volts (V) using a **voltmeter**. A voltmeter is always connected across the component. We say the voltmeter is connected in **parallel** (Figure 2.2). Circuit symbols are shown in Figure 2.1.

For an electric current to flow, there needs to be a closed circuit (complete loop) and a source of potential difference.

Potential difference is sometimes referred to as voltage.

1 volt is the energy transferred when 1 coulomb of charge moves through a component. 1 V = 1 J/C. If a 12 V battery is used to light a lamp, each coulomb of charge going from the battery receives 12 J of energy.

3. **Write two things that are needed for there to be an electric current.**

4. **A 6 V battery passes a current of 1 A through a lamp for 1 minute. Calculate how much energy is transferred from the battery to the lamp.**

Figure 2.1 Circuit symbols

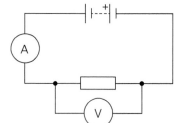

Figure 2.2 Measuring the pd across a resistor using a voltmeter

Current, resistance and potential difference

Electrons are 'pushed' around a circuit by a battery. They bump into the metal ions in the resistor. Energy is transferred to the metal ions, so they vibrate more and the resistor gets hotter. The increased vibrations of the ions held in their fixed lattice make it harder for the electrons to travel through the resistor, so its resistance increases (Figure 2.3).

🔘 metal ions in the resistor

⚪ electrons collide with the metal ions

Figure 2.3 The movement of electrons in a wire carrying a current

The filament in a lamp connected in a circuit becomes so hot it emits light.

Note that the net direction in which the electrons move is opposite to the direction of the conventional current. The conventional current direction, from positive to negative, was well established before scientists understood that the electrons actually moved from negative to positive. So they did not change it.

Figure 2.4 Circuit with variable resistor and lamp

5 **Explain why the bulb in Figure 2.4 gets hot.**

6 **The circuit shown in Figure 2.5 includes a variable resistor. Explain how the variable resistor can be used as a dimmer switch.**

Figure 2.5

Current, *I*, **resistance**, *R* and potential difference, *V* are linked by the equation:

potential difference, *V* = current, *I* × resistance, *R*

(in volts, V)   (in amperes, A) (in ohms, Ω)

$$V = IR$$

Example: Calculate the potential difference across a 5 Ω resistor when the current through it is 2 A.

$V = IR = 2 \times 5 = 10$ V.

7 **Calculate the resistance of a car headlamp when the supply potential difference is 12 V and the current is 3 A.**

8 **Calculate the potential difference across a 6 Ω resistor when the current through it is 1.5 A.**

Series and parallel circuits

Learning objectives:

- recognise series and parallel circuits
- describe the changes in the current and potential difference in series and parallel circuits.

KEY WORDS

parallel circuit
series circuit

All the electrical appliances in a home are connected in a parallel circuit. If they were connected in series, you would need to switch on every single appliance in order to watch TV.

Lamps in series and parallel

In the **series circuit** in Figure 2.6 the lamps are connected next to each other and form a single loop with the battery and the switch. In the **parallel circuit** both sides of the lamps are connected to each other – a little like the rungs of a ladder.

When they are shining, the lamps connected in parallel are brighter than lamps connected in series.

If an extra lamp is added to the series circuit, then all of the lamps in the circuit are even dimmer. If an extra lamp is added to the parallel circuit, the lamps are the same brightness as before.

1. **None of the lamps in Figure 2.6 are currently shining. State what you would have to do to the circuits to make the lamps shine.**

2. **A third lamp is added to the series circuit. Describe what happens to the brightness of the two lamps that were already in the circuit.**

3. **Suggest what would happen if one bulb was unscrewed in each circuit.**

Series circuit

Parallel circuit

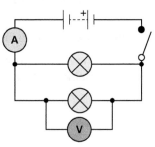

Figure 2.6 A series circuit and a parallel circuit

Resistors in series

In the series circuit in Figure 2.7 the current has to pass through *both* resistors, R_1 *and* R_2. There is nowhere else for it to go. This means that the readings on all of the ammeters are the same.

When components are connected in series, the same current flows through each component. The size of the current depends on the total resistance of the components.

For components in series, the total resistance is the sum of all of the resistances. The total resistance of the circuit in Figure 2.7 is $R_1 + R_2$.

The potential difference of the power supply is shared between the components. This means that the reading of voltmeter V_1 plus the reading of voltmeter V_2 would equal the potential difference of the battery.

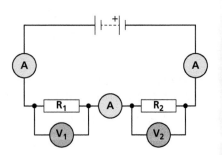

Figure 2.7 A series circuit

4 A motor, a lamp and a 12 V battery are connected in series. The resistance of the motor is 10 Ω and the resistance of the lamp is 20 Ω. The current through the lamp is 0.4 A.

a Determine the current through the motor.

b Calculate the total resistance of the circuit.

c If the potential difference across the motor is 4 V, what is the potential difference across the lamp?

d Suggest how the current would change if the lamp was replaced with a 50 Ω resistor.

Resistors in parallel

In the parallel circuit in Figure 2.8, the current can pass through either R_1 or R_2 in the circuit. This means that the reading on ammeter A_1 is equal to the sum of the readings on ammeters A_2 and A_3.

The potential difference of the power supply is the same as the potential difference across each component. So the reading of both voltmeters V_1 and V_2 would be the same and would equal the potential difference of the power supply.

Adding a resistor in series increases the total resistance because the electric charge has to pass through another component. Adding a resistor in parallel decreases the total resistance because you are providing an alternative path for the electric charge. The total resistance of a parallel circuit is always smaller than the smallest resistance of any component.

Figure 2.8 A parallel circuit

5 The 10 Ω motor, 20 Ω lamp and 12 V battery from Q4 are now connected in parallel. A current of 1.8 A passes through the battery and a current of 1.2 A passes through the motor.

a Determine the current through the lamp.

b Calculate the potential difference across the motor.

c Explain whether the total resistance of this circuit is greater or smaller than 10 Ω.

d A further resistor is added in parallel to the motor and the lamp. Explain what happens to the size of the current passing through the battery.

DID YOU KNOW?

A current of 1 A means that more than 6 000 000 000 000 000 000 electrons pass each point every second. This is only a small fraction of the electrons in the wire!

Investigating circuits

Learning objectives:

- use series circuits to test components and make measurements
- carry out calculations on series circuits.

KEY WORDS

ammeter
equivalent
    resistance

When a sports match is televised it can take 24 km of electrical cabling to connect up the TV cameras and the studio. If the equipment goes wrong, engineers need to check quickly that the cables are working. How can they do this?

Circuits for testing and measuring

You can use the circuit in Figure 2.9 to check if a component or an electrical cable conducts electricity easily. The buzzer should sound when the cable or the component is attached to the terminals.

1 **Explain how the circuit in Figure 2.9 works.**

The circuit in Figure 2.10 is used to investigate the resistance of a component. You connect the component between the terminals. This circuit can be used to investigate lamps and diodes as well as components that measure temperature and light intensity.

The **ammeter** measures the current passing through the component and the voltmeter measures the potential difference across the component. Ammeters are always connected in series with the component, and voltmeters are always connected in parallel. Voltmeters have a very high resistance, which means that only a very small current flows through a voltmeter. Ammeters have a very low resistance, which means that they do not have very much effect on the resistance of the circuit.

You can change the current by altering the resistance of the variable resistor. The resistance is usually altered by moving a slider or by turning a dial.

2 **An electric heater is placed between the terminals of the circuit in Figure 2.10. The ammeter reading is 2 A and the voltmeter reading is 12 V.**

   a **Calculate the resistance of the heater.**

   b **Describe how you could alter the circuit so that a current of 1 A passes through the heater.**

Figure 2.9 A circuit for testing components and cables

REMEMBER!

The resistance of a component equals the potential difference divided by the current.

Figure 2.10 A circuit to measure the resistance of a component

Circuit calculations

These rules help you to calculate currents, potential differences and resistances in circuits.

For resistors in series, the total potential difference is the sum of the potential differences across the resistors and the current is the same through all of the resistors. The total resistance is the sum of the resistances of the resistors.

For resistors in parallel, the potential difference across each resistor is identical, but the total current is the sum of the currents that pass through each of the resistors.

3 A resistor, an ammeter and a voltmeter are connected in series with a 12 V power supply. The ammeter shows the current as 0 A. Suggest what is wrong with the circuit.

4 The potential difference across a resistor is 12 V and the current is 0.6 A. What is the value of its resistance?

5 A 5 Ω and a 7 Ω resistor are connected in series with a 6 V battery. Calculate the current in the circuit.

6 A 3 Ω and a 6 Ω resistor are connected in series with a 12 V battery. What is the potential difference across the 3 Ω resistor?

7 A 3 Ω and a 6 Ω resistor are connected in series with a battery. A current of 1 A passes through the 3 Ω resistor. Determine the potential difference of the battery.

8 A 4 Ω resistor is placed in series with another resistor and a 12 V battery. The potential difference across the 4 Ω resistor is 8 V. Determine the resistance of the other resistor.

Equivalent circuits

Sometimes you can simplify circuit calculations by replacing all the components in a circuit with a single resistor (Figure 2.11). The single resistor needs to have the **equivalent resistance** of the components in the circuit. You can then work out the current passing through the power supply.

9 A 12 V car battery is supplying a current of 60 A to the electric components in a car. The driver then switches on the sound system and a larger current passes through the battery. What happens to the equivalent resistance of the circuit?

10 A 12 Ω motor is connected in parallel with a 6 Ω lamp. Together these are connected in series with a 5 Ω resistor and a 9 V battery. The equivalent resistance of the motor, lamp and resistor is 9 Ω. Calculate the current passing through the battery.

DID YOU KNOW?

When you make a series circuit with a 1.5 V battery, a torch bulb and 2 m of connecting wire, it will take about 2 days for an electron to go around the circuit.

Figure 2.11 These circuits draw the same current from the battery

Circuit components

Learning objectives:

- set up a circuit to investigate resistance
- investigate the changing resistance of a filament lamp
- compare the properties of a resistor and filament lamp.

New light bulbs have been introduced to replace the filament bulb. The so-called 'energy saver' light bulb lasts longer and is more economical to use, but it has the disadvantage that it contains mercury, which is toxic.

Measuring resistance

The circuit shown in Figure 2.12 can be used to measure the resistance of a fixed resistor. As the variable resistor is changed, the readings on the ammeter and voltmeter are recorded. A graph of current (*I*) against potential difference (*V*) is plotted. A straight line through the origin shows that current is proportional to potential difference (Figure 2.13). Such resistors are ohmic – they obey Ohm's law. Their resistance is constant. The resistance is equal to 1/gradient of an *I–V* graph. Copper wire and all other metals give this shape of graph as long as the temperature does not change.

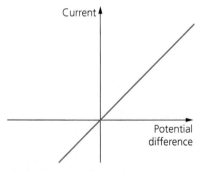

Figure 2.12 This circuit can be used to measure the resistance of a resistor

1. **What does a straight line graph through the origin tell you about the quantities plotted?**

2. **Which meter is connected in parallel, the ammeter or the voltmeter?**

The changing resistance of a filament lamp

If you switch on a light bulb using a dimmer switch, you will see that you can change the brightness of the bulb. This is because the higher the current, the higher the temperature of the filament. The hotter the bulb, the whiter and brighter the light from it becomes.

If the fixed resistor in Figure 2.12 is replaced by a **filament bulb**, the corresponding graph of current against potential difference is no longer a straight line. This is because the resistance of the filament bulb changes as its temperature changes. In Figure 2.15 the resistance is different for each value of potential difference and current.

When the filament in a bulb gets hot, two things happen. The free electrons move faster, and the metal ions in the filament vibrate more, taking up more space. As the atoms take up more space, the electrons collide with them more often, so the resistance and temperature of the bulb increase. This is why the resistance of a filament bulb increases with temperature.

Figure 2.13 *I–V* graph for an ohmic conductor

The filament is made of tungsten as tungsten does not melt and evaporates very little at the typical filament bulb operating temperature of 2000 °C. An inert gas such as nitrogen or argon is usually included in the bulb to prevent the evaporation of the tungsten.

3 **Explain how you know that the filament lamp is a non-ohmic conductor.**

4 **The filament in a bulb is made from tungsten. Tungsten, like other metals, obeys Ohm's law. Why is the I–V graph for a filament lamp not a straight line?**

Comparing I–V graphs

A fixed resistor at constant temperature produces a straight line I–V graph (Figure 2.13), showing the resistance is constant. The value of the resistance is equal to the inverse of the gradient of the I–V graph.

The filament of a lamp is a heating element that gets so hot that it emits light. This huge temperature change means that the filament is non-ohmic – its resistance increases as the temperature increases. The I–V graph is a curve (Figure 2.15) – it is nonlinear. The resistance of the bulb at different potential differences can only be found from instantaneous I–V values, not from the gradient.

> **DID YOU KNOW?**
>
> The average filament light bulb has a lifetime of about 1000 hours. The tungsten used to make the filament evaporates at 2500 °C.

Figure 2.14 Coiled tungsten filament lamp

> **KEY INFORMATION**
>
> The resistance of a non-ohmic conductor is found from instantaneous values, not the gradient of the graph. A graph of current against potential difference is called an I–V characteristic of the component.

Figure 2.15 The changing slope of this graph shows that the resistance of the filament lamp increases as the current increases

5 a **Calculate the resistance at 1 V and 6 V in Figure 2.15.**

b **Sketch a graph of resistance against time for the filament lamp immediately after it is switched on.**

REQUIRED PRACTICAL

Investigate, using circuit diagrams to construct circuits, the *I–V* characteristics of a filament lamp, a diode and a resistor at constant temperature

KEY WORDS

dependent variable
diode
filament lamp
independent variable
ohmic conductor
Ohm's law
resistor

Learning objectives:

- understand how an experiment can be designed to test an idea
- evaluate how an experimental procedure can yield more accurate data
- interpret and explain graphs using scientific ideas.

Some components have a constant resistance. When we apply a potential difference across them current will flow. If we double the potential difference, the current doubles. We call these components ohmic. Other components do not have a constant resistance – increasing the potential difference might alter the current flow but it does not change proportionately. These are called non-ohmic. We can tell which are which by testing them, plotting graphs of the data and looking at the shape of the graph.

These pages are designed ❶ to help you think about aspects of the investigation rather than to guide you through it step by step.

Designing a circuit to test the components

The circuit shown in the figure can be used to test components to see whether their resistance changes. The component is represented by the rectangle (this is the symbol for a resistor and the component has some resistance).

The two variables are potential difference and current.

❶ **Why are the ammeter and the voltmeter in the positions shown in the circuit?**

❷ **State the independent variable and the dependent variable.**

Figure 2.16 Circuit diagram for testing components

Gathering accurate data

The resistance of **ohmic conductors** can increase when their temperature increases. This is a problem with this experiment because one of the effects of passing a current through something is that its temperature increases. This has to be allowed for in the way the experiment is carried out.

3 Why should the power supply be turned off between readings?

Analysing the data

Gathering readings for potential difference and current means that they can be plotted as points on a graph. We can then draw a line of best fit for each component tested. Potential difference can be applied either way round so negative values can be gathered as well as positive. Therefore the axes need to have negative values as well as positive ones.

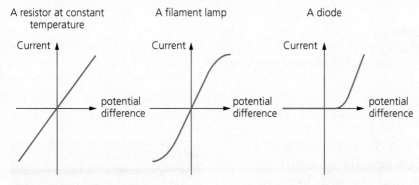

Figure 2.17

By looking at the shape of the graph we can see whether the component is ohmic. If it is, then the current will be directly proportional to the potential difference.

4 Look at the graph of the resistor. Describe the relationship between current and potential difference.

5 Look at the graph of the readings from the lamp. Explain what this shows.

6 Explain what the graph tells us about the resistance of a diode.

DID YOU KNOW?

The first diodes weren't the tiny semiconductor devices used nowadays but large glass valves which took several minutes to heat up and glowed.

REQUIRED PRACTICAL

Use circuit diagrams to set up and check appropriate circuits to investigate the factors affecting the resistance of electrical circuits, including the length of a wire at constant temperature and combinations of resistors in series and parallel

KEY WORDS

current
parallel
potential
    difference
resistance
series

Learning objectives:

- use a circuit to determine resistance
- gather valid data to use in calculations
- apply the circuit to determine the resistance of combinations of components.

We can use a circuit to determine the resistance of a component, as resistance can be calculated from measuring potential difference and current. We can then see how the resistance is affected by factors such as the length of a wire or when several components are combined.

These pages are designed ❶ to help you think about aspects of the investigation rather than to guide you through it step by step.

Using a circuit to get useful data

The **resistance** of a component, such as a piece of wire, can be calculated using the equation:

resistance = **potential difference** ÷ **current**

$$R = \frac{V}{I}$$

If we set up a circuit with an ammeter and a voltmeter in it, we can record the data to calculate the resistance. The circuit we can use is shown in Figure 2.18. The rectangle represents the component being tested, such as a length of wire.

① **Explain what you would expect to happen to the current passing through the component as the potential difference across it is increased.**

② **Describe how the potential difference across the component is altered in the circuit shown.**

③ **If the current passing through the component increases, describe what will happen to its temperature.**

Figure 2.18 Circuit diagram for measuring potential difference across a component and the current passing through it

Length of a wire and its resistance

When the component being tested is a length of wire, we can find out how the resistance changes when the length is altered. For each length of wire, we can record the potential difference across the wire and current passing through it and use them to calculate the resistance. We can then plot a graph of resistance against length of the wire to show how changing the length of the wire affects the resistance.

One of the factors that can affect the accuracy of the results is temperature. As more current passes through the wire it gets hotter and this alters the resistance. It is important to avoid increasing the thermal energy store of the wire.

4 In this experiment, state what readings would be taken and what calculations would be done.

5 a Predict what effect the length of a wire will have on its resistance.

b Sketch a graph showing your prediction.

6 Suggest a good way of stopping the heating effect of the current affecting the results too much.

Investigating combinations of components

We can also join components together and see what the combined resistance is. We can connect them in **series**, as shown in Figure 2.19. We can then measure the potential difference across them and the current passing through and calculate the combined resistance of the resistors in series.

We can also do this with components in **parallel**, as shown in Figure 2.20. This will enable us to investigate what the combined resistance of the resistors in parallel is.

7 a Draw circuit diagrams to show how measurements could be taken to calculate the resistance of two components in series and in parallel.

b For both series and parallel diagrams, predict what you would expect the combined resistance to be, compared with the resistance of the individual components.

8 A student connected two resistors in turn to the circuit in Figure 2.18. The first resistor produced a current of 0.10 A and a p.d. of 6.0 V. The second resistor produced a current of 0.20 A and a p.d. of 3.0 V. When the student connected the resistors in series, they produced a current of 0.05 A and a p.d. of 3.9 V.

a Explain why the result for the resistors in series was unexpected.

b Suggest a reason for the unexpected result.

> **REMEMBER!**
> ....
> The greater the resistance, the higher the potential difference is needed to make a certain current pass.

Figure 2.19 Resistors in series

Figure 2.20 Resistors in parallel

> **DID YOU KNOW?**
> ....
> The equation $V = IR$ is sometimes known as Ohm's law. This is not strictly correct because the equation applies to any component, whereas Ohm's law only applies to certain components, and then only if the temperature is kept constant.

Control circuits

Learning objectives:

- use a thermistor and a light-dependent resistor (LDR)
- investigate the properties of thermistors, LDRs and diodes.

KEY WORDS
....
diode
light-dependent
  resistor (LDR)
sensors
thermistor

LDRs are placed on top of street lights to turn them on when it gets dark.

Control circuits

Control circuits use components to detect changes. These components are called **sensors**.

A **thermistor** (Figure 2.21) is a temperature-dependent resistor. Its resistance changes a lot as temperature changes. At low temperatures its resistance is high. As the temperature increases its resistance decreases.

A **light-dependent resistor (LDR)** is a component whose resistance changes a lot as light intensity changes. When it is light the resistance of the LDR is low. When it is dark the resistance of the LDR is very high.

1. **What property of an LDR changes as the light level changes?**

2. **What happens when the temperature of a thermistor increases?**

Figure 2.21 Thermistor

The properties of thermistors

The resistance of a thermistor decreases as the temperature increases. Each thermistor has its own characteristics, but the resistance of a typical thermistor changes from 2000 Ω at −20 °C to 200 Ω at +20 °C.

A thermistor is made from a semiconductor. A semiconductor is neither a good conductor nor an insulator. When a semiconductor is heated it can conduct more easily. This is because the rise in temperature releases more free electrons to carry the current. The higher the temperature the lower the resistance (Figure 2.22).

The resistance of a thermistor is highest when cold. It can be used to:

- turn on a heater when it gets cold, either in the house or in a greenhouse
- act as a fire alarm
- keep a fish tank from becoming too cold.

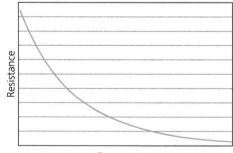

Figure 2.22 Graph of resistance against temperature for a thermistor

3 Explain how you know that a thermistor is not an ohmic conductor.

4 Explain how Figure 2.22 shows that a thermistor's resistance decreases when the temperature increases.

The properties of light-dependent resistors

In bright sunlight an LDR has a resistance of about 100 Ω. When it is dark the resistance of the LDR becomes very large (Figure 2.23). It can be over 10 MΩ (10 000 000 Ω) in the dark.

An LDR connected in series with a battery and an ammeter can be used to make a simple light meter.

When it is bright, the resistance of the LDR is low and the reading on the ammeter is high. When it is dark, the resistance of the LDR is high and the reading on the ammeter is low.

This can be used by a cricket umpire to decide whether it is too dark to carry on playing safely.

5 Describe what happens to the current if you cover and uncover an LDR when a bright light is shining on it.

The properties of a diode

A **diode** is a component that only allows a current to flow in one direction – the direction in which the arrow points in the circuit symbol (Figure 2.24).

The current–potential difference characteristics for a diode (Figure 2.25) can be found using a circuit similar to the one used to draw the I–V graph for a filament lamp.

Most diodes start to conduct when the potential difference across them is about 0.6 V. The steep slope of the graph shows that current passes easily through the diode when it is conducting. With a negative potential difference, very little current flows.

6 Explain what the I–V graph for a diode tells you about the resistance of the diode when the potential difference is negative.

7 Explain why you often need another resistor to protect a diode in a circuit.

DID YOU KNOW?

Some incubators for newborn babies use thermistors that detect a 0.1°C change in temperature.

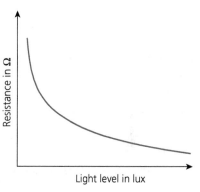

Figure 2.23 Change in resistance with light level in an LDR

REMEMBER!

The resistance of an <u>L</u>DR is <u>L</u>ow in the <u>L</u>ight.

direction of current

Figure 2.24 The arrow on the diode symbol tells you which way the current passes through it

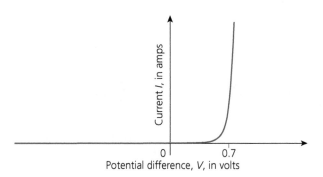

Figure 2.25 I–V graph for a diode

Electricity in the home

Learning objectives:

- recall that the domestic supply in the UK is a.c. at 50 Hz and about 230 V
- describe the main features of live, neutral and earth wires.

KEY WORDS

earth
fuse
live
neutral

The live wire in a mains supply is dangerous, even when the switch is open. Connecting it to earth can cause fire or injury. We need to understand how to use electricity safely.

Domestic electricity supply

A cell or battery has two terminals, positive and negative. The current is d.c., which means that it always passes in the same direction.

Mains electricity differs in two ways (Figure 2.26):

- The current alternates, that is, it changes direction. It has a frequency of 50 Hz.
- It has a much higher potential difference (about 230 V).

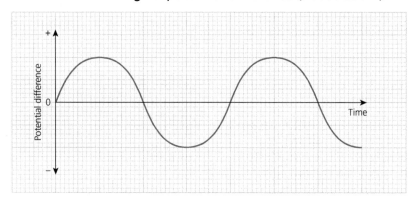

Figure 2.26 The potential difference variation from the mains

① **Describe the difference between a direct and an alternating potential difference.**

② **The mains electricity in the USA has a potential difference of 120V and a frequency of 60Hz. Describe how Figure 2.26 would change for the USA.**

Connecting a three-pin plug

Live, neutral and **earth** wires can be seen in a plug (Figure 2.27). If the appliance is working properly, there should be no current in the earth wire.

The three wires inside the mains cable are colour-coded:

- brown is connected to the live terminal (L)
- blue is connected to the neutral terminal (N)
- green/yellow stripe is connected to the earth terminal (E).

Figure 2.27 What colour is the earth wire?

3. Explain why most electric wires in the home are covered in plastic.

4. Suggest why the three wires have to be very different colours.

Live, neutral and earth wires

Our bodies are at Earth potential – there is no potential difference between our bodies and the Earth. If the casing of a faulty appliance becomes live, the potential difference between it and Earth is 230 V. If a person touches it, there is a complete circuit and current passes through the person's body to Earth. The person receives an electric shock. If the appliance is earthed, it is connected to the Earth or ground (Figure 2.28). Any charge in it flows safely down to the ground through the low-resistance earth wire. This stops a person receiving an electric shock if they touch the live case of a faulty appliance.

Figure 2.28 The arrangement of wires in a metal-cased appliance

Figure 2.29 Double insulation symbol

The mains electricity supply usually comes from a power station. Two wires connect a house to a power station – live and neutral.

- The live wire carries a high potential difference into and around the house. The **fuse** in the plug (F in Figure 2.27) is always connected to the live wire.
- The neutral wire provides a return path to the local substation. The neutral wire is earthed and so is at, or close to, earth potential (0 V). There is no current in the neutral wire until an electrical appliance is connected.
- The earth wire is a safety wire. It is connected to the metal case of an appliance to prevent it becoming charged if touched by a live wire. It provides a low-resistance path to the ground. There is normally no current in it.

5. Explain why a battery-powered torch has two connections to its power supply but a mains lamp has three.

6. Describe the function of the earth wire. Explain whether the current is high or low when there is a fault and how this makes the appliance safe.

DID YOU KNOW?

A double-insulated appliance does not need an earth connection (Figure 2.29). It has a plastic case with no electrical connections to it, so the case cannot become live.

REMEMBER!

A fuse is always connected in the live wire. If the current becomes higher than the fuse's rating, the wire in the fuse will melt and switch off the circuit.

Transmitting electricity

Learning objectives:

- describe how electricity is transmitted using the National Grid
- explain why electrical power is transmitted at high potential differences
- understand the role of transformers.

KEY WORDS

National Grid
transformer

In the USA, the potential difference used is 120 V instead of 230 V as in the UK. This means the wires have to carry about twice the current to make appliances work.

The National Grid

When electricity was first delivered to homes, each town had its own local power station. If the power station broke down, the town did not receive any electric power. Each power station produced electricity at a different potential difference. This meant that electric appliances, such as light bulbs, would only work in one town. If you moved house, you would have to buy new ones.

The **National Grid** is a collection of power cables and **transformers** that connect power stations to factories and houses across Great Britain. Everything is connected up in a grid so that electrical power can be transferred along many different routes. This means that the electrical power in your house can come from lots of different power stations.

Figure 2.30 Power cables connected in the National Grid

1. State an advantage of connecting your house to the National Grid rather than just connecting it up to a local power station.

2. Explain what the words National and Grid mean when referring to the transmission of electrical power.

Changing the potential difference

The potential difference of the domestic UK mains supply is 230 V. This means that there is a potential difference of 230 V between the live wires and the earth wires in a house.

Electrical power is transmitted across the country at 400 000 V. The potential difference between a live power line and the earth is very large.

3. Explain why it would not be a good idea for the potential difference to be 400 000 V in a domestic electricity supply.

An electric current passing through the National Grid's power cables heats up the cables. Energy is being transferred to the thermal energy stores of the surroundings rather than useful energy stores in houses and factories.

Figure 2.31 The National Grid

With a higher current, more energy is wasted and the National Grid becomes less efficient. For the same electrical power, increasing the potential difference reduces the current. So using a high potential difference makes the National Grid more efficient.

4 **Suggest why it is important that energy wasted by the National Grid is minimised.**

5 **How does increasing the potential difference make the National Grid more efficient?**

Transformers

Transformers are devices that can change the potential difference. They are made from two coils of wire with some iron passing between them. Varying the number of turns on each coil changes the potential difference.

Figure 2.32 Step-up transformers are installed close to the power stations

Step-up transformers increase the potential difference. They are connected between the power stations and the National Grid (Figure 2.31). Step-down transformers decrease the potential difference.

6 **State where step-down transformers are connected in the National Grid.**

7 **Transformers have no moving parts. Suggest why this means that they are very efficient.**

8 **Suggest why step-up transformers are placed as close to power stations as possible (Figures 2.31 and 2.32).**

9 **Explain why the birds on the high potential difference power lines in Figure 2.33 are safe.**

Figure 2.33 Birds on power lines

Power and energy transfers

KEY WORD
....
power

Learning objectives:

- describe the energy transfers in different domestic appliances
- describe power as a rate of energy transfer
- calculate the energy transferred.

Much more energy is transferred when you heat a room than when you light a room.

Energy transfers

Electrical devices that we use every day are designed to transfer energy. All electrical appliances transfer energy. But different appliances transfer energy in different ways. They transfer energy from the a.c. mains supply or stores such as batteries to stores such as the kinetic energy store of a motor or the thermal energy store of hot water in a kettle.

1 **State the energy transfers and stores when a kettle is used to heat water.**

Figure 2.34 A hairdryer

Power and energy transferred

Consider a hairdryer (Figure 2.34). The hairdryer receives 1500 J of energy each second from the mains supply. It transfers 1500 J of energy per second from the mains supply to two main energy stores: thermal energy stored in the air and kinetic energy in the moving air.

The **power** is the amount of energy transferred each second. The units are joules per second, or watts (W). As the hairdryer transfers 1500 J each second, its power is 1500 W or 1.5 kW.

2 **An electric drill (Figure 2.35) connected to the a.c. mains transfers 400 J every second.**

  a **Describe how the drill transfers energy and the stores it transfers energy to.**
  b **State the power of the drill.**

Figure 2.35 An electric drill

The amount of energy transferred by an appliance depends on its power and the length of time it is used. We can use this equation to calculate the amount of energy transferred.

Energy transferred (in joules, J) = power (in watts, W) × time (in seconds, s)

$$E \qquad = \qquad P \qquad t$$

Example:

The hairdryer in Figure 2.34 is used for 5 minutes. Calculate the total energy transferred by the hairdryer.

$E = Pt$

$= 1500 \text{ W} \times (5 \times 60) \text{ s}$

$= 450\ 000 \text{ J (or 450 kJ)}$

3 An electric oven with a power rating of 2.5 kW is switched on for 45 minutes.

Calculate the total energy transferred by the oven.

4 A hairdryer transfers 10 000 J of energy from the a.c. mains supply in 5 s. Calculate its power.

Charge and energy transferred

When charge flows in a circuit, electrical work is done. We can calculate the amount of energy transferred by electrical work using the equation:

energy transferred, E = charge flow, Q × potential difference, V

(in joules, J)   (in coulombs, C)   (in volts, V)

$E = QV$

Example:

A charge of 50 C flows through a device with a potential difference across the device of 12 V.

Calculate the total energy transferred.

$E = QV$

$= 50 \text{ C} \times 12 \text{ V}$

$= 600 \text{ J}$

DID YOU KNOW?

Homes and offices are supplied with electricity at 230 V, but small factories have an 11 000 V supply and large factories 33 000 V.

5 A charge of 30 C flows through a TV which is connected to the mains supply of 230 V.

Calculate the total energy transferred.

6 A device transfers a total of 1800 J with a charge of 75 C.

Calculate the potential difference across the device.

7 A home appliance has a power of 1150 W and is switched on for 5 minutes.

a Determine how much charge flows through the appliance.

b Calculate the amount of charge that passes through a 415 V factory appliance when the same amount of energy is transferred.

Calculating power

Learning objectives:

- calculate power
- use power equations to solve problems
- consider power ratings and changes in stored energy.

We use the word power a lot – 'a powerful idea' or 'a powerful piece of music'. However, in science, we use it in a very specific way – as a measure of how quickly energy is transferred. Unlike ideas or music, this power can be calculated.

Calculating power

The **power** transfer in any component is related to the potential difference across it and the current passing through it. We can calculate power using the equation:

power, P = potential difference, V × current, I

(in watts, W)   (in volts, V)   (in amps, A)

$P = VI$

When a current passes through a resistor, such as a kettle element, it has a heating effect. Work is done by the electrons which is transferred to thermal energy in the element.

As $V = IR$, so $P = (IR) \times I = I^2R$

So the power transfer is also given by the equation:

power   =   (current)²   ×   resistance

(in watts, W)   (in amps, A)²   (in ohms, Ω)

$P = I^2R$

① An electric heater takes a current of 4 A when connected to a 230 V supply.

  a Calculate its power.

  b Calculate its resistance.

② A lamp has a power of 36 W when connected to a 12 V supply.

  a Calculate the current through the lamp.

  b Calculate the resistance of the lamp.

Heating up

We can use equations for power and energy transfer to solve problems.

Example: Jo boils a kettle of water to make a cup of tea (Figure 2.36). The kettle has a power rating of 2.4 kW.

The mains supply is 230 V. Calculate:

a the current in the kettle element

b the resistance of the kettle element.

Answer:

a $P = VI$

  Rearrange the equation to make I the subject:

  $I = P \div V$
  $= 2400 \text{ W} \div 230 \text{ V}$
  $= 10.4 \text{ A}$

b $P = I^2R$

  resistance of element, R
  $= P \div I^2$
  $= 2400 \div (10.4)^2$
  $= 22.2 \text{ Ω}$

Figure 2.36 An electric kettle

Example:

An electric kettle connected to the 230 V mains supply draws a current of 10 A. It contains 2 kg of water. Calculate the rise in temperature of the water when the kettle is switched on for 1 minute.

The specific heat capacity of water is 4200 J/kg °C

Power of kettle, $P = VI = 230$ V $\times$ 10 A $= 2300$ W

Energy transferred in 1 minute (60 s) $= Pt$

$= 2300$ W $\times$ 60 s $= 138\ 000$ J

If we assume all this energy is given to the 2 kg of water in the kettle, we can calculate the rise in temperature, $\Delta\theta$. Also, see topic 1.5.

Energy transferred to water $= mc\ \Delta\theta$

$138\ 000$ J $= 2$ kg $\times 4200$ J/kg °C $\times \Delta\theta$

$\Delta\theta = 138\ 000 \div (2 \times 4200) = 16.4$ °C

3 In the example above it was assumed that all the energy transferred by the electric current is transferred into thermal energy of the water. Suggest what other stores the energy might be transferred to.

4 Al has an outdoor swimming pool. It is 15 m long, 10 m wide and 2 m deep. The density of water is 1000 kg/m³.

   a Calculate the mass of water in the pool.

   b Al wants to warm the water from 17 °C to 22 °C.
   Calculate how much energy is transferred.

   c The power of the heater is 2 kW. Calculate how long it takes to raise the temperature of the water.

Changes in stored energy

A more powerful appliance can transfer energy more quickly.

A battery-operated toy car with a power rating of 5 W transfers 5 J every second. Energy is transferred from the store of chemical energy in the battery to the store of kinetic energy in the toy car. Although the total amount of energy is conserved, the decrease in the energy store of the battery does not equal the increase in the kinetic energy store of the car. The toy does work against friction, so the energy that is dissipated is transferred to the thermal energy store of the surroundings.

An electric cooker with a power rating of 2 kW transfers 2 kJ every second. The energy transferred by the electric current increases the thermal energy stored in the food, the saucepan and the surroundings.

5 Describe how different stores of energy change when these appliances are in use.

   a A microwave oven with a power rating of 800 W.

   b A vacuum cleaner with a power rating of 1.6 kW.

Figure 2.37 Energy is transferred between stores as this car moves

Figure 2.38 Cooking involves energy being transferred from one store to another

KEY CONCEPT

What's the difference between potential difference and current?

Learning objectives:

- understand and be able to apply the concepts of current and potential difference
- use these concepts to explain various situations.

When we're exploring and using electrical circuits it's useful to be able to measure things. This enables us to explain why electricity is sometimes really safe and sometimes lethally dangerous. It isn't simply a case of saying that 'there's more electricity in one than the other'.

Potential difference and current

To understand what is going on, we need to think about two quantities, **potential difference** and **current**. These are not the same; understanding the difference will help make sense of a lot of things to do with circuits.

Current is a flow of **charge**. If you set up a simple circuit with battery, wires and a bulb, the bulb lights because there is a current in the circuit. Current is a flow of electrons moving through the wires. Current is measured in amperes (A).

Potential difference is the work done in moving a unit of charge. It is an indication of how much energy is transferred to a unit charge when charge moves between two points, such as between the terminals of a battery. Potential difference is measured in volts (V). Potential difference is often referred to as voltage and both terms can be used, but the appropriate scientific term is potential difference. A 1.5 V battery does not transfer much energy to each unit of charge. In Figure 2.39, if you touch the two terminals you won't feel anything. A 12 V battery (such as that used in a car) transfers more energy to each unit of charge, and the mains electricity supply (230 V) transfers much more energy to each unit charge.

Figure 2.39 A 1.5 V battery

1 Trucks have electrical systems that run on 24 V. How could you produce this using two car batteries?

The difference between potential difference and current

Potential difference is the **energy transferred** per coulomb of charge between two points. Current is the flow of electrical charge. The size of the electric current is the rate of flow of electrical charge.

The bulb in the torch shown in Figure 2.40 is designed to use 4.5 V and carry 750 mA of current. The energy transferred by the current is enough to make the bulb glow, but not so high that the bulb would blow (break).

The electric heater shown in Figure 2.41 is designed to use mains potential difference (230 V) and carry 8 A. Each coulomb of charge is carrying more energy and there is also more electrical charge flowing per second.

When lightning strikes, both the potential difference and current are huge. A thunderstorm can generate a potential difference of up to 500 000 V and the current from lightning can reach thousands of amps.

So why can someone touch the charged dome of a Van de Graaff generator and not be in danger? The potential difference is high (even a small generator designed by schools can produce up to 100 000 V) but the discharge current is tiny, usually only a few milliamps. The high potential difference produces the spectacular effects but the low current means it's safe.

Figure 2.40 A torch

Figure 2.41 An electric heater

2 Is it true to say that the highest potential differences are always the most dangerous?

3 Why do electricians sometimes say, 'It's the volts that jolt but the current that kills.'

Why are potential difference and current important ideas?

Electrical **power** shows how quickly energy is being transferred; it is calculated from potential difference times current: $P = VI$. Increasing either V or I means more power.

Figure 2.42 An electric oven

Resistance shows how hard the current is being opposed. A greater resistance means that there is less current (if the potential difference is the same). Sometimes we want a high current to pass through a component, such as the heating element in an electric oven (Figure 2.42). An electric oven can have a power rating of about 4 kW and operate at up to 30 A. On other occasions we want the current to be very small, such as for a light bulb. The electric oven and light bulb both operate from the mains, but the light bulb has a much higher resistance. Resistance is calculated from potential difference divided by current: $R = \frac{V}{I}$.

4 What is the power rating of a bulb working on the mains potential difference of 230 V and drawing a current of 0.05 A?

5 What would the resistance of this bulb be?

MATHS SKILLS

Using formulae and understanding graphs

Learning objectives:

- recognise how algebraic equations define the relationships between variables
- solve simple algebraic equations by substituting numerical values
- describe relationships expressed in graphical form.

KEY WORDS

algebraic equation
constant of
    proportionality
directly
    proportional
linear relationship

Mathematics helps you to express abstract concepts and ideas in a more concrete and helpful way.

Algebraic equations and relationships

Algebraic equations show relationships between variables, which are represented as letters. For example, the relationship between potential difference (V), current (I) and resistance (R):

$V = IR$, where:

V = potential difference in volts, V

I = current in amps, A

R = resistance in ohms, Ω

From the equation, you can see that if the resistance R is constant, the bigger the potential difference V between two points in a circuit, the bigger the current I. The current through a conductor between two points is **directly proportional** to the potential difference across the two points. This is written mathematically as:

$V \propto I$, where the symbol $\propto$ means 'proportional to'.

1 **a** Calculate the potential difference across a component of resistance 100 Ω when the current is 10 A.

 b Calculate the potential difference across a component of resistance 3 kΩ when the current is 5 A.

2 Show how you would rearrange the equation $V = IR$ to calculate the resistance R of a component.

REMEMBER!

To express very large quantities, use larger multiples or smaller submultiples of the base unit. For example, 1000 Ω is usually written as 1 kΩ, and 2500 Ω can be written as 2.5 kΩ. Here, 'k' means kilo, which is 10^3 or 1000. But remember – in calculations, always use the base unit (in this example, ohms): 1000 Ω and 2500 Ω.

Power and energy transfer in circuits

The equation for power is:

power = potential difference × current

and the algebraic equation is:

$P = VI$, where:

P is power in watts, W

V is potential difference in volts, V

I is current in amps, A

The same relationship can also be expressed by substituting IR for V, as $V = IR$. The expression becomes:

$P = (IR) \times I$

which can be written as $P = I^2R$.

3 Calculate the power of a motor supplied with a potential difference of 230 V and a current of 5 A.

4 How would you rearrange the equation to calculate the current I when you are given the potential difference V and the power P?

5 Calculate the power of a motor supplied with a current of 5 A if the resistance is 1000 Ω.

Describing relationships expressed in graphical form

Figure 2.43 shows that there is a **linear relationship** between potential difference and current through an ohmic conductor at constant temperature – the graph is a straight line. Because the straight line goes through the origin, we can also say that current is directly proportional to the potential difference, $V \propto I$.

We can insert a **constant of proportionality** (k) to describe the relationship between V and I:

$V = kI$

In Figure 2.43, the reciprocal of the slope or gradient of the line (1/gradient) is equal to the constant of proportionality, which in this graph is the resistance in the circuit, R. The straight line indicates that the resistance is constant (it does not change).

The relationship between potential difference and current flowing through a filament lamp is different (Figure 2.44). Initially, at low values of V and I, the gradient is straight, but then it quickly becomes a curve. This indicates that the gradient is changing, which means that the resistance is changing.

The resistance of a filament lamp increases as the temperature of its filament increases. As a result, the current flowing through a filament lamp is not directly proportional to the potential difference across it.

6 What does the slope of a straight-line graph indicate?

7 Looking at a graph, how would you know if the relationship is not directly proportional?

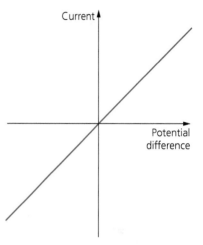

Figure 2.43 I–V graph for an ohmic conductor at constant temperature

---

KEY INFORMATION

Note also that the values of potential difference and current can also be negative, so the line stretches back into the negative quadrant.

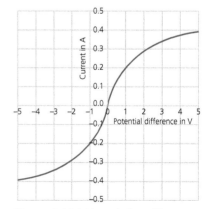

Figure 2.44 I–V graph for a filament lamp

Check your progress

You should be able to:

Recall that an electric current is a flow of electrical charge and is measured in amperes (A) → Remember that charge is measured in coulombs (C) and recall and use the equation $Q = It$ → Explain the concept that current is the rate of flow of charge. Rearrange and apply the equation $Q = It$

Recognise and use electric circuit symbols in circuit diagrams → Draw and recognise series and parallel circuits. Compare the brightness of lamps connected in series and parallel → Recall that the current in a series circuit is always the same and that the total current in a parallel circuit is the sum of the currents through each branch

Recall that the current through a component depends on the resistance of the component and the potential difference across it → Recall and apply the equation $V = IR$ and for series circuits $R_{total} = R_1 + R_2$ → Explain the effect of adding more resistors to series and parallel circuits

Set up a circuit to investigate the relationship between V, I and R for a fixed resistor → Draw I–V graphs for a fixed resistor → Analyse and interpret I–V graphs for a fixed resistor

State the main properties of a diode, a thermistor and a light-dependent resistor (LDR) → Describe the behaviour of a thermistor and LDR in terms of changes to their resistance → Describe applications of diodes, thermistors and LDRs and explain their uses

Draw I–V graphs for filament lamp → Explain the properties of components using I–V graphs → Use I–V graphs to determine whether the characteristics of components are ohmic or non-ohmic

Recall that cells and batteries produce low-voltage direct current → Recall that domestic supply in the UK is 230 V a.c. and 50 Hz → Explain the difference between direct and alternating potential difference

Identify live, neutral and earth wires by their colour-coded insulation → Explain why a live wire may be dangerous even when a switch in the main circuit is open → Explain the dangers of providing any connection between the live wire and earth or our bodies

Recall that the National Grid is a system of cables and transformers linking power stations to consumers → Describe how step-up and step-down transformers change the potential difference in the National Grid → Explain why electrical power is transmitted at high voltages in the National Grid

Understand that everyday electrical appliances bring about energy transfer → Recall and use the equation energy transferred $E = Pt$ → Recall and apply the equation energy transferred $E = QV$

Recall that power is measured in watts (W) and 1 kW = 1000 W → Recall and use the equation $P = V \times I$ → Recall and apply the equation $P = I^2R$

Worked example

The diagram below shows a circuit used to investigate the resistance of a piece of thin wire.

power pack

A

C

thin wire

B

1   **Name the three components in the circuit labelled A, B and C.**

A is an ammeter, B is a voltmeter and C is a thermistor.

> A and B are correct, but C is a variable resistor.

2   **Give the purpose of component C.**

To regulate the temperature.

> Component C is used to change the potential difference across the test material.

3   **The student recorded the potential difference across the thin wire and the current passing through it. She plotted her results on a graph. Explain which variable she should plot on each axis.**

She should plot potential difference on the x-axis and current on the y-axis.

> This is correct, but the explanation has not been given. Potential difference is plotted on the x-axis because it is the independent variable, and current is plotted on the y-axis because it is the dependent variable.

4   **The student increased the potential difference to 12 V. Explain what you think would have happened.**

The wire gets very hot.

> The wire got hot because of the large current passing through it. Large currents transfer lots of energy.

5   **Explain how you would expect the graph to look if the wire had been replaced by a filament lamp.**

The same

> The line would initially be straight but then curve with a shallower gradient as the temperature of the filament increases.

End of chapter questions

Getting started

1 Write the colour of the insulation on the earth wire in a three-pin plug. `1 Mark`

2 Draw the circuit symbol for a voltmeter. `1 Mark`

3 State whether the ammeter should be connected in series or parallel when measuring an electric current. `1 Mark`

4 Describe what we mean by the National Grid. `2 Marks`

5 Calculate the current when 100 C of charge flows in 20 s. `2 Marks`

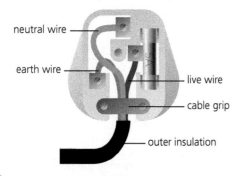

neutral wire
earth wire
live wire
cable grip
outer insulation

6 Describe what is wrong with the wiring in the plug diagram above. `2 Marks`

7 Which of these correctly describes a diode? `1 Mark`

   a It glows brighter if more current flows through it.

   b It only allows current to flow through it in one direction.

   c It reverses the direction in which current flows.

   d It shows how much current is flowing.

Going further

8 Draw the circuit symbol for a thermistor. `1 Mark`

9 A charged object produces an **electric field**. Describe what is meant by an electric field. `2 Marks`

10 Give the frequency and voltage of the domestic mains supply in the UK. `2 Marks`

11 Suggest what will happen to the brightness of the lamps and the current in a series circuit if an additional lamp is added. `2 Marks`

12 A 2 kW kettle is attached to a 230 V mains supply. Calculate the current through the kettle. `2 Marks`

13 Which of these explains why high voltage is used to transmit electricity over long distances? `1 Mark`

   a It increases the current flow.

   b It warms the atmosphere.

   c It reduces the energy losses.

   d The generator produces it at that high voltage.

More challenging

14 What happens to the resistance of an LDR when the light level is decreased? `1 Mark`

15 Why does a person gets an electric shock if they touch the exposed metal of a damaged electrical cable when they are earthed? `1 Mark`

16 Explain how a fuse acts as a safety device. `2 Marks`

17 Draw a circuit diagram of a circuit you could use to find the resistance of a short piece of nichrome wire. `2 Marks`

18 Calculate the current through a lamp of resistance 8 Ω when connected to a 12 V battery. `2 Marks`

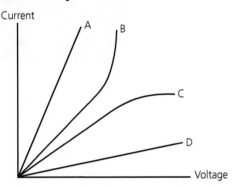

19 The current–voltage characteristics for four components, A–D, were investigated and the results drawn on the graph above. Which component was a filament lamp and which was a high-value resistor? `2 Marks`

Most demanding

20 Give power as an equation in terms of current and resistance. `1 Mark`

21 Explain the effect of adding resistors in series and in parallel on the total resistance of a circuit. `2 Marks`

22 Calculate the energy transferred in 1 minute by a 60 W light bulb connected to a 230 V mains supply. `2 Marks`

23 Four appliances were switched on for various times. Incomplete information about each and how long they were on for is shown in the table below. Which appliance transferred the most energy in the time given and how much energy was transferred? `2 Marks`

Appliance	Power rating (W)	Current (A)	Voltage (V)	Time left on (s)
Kettle	3000	12		20
Microwave	920		230	60
Torch		5	12	200
Food mixer		6	230	50

24 In certain places the National Grid transmits electricity at a potential difference of 44 kV. Evaluate the use of a high potential difference when transmitting electrical power. `3 Marks`

`Total: 40 Marks`

PARTICLE MODEL OF MATTER

IDEAS YOU HAVE MET BEFORE:

ENERGY CHANGES AND TRANSFERS

- The concept of heating and thermal equilibrium
- The temperature difference between two objects leads to energy transfer from the hotter to the cooler one

CHANGES OF STATE

- There are similarities and differences between solids, liquids and gases
- Energy has to be supplied to melt a solid or to boil a liquid

PRESSURE OF A GAS

- Atmospheric pressure decreases as the height above sea level increases.
- In a gas the particles are far apart and move freely.
- Pressure is measured in pascals (Pa). 1 Pa = 1 N/m^2.

IN THIS CHAPTER YOU WILL FIND OUT ABOUT:

WHAT USES ARE MADE OF THE HIGH SPECIFIC HEAT CAPACITY OF WATER?

- The specific heat capacity, c, is the energy required to raise the temperature of 1 kg of an object by 1 °C. The unit for c is J/kg °C.
- Water has a very high specific heat capacity. A lot of energy is needed to heat the water in a radiator or hot water bottle.
- The internal energy of the system is the total amount of kinetic energy and potential energy.

WHAT ARE THE SPECIFIC LATENT HEAT OF VAPORISATION AND THE SPECIFIC LATENT HEAT OF FUSION?

- A particle model is used to show that mass is conserved when changing state.
- The specific latent heat of fusion is the energy required to change 1 kg of an object from a solid to a liquid without a change in temperature.
- The specific latent heat of vaporisation is the energy required to change 1 kg of an object from a liquid to a gas without a change in temperature.

WHAT HAPPENS TO THE PRESSURE OF A GAS WHEN IT IS HEATED, KEEPING THE VOLUME CONSTANT?

- An increase in temperature increases the kinetic energy of the gas particles.
- The particles move faster, colliding more often and with greater force on the walls of their container. The pressure of the gas increases.

Density

Learning objectives

- use the particle model to explain the different states of matter and differences in density
- calculate density.

KEY WORDS

bonds
density
gas
liquid
particle model
solid

Inspectors measure the density of milk and beer to see whether they have been watered down.

States of matter

A **solid** has a fixed size and shape. The particles vibrate to and fro but cannot change their positions. They are held together by strong forces of attraction called **bonds**.

A **liquid** has a fixed size but not a fixed shape. It takes the shape of its container. The bonds between particles are less strong than in a solid. The particles are close together and attract each other. They move around but have no regular pattern.

A **gas** has no fixed size or shape. Its particles move randomly and fill the space available. The particles are well spaced out and virtually free of any attractions. They move quickly, colliding with each other and the walls of their container.

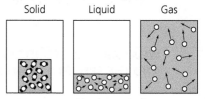

Figure 3.1 **Particle model** of particles in a solid, liquid and gas

1 Which state does each of the following describe?

  a   fixed shape and volume

  b   particles move around freely at high speed

  c   fixed volume but no fixed shape

Differences in density

Some people say 'lead is heavier than iron'. What they mean is that a piece of lead is heavier than a piece of iron of the same volume. **Density** compares the mass of materials with the same volume. Lead is denser than iron.

Densities of different materials

Substance	Density in kg/m³
gold	19 000
iron	8000
lead	11 000
cork	250
mercury	13 600
water	1000
petrol	800
air	1.3

In general, the liquids in the table on page 78 have densities lower than solids but higher than gases, but there are exceptions. The reason for the lower density is that the particles in a liquid are not as tightly packed as the particles of a solid (Figure 3.1).

The particles in a gas are more spread out, unless compressed. Gases have very low densities.

Mercury and cork do not follow the pattern. Mercury is a very dense liquid. Cork is a solid with a low density.

2 **Explain why solids usually have a higher density than liquids and gases.**

3 **Explain why gases have a low density.**

Density

Density is the mass of unit volume of a substance. It is given by the equation:

$$\text{density} = \frac{\text{mass (in kg)}}{\text{volume (in m}^3\text{)}}$$

$$\rho = \frac{m}{V}$$

where mass is in kg, volume in m^3 and density is in kg/m^3.

Density is also given in g/cm^3 where mass is in g and volume is in cm^3.

$1\ g/cm^3 = 1000\ kg/m^3$

Example: Calculate the mass of 3 m^3 of water. The density of water is 1000 kg/m^3.

$$\rho = \frac{m}{V}$$

Rearrange the equation to give:

$$m = \rho V$$

$$= 1000\ kg/m^3 \times 3\ m^3$$

$$= 3000\ kg$$

4 **a** **Calculate the density of a 5400 kg block of aluminium with a volume of 2 m^3.**

  b **Calculate the mass of steel having the same volume as the aluminium block. Density of steel = 7700 kg/m^3.**

  c **Explain why aluminium is used to build aeroplanes rather than steel (Figure 3.2).**

5 **Calculate the mass of air in a room 5 m by 4 m by 3 m. The density of air is 1.3 kg/m^3.**

6 **Suggest why cork floats in water, but iron sinks.**

7 **Explain what happens to the density of air in a bicycle tyre when someone sits on the bicycle.**

8 **Explain why a density of 1 g/cm^3 is the same as a density of 1000 kg/m^3.**

Figure 3.2 Materials used in aeroplanes have to be light but strong

REQUIRED PRACTICAL

To investigate the densities of regular and irregular solid objects and liquids

KEY WORDS

density
resolution
significant figures

Learning objectives:

- interpret observations and data
- use spatial models to solve problems
- plan experiments and devise procedures
- use an appropriate number of significant figures in measurements and calculations.

There is a great story about how scientists learnt how to measure density. Density is worked out knowing the mass of an object and the volume it occupies. Measuring the volume is easy enough if the object is a regular shape such as a cube but what if it was, say, a crown?

This problem was given to Archimedes, a clever man who lived thousands of years ago in Greece. The king had ordered a new crown to be made but suspected the craftsman had mixed a cheaper metal with the gold. Measuring the density would reveal if the gold was pure, but how could the volume be found? Archimedes realised that by carefully immersing the crown in a full can of water, the water that overflowed would have the same volume as the crown.

Apparently he shouted 'Eureka!' ('I have found it!') and the cans used in practical investigations are known as Eureka cans in recognition of this.

These pages are designed ❶ to help you think about aspects of the investigation rather than to guide you through it step by step.

Figure 3.3 Archimedes making his discovery

Measuring the density of a liquid

The **density** of any substance can be worked out using the formula:

$$\text{density} = \frac{\text{mass}}{\text{volume}}$$

If mass is measured in grams (g) and volume in cubic centimetres (cm^3), the density will be in g/cm^3.

Measuring the density of a liquid can be done by pouring the liquid into a measuring cylinder to find its volume and using a balance to find the mass. The results might look rather like those in the table.

Liquid	Mass (g)	Volume (cm^3)
coconut oil	18.5	20
acetone	19.6	25
sea water	51.3	50

Density of different liquids

1. Explain why you would not get the mass of the liquid by just putting the measuring cylinder with the liquid on the balance and recording the reading.

2. Suggest what you could do to get the mass of the liquid.

3. Calculate the density of each of the liquids in the table.

Measuring the density of a regular solid

Solids, of course, have their own shape. If that shape is a regular one, we can calculate the volume by measuring dimensions and then using the correct equation. For example, if the solid was a cuboid, the volume would be length multiplied by width multiplied by height. The mass would be divided by this to get the density.

For example, if a 2.0 cm cube of soft rubber had a mass of 8.82 g, its volume would be 2.0 cm × 2.0 cm × 2.0 cm, which is 8.0 cm^3, and the density would be 8.82 g / 8.0 cm^3, which is 1.1 g/cm^3.

The answer can only have the same number of **significant figures** as the measurement with the least number of significant figures (in this case 8.0 – it has two significant figures).

Material	Mass (g)	Length (cm)	Width (cm)	Height (cm)
cork	3	2.0	2.0	3.0
oak	17	2.0	3.0	4.0
tin	364	2.5	2.5	8.0

Quantities of three materials

4. Look at the table. What is the volume of the piece of cork?

5. Determine the density.

6. What are the densities of the other two materials?

7. Explain why it is incorrect to use 0.70833333 g/cm^3 as the answer for the density of oak.

Measuring the density of an irregular solid

This is, of course, the problem that Archimedes was trying to solve, and his solution (apparently inspired by getting into a bath tub that was too full) was to use the idea of displacement. The solid will displace the same volume of water as its own volume. If there's room in the container, it rises. If not, it overflows.

Imagine trying to see whether a gold necklace was pure. Knowing that the density of gold is 19.29 g/cm^3, being able to dangle the necklace on a thread and having a glass of water full to the brim, you could carry out a simple experiment.

8. What procedure would you follow?

9. What measurements would you need to take?

10. What calculation would you then perform?

11. Why would this experiment not be very accurate?

Figure 3.4 How could you find out if this is pure gold?

Changes of state

Learning objectives

- describe how, when substances change state, mass is conserved
- describe energy transfer in changes of state
- explain changes of state in terms of particles.

When a liquid boils, the energy transferred to the liquid gives the molecules enough energy to break away from the surface.

Conservation of mass

When substances change state, mass is **conserved.** If you start with 1 kg of ice and melt it, you will have 1 kg of water. Nothing has been added or removed. The process is reversible. If you freeze the 1 kg of water you will end up with 1 kg of ice again.

This is an important idea as it shows that when the state of something is altered, no material has gone away or has been added. There are the same number of particles of the substance there. It is the arrangement that has been changed, not the amount. It also shows that material has the same mass, even though it might have changed state. Boiling 1 kg of water will produce 1 kg of steam.

DID YOU KNOW?

Dry ice is frozen carbon dioxide which turns directly from a solid to a gas at a temperature of −78.5 °C. The fog you see is a mixture of cold carbon dioxide gas and cold, humid air, created as the dry ice sublimates (Figure 3.5).

1 What type of change occurs when a substance changes from liquid to solid?

Changing state

Changes of state occur when substances change from one state to another. The processes of changing from one state to another are:

- **melting:** changing from solid to liquid
- **freezing:** changing from liquid to solid
- **boiling:** changing from liquid to gas at the boiling point
- **evaporating:** changing from liquid to gas when the temperature of the liquid is lower than the boiling point
- **condensing:** changing from gas to liquid
- **sublimating:** changing from solid to gas without going through the liquid state.

Changes of state are physical changes. Unlike a chemical change, the change does not produce a new substance. If the change is reversed, the substance recovers its original properties.

2 Suggest how you could prove that mass is conserved when ice melts.

Figure 3.5 Dry ice sublimates

3. Give an example of a change of state. Specify the material involved.

4. We often say 'it is freezing' when the temperature is cold outside. Explain why this is not an accurate statement.

Explaining changes of state

When a substance changes state, energy is transferred to change the arrangement of the particles.

When a substance melts, such as ice changing to water, energy must be transferred to the ice to change its state from solid to liquid.

In the solid state, such as ice, the particles are close-packed with strong bonds between them. Energy must be provided to weaken these bonds and allow the particles to move more freely in the liquid state (water). To change into a gas (steam) a lot of energy must be provided to break the bonds between the particles and allow the gas particles to spread out, filling the available space.

When a liquid cools down, the particles decrease their kinetic energy, allowing them to come closer together and form bonds (freezing). Energy is released to the surroundings. Energy is also released when a gas condenses to form a liquid.

Evaporation produces cooling (Figure 3.6). As a liquid warms up, the average speed of the molecules in it increases. But not all the molecules in the liquid will be travelling at the same speed (Figure 3.7). It is the faster molecules with more energy which escape from the surface of the liquid, leaving behind the slower molecules with less energy (Figure 3.8).

5. Explain why you hang out washing rather than leaving it in a pile to dry.

6. Explain why evaporation produces cooling.

7. Suggest why being burnt by steam is worse than being burnt by hot water.

8. Explain how sweating can help to reduce body temperature.

Figure 3.6 The sand in this pot is wet. Evaporation transfers thermal energy away from the inner pot and keeps the food cool

Figure 3.7 The molecules in a liquid do not all travel at the same speed

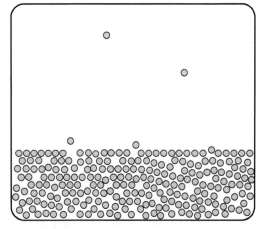

Figure 3.8 Evaporation from the surface of a liquid

Internal energy

Learning objectives

- describe the particle model of matter
- understand what is meant by the internal energy of a system
- describe the effect of heating on the energy stored within a system.

KEY WORDS

internal energy
particle model

In air, the molecules of the gases hitting your face have an average speed of about 1600 km/h.

Particle model

Everything is made of small particles (atoms or molecules). This is the **particle model**.

The sizes of these particles are different for different materials. The particles are very hard. They cannot be squashed or stretched. But the distance between them can change. The particles are always moving. The higher the temperature, the faster they move.

At the same temperature, all particles have the same average kinetic energy. This means that heavy particles move slowly and light particles move quickly.

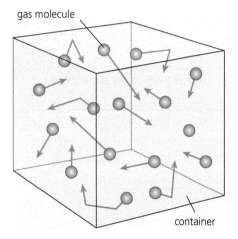

gas molecule

container

Figure 3.9 The gas particles in this container all have the same average kinetic energy

1. Explain why the particles in solids, liquids and gases have kinetic energy.

2. Compare the speeds of heavy particles and light particles when they are at the same temperature.

Internal energy

The particles in solids, liquids and gases have kinetic energy because they are always moving. They also have potential energy because their motion keeps them separated.

This opposes the forces trying to pull them together. The particles in gases have the most potential energy because they are furthest apart. The **internal energy** of a system is the total kinetic energy and potential energy of all the particles in the system.

3 Explain why the particles in solids, liquids and gases have potential energy.

4 What is the internal energy of an object?

Changes in internal energy

The hotter a material is, the faster its particles move and the more kinetic energy they have. If a hot object is in contact with a cold one, energy is transferred between the two objects. When both are at the same temperature there is no further exchange of energy between them.

You can cool a glass of water by adding ice cubes to it. The faster moving molecules of water transfer energy to the ice. The internal energy store of the water decreases and the water cools down. The internal energy store of the ice increases and the ice melts.

Heating changes the energy stored in a system. It increases the energy of the particles that make it up. The increase of the internal energy store can have two effects.

When ice melts the internal energy store of the ice increases. When there is a change of state there is no change in temperature. The increase in internal energy is used to weaken the bonds, for instance, changing a solid to a liquid.

If we carry on heating the melted ice, the internal energy store increases further, causing the temperature of the water to increase.

5 What happens to the internal energy of a system when it is heated?

6 A glass jar containing water is moved from inside a house to outside the house, where the temperature is –2 °C. Describe what happens to the internal energy of the glass and water.

7 Water can exist both in the liquid and the gaseous state at 100 °C.

  a Compare the amount of internal energy in steam at 100 °C with that of water at the same temperature.

  b Justify why using steam to power engines is more useful than using hot water.

DID YOU KNOW?

Water is unusual in that it expands as it freezes. It is most dense at 4 °C (Figure 3.10). When a pond freezes over, there is a layer of denser water at the bottom where fish can survive.

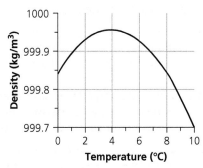

Figure 3.10 Water is most dense at 4 °C

Specific heat capacity

KEY WORDS

specific heat capacity

Learning objectives:

- describe the effect of increasing the temperature of a system in terms of particles
- state the factors that are affected by an increase in temperature of a substance
- explain specific heat capacity.

A cup of water at 50 °C and a bath of water at 50 °C have the same temperature but the bath of water has a greater store of thermal energy.

Heating up

When a liquid is heated, the particles move faster. They gain kinetic energy and the temperature rises. The particles are close together and attract each other strongly. Their motion opposes the forces of attraction and keeps them separated. As they are moving faster, they also separate a bit more and gain potential energy. So the liquid has more kinetic energy and more potential energy. Its internal energy has increased.

1 Describe two changes that happen to the particles when a liquid is heated.

Increasing temperature

When a liquid is heated, its temperature increases. The temperature rise depends on:

- the mass of liquid heated
- the liquid being heated
- the energy input to the system.

2 Dan is heating a large saucepan of water to boiling point. Explain why more energy is needed to do this than to heat a cup of water to the same temperature.

3 Milk does not need as much energy to raise its temperature by 10 °C as the same mass of water. Will hot milk give out less energy than the same amount of water at the same temperature when it cools down? Explain your answer.

Specific heat capacity

When an object is heated, energy is transferred and its temperature rises. The amount of energy needed to change the temperature of an object depends on the material the object is made from. This property is called the **specific heat capacity**.

MAKING LINKS

Chapter 1 has already introduced the idea of calculating the amount of energy in a system's energy store as its temperature changes. This is the same concept, but now we are looking at temperature change within the wider picture of internal energy and energy transfers.

Remember from topic 1.5 that the specific heat capacity of a substance is the energy needed to raise the temperature of 1 kg of the substance by 1 °C. It is given by the equation:

change in thermal energy = mass × specific heat capacity
× temperature change

$$\Delta E = mc\,\Delta\theta$$

where ΔE is in J, m is in kg, c is in J/kg°C and $\Delta\theta$ is in °C.

Example: A change in thermal energy of 18 kJ of energy was supplied to a 2 kg steel block and raised its temperature from 20 °C to 40 °C. Calculate the specific heat capacity of steel.

$$\Delta E = mc\,\Delta\theta$$

$$\Delta E = 18\,\text{kJ} = 18\,000\,\text{J}$$

$$m = 2\,\text{kg}$$

$$\Delta\theta = (40 - 20) = 20\,°C$$

Specific heat capacity, $c = \Delta E \div (m\,\Delta\theta)$

$$= 18\,000\,\text{J} \div (2\,\text{kg} \times 20\,°C) = 450\,\text{J/kg°C}$$

Figure 3.11 A domestic radiator contains water which is heated by a boiler

Material	Specific heat capacity in J/kg°C
water	4200
ice	2100
aluminium	880
copper	380

Specific heat capacities of some materials

Water has a very high specific heat capacity. This means that, for a given mass, it absorbs a lot of energy when its temperature increases. It also gives out a lot of energy when it cools down.

4 Calculate how much energy is needed to heat 100 g of water from 10 °C to 40 °C.

5 Water has a very high specific heat capacity. Describe a practical use of this.

6 A 2 kW electric heater supplies energy to a 0.5 kg copper kettle containing 1 kg of water.
   a Calculate the time taken to raise the temperature by 10 °C.
   b What have you assumed in doing this calculation?

7 Suggest why copper saucepans are sometimes used for cooking.

DID YOU KNOW?

Water needs lots of energy to heat it up and gives out lots of energy when it cools down. This is why a hot-water bottle is so effective in warming a bed. An equal mass of mercury would store only 1/30th as much energy, but would take only $\frac{1}{13}$th of the volume!

KEY INFORMATION

Power (in watts, W) = energy (in J) / time (in s).

COMMON MISCONCEPTION

Do not confuse thermal energy transfer and temperature. Temperature is how hot an object is. A change in thermal energy does not always produce a change in temperature.

Latent heat

Learning objectives

- explain what is meant by latent heat
- describe how when a change of state occurs it changes the energy stored but not the temperature
- perform calculations involving specific latent heat.

The latent heat of water is responsible for tornados, hurricanes and the fact that snow takes a long time to melt.

Latent heat

When you heat a solid, such as a lump of ice, its temperature rises until it starts to change to a liquid. At its melting point, the temperature stays the same until all the ice has melted (Figure 3.12).

The temperature of the liquid then rises until it starts to change into a gas. At its boiling point, the temperature stays the same until all the liquid has turned into a gas. The temperature then starts to rise again.

Latent heat is the energy needed for a substance to change the state of a substance without a change in temperature.

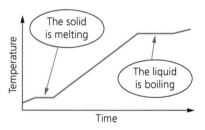

Figure 3.12 Temperature–time graph for heating a substance

1. **Describe what is happening when the graph flattens out.**

2. **Energy is needed to turn water into steam. Suggest how the particle model explains this.**

Changes of state

The amount of energy needed to change the state of a sample of a substance, without a change in temperature, depends on the mass of the sample and the type of substance. All substances have a property called **specific latent heat**.

The specific latent heat is the amount of energy needed to change the state of 1 kg of a substance without a change in temperature. Its unit is J/kg. It is given by the equation:

$E = mL$

where E = energy for a change of state in J

m = mass in kg

L = specific latent heat in J/kg.

Specific latent heat of fusion refers to a change of state from solid to liquid. **Specific latent heat of vaporisation** refers to a change of state from liquid to vapour.

Some specific latent heats

Change of state	Specific latent heat in J/kg
ice to water	340 000
water to steam	2 260 000

The specific latent heat of vaporisation is much greater than the specific latent heat of fusion. Most of this energy is used to separate the particles so they can form a gas, but some is required to push back the atmosphere as the gas forms.

3 Explain why there is no change in temperature when a block of ice melts.

4 Why is the specific latent heat of vaporisation much greater than the specific latent heat of fusion?

Latent heat calculations

(In these calculations use the specific heat capacities given in the table above.)

Many calculations of specific and latent heat require you to find the energy needed to change the state as well as the temperature of an object. This involves using both specific heat capacity and latent heat equations:

$$\Delta E = mc\Delta\theta \qquad E = mL$$

5 Calculate the energy transferred from a glass of water to just melt 100 g of ice cubes at 0 °C.

6 a Calculate the total energy transferred when 200 g of ice cubes at 0 °C are changed to steam at 100 °C. (Hint: Use the equation for specific heat capacity as well as the equation for specific latent heat.)

   b Sketch and label a temperature–time graph for this transfer.

7 A block of ice at −2 °C was heated. After 7304 J of energy were transferred to the ice, the ice had melted and reached a temperature of 5 °C. Calculate the mass of the ice.

DID YOU KNOW?

A jet of steam releases latent heat when it condenses (changes to a liquid). This can be used to heat drinks quickly (Figure 3.13).

Figure 3.13 Machines in cafes use steam to heat milk quickly

COMMON MISCONCEPTION

Heating does not always involve a change in temperature. When a change of state occurs, the energy supplied changes the energy stored (internal energy) but not the temperature.

Particle motion in gases

Learning objectives:

- relate the temperature of a gas to the average kinetic energy of the particles
- explain how a gas has a pressure
- explain that changing the temperature of a gas held at constant volume changes its pressure.

KEY WORDS

gas pressure
randomly

Inside a rocket some of the fast-moving gas particles colliding with the walls create a force. The fast-moving gas particles moving out of the bottom of the rocket propel the rocket upwards, like in Figure 3.14.

Temperature and pressure of a gas

The particles in a gas move around **randomly**. These particles have kinetic energy. They move about freely at high speed.

The higher the temperature, the faster the particles move and the more kinetic energy they have. The temperature of a gas is related to the average kinetic energy of the molecules. As the temperature increases, the particles move faster. They gain more kinetic energy.

Figure 3.14 The Soyuz MS-01 spacecraft launch

1 **What happens to the molecules of a gas when the gas is heated?**

2 **How does the particle model explain temperature?**

The molecules of a gas collide with each other as well as with the walls of their container (Figure 3.15). When they hit a wall there is a force on the wall. Pressure is equal to the force on the wall divided by the area over which the force acts. The total force exerted by all the molecules inside the container that strike a unit area of the wall is the **gas pressure**.

3 **Describe, in terms of particles, how a gas exerts a pressure.**

4 **Suggest why the pressure inside a bicycle tyre increases when you pump more air into it.**

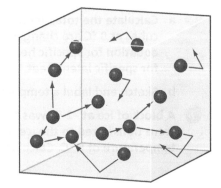

Figure 3.15 When gas particles hit a wall of their container there is a force on the wall. This force is what causes the pressure of the gas.

Changing the temperature of a gas

Air is sealed in a container (Figure 3.16). If we keep the mass and volume of the air constant, an increase in the temperature will increase the pressure of the gas.

Figure 3.16 Heating air in a sealed container

There are the same number of particles because the container is sealed, and there is the same mass of gas. As the container is sealed the volume of gas is also constant. As the particles have more energy, they move faster, hitting the walls more often and with greater force, increasing the pressure.

5 How do we know that the mass of gas is constant?

6 Explain, using ideas about energy, why the pressure of gas increases if it gets hotter.

REMEMBER!

Gas particles collide with each other and with the walls of their container, but only collisions of particles with the walls contribute to the pressure of a gas.

KEY CONCEPT

Particle model and changes of state

Learning objectives:

- use the particle model to explain states of matter
- use ideas about energy and bonds to explain changes of state
- explain the relationship between temperature and energy.

KEY WORDS

bonds
fusion
internal energy
latent heat
matter
particle model
vaporisation

Everything on Earth is made of matter, but that matter isn't always the same. Matter can exist in three different states: solid, liquid, gas. The particle model of matter helps us understand the differences between those states.

Solid   Liquid   Gas

Add thermal energy

Figure 3.17 States of matter

Solids, liquids and gases

All **matter** is made up of atoms and molecules, but it is the way these atoms and molecules are held together that determines whether a substance is solid, liquid or gas. In a solid the atoms are held tightly together forming strong regular shapes. In a liquid the atoms are held much more loosely, which is why liquids can flow. In a gas the atoms and molecules are free to move about on their own.

What determines the state of matter is the strength with which the atoms and molecules are held together by their **bonds**.

All atoms also vibrate. Even in a solid, where the atoms are held together in a tight structure, every single atom is moving backwards and forwards next to its neighbour.

To get a solid to become a liquid, energy has to be added to the substance (Figure 3.17). Energy increases the vibrations of the atoms. As the vibrations increase, the bonds that hold the atoms are stretched and the atoms are pushed further apart from each other (Figure 3.18).

Adding more energy to the solid increases the vibrations even more until there comes a point where the bonds can no longer hold together. Many bonds break and the atoms are free to move – the solid has become a liquid. Adding yet more energy breaks all the bonds completely and the atoms escape into the atmosphere. The liquid becomes a gas.

Cold

Hot

Figure 3.18 Vibrations in hot and cold solids

1. State the difference between a solid and a liquid.

2. Explain why solids expand as they are heated.

3. Explain what happens to the internal energy of a solid as it is heated.

Change of state and change in temperature

The state of matter depends on the amount of energy inside it. Heating a substance increases the amount of **internal energy** and this either raises the temperature of the system or produces a change of state. The process also works in reverse. If you take energy out of the substance it will either decrease the temperature of the system or change state from a gas back to a liquid or from a liquid to a solid (Figure 3.19).

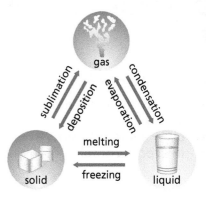

Figure 3.19 Changing between states of matter

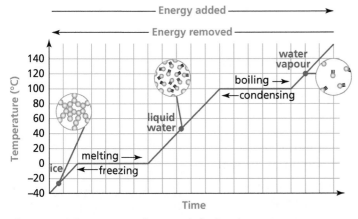

Figure 3.20 Temperature–time graph for heating water

When you heat a substance there are stages where you just get a rise in temperature and then stages where you get a change of state.

Follow the steps on the graph in Figure 3.20 which shows the three states of water: ice, liquid and water vapour.

Start with ice at –40 °C. As you heat the ice it gets warmer, but is still a solid. The slope of the graph shows the increasing temperature. Then at 0 °C energy is still being put into the ice, but there is no increase in temperature. The graph now shows a level straight line. This is where the energy is being absorbed by the substance to change it into the next state: liquid water. The amount of energy needed to change the state from solid to liquid is called the specific **latent heat** of **fusion**.

Once the ice has melted into water the temperature begins to rise again. The line on the graph is sloping upwards. When the temperature reaches 100 °C we get the second change in state. Energy is absorbed but there is no rise in temperature. The amount of energy required to change the state from liquid to water vapour is called the specific latent heat of **vaporisation**.

④ **Ethanol freezes at –114 °C and boils at 78 °C. Draw a temperature–time diagram for heating ethanol from –120 °C to 100 °C.**

⑤ **Explain what a line sloping down from left to right on a temperature–time graph means.**

MATHS SKILLS

Drawing and interpreting graphs

Learning objectives:

- plot a graph of temperature against time, choosing a suitable scale
- draw a line of best fit (which may be a curve)
- interpret a graph, of temperature against time.

A graph of temperature against time for a substance can show quite a lot about what is going on. If we know how to read a graph, we can work out what that might be.

Drawing a graph

To set out the axes for a graph, the **range** of values has to be identified. The maximum and minimum values should be known.

The number of units per square on the graph paper should be chosen with care. It's essential to select a **scale** that is easy to interpret. One that uses five large squares for 100 units is much easier to interpret than a scale that has, say, three large squares for 100 units. Sometimes it is better to use a smaller scale (e.g. two large squares for 100 units) and have a scale that is easier to interpret than to try to fill the page.

KEY INFORMATION
....
Suitable scales are 1, 2, 5 and 10 (or multiples of 10) units per square.

A group of students conducted an experiment where they recorded the temperature of stearic acid every minute as it cooled down from 95 °C. The results are shown in the table.

Results from experiment on cooling stearic acid

Time (min)	Temperature (°C)	Time (min)	Temperature in (°C)
0:00	95.0	8:00	68.1
1:00	90.9	9:00	68.1
2:00	86.3	10:00	67.9
3:00	80.7	11:00	67.3
4:00	73.0	12:00	64.2
5:00	68.1	13:00	58.4
6:00	68.0	14:00	48.2
7:00	68.1	15:00	35.9
		16:00	25.0

MATHS
....
Some graphs will have a **line or curve of best fit**. A line of best fit goes roughly through the centre of all the plotted points. It does not go through all the points. The line of best fit could be a curve. If all the points fall close to the line (or curve), it suggests that the variables are closely linked. Look at the points carefully and see what would fit them well.

1. What are the maximum and minimum values that need to be plotted?

2. Draw and label axes for plotting this data set.

3. Plot the points and draw a line of best fit.

4. Describe the features of the line of best fit.

Interpreting a graph

The graph in Figure 3.21 shows temperature against time for heating a lump of paraffin wax. The temperature was recorded using a data logger. The rate at which energy was supplied to the wax stayed constant. The graph shows that the temperature of the solid wax increased until about 7 minutes and then stopped rising. It then started rising again at about 15 minutes.

Figure 3.21 Graph of temperature against time for heating paraffin wax

5 **Why is there a curve and not a straight line when the energy is being supplied at a constant rate?**

6 **What is happening between 7 and 15 minutes?**

7 **What is the melting point of paraffin wax?**

Understanding the shape of the line

This graph shows a really important point. While the wax is melting, energy is being supplied but the temperature isn't changing. The energy being supplied is being used to change the state of the wax and while this is happening the temperature stays the same.

Now look at the graph you drew of temperature against time for stearic acid. This was cooling down, but there are similarities.

8 **Suggest an explanation for the shape of the graph.**

9 **What is happening between about 5 and 9 minutes?**

10 **What is the melting point of stearic acid?**

11 **Describe the shape of the graph with reference to what is happening with regard to the internal energy of the stearic acid.**

12 **Label the regions of the graphs for stearic acid and paraffin wax to show what is happening to the kinetic energy and the potential energy of the particles.**

13 **Explain how the shape of the graph in Figure 3.21 would change for a substance that had the same melting point but had a smaller specific heat capacity and a larger latent heat of fusion. Assume everything else (such as the mass of the substance and the heater) remains the same.**

Check your progress

You should be able to:

Use density = mass/volume to calculate density
→
Use particle diagrams to communicate ideas about relative densities of different states
Use the density equation to calculate mass and volume
→
Link the particle model for solids, liquids and gases with density values in terms of the arrangements of the atoms or molecules

Describe changes of state as physical changes
→
State that mass is conserved when substances change state
Explain that changes of state are physical, not chemical, changes because the material recovers its original properties if the change is reversed
→
Explain how changes of state conserve mass

Describe how heating raises the temperature of a system
→
Describe that heating raises the temperature or changes the state of a system but not at the same time
→
Explain that internal energy is the total kinetic energy and potential energy of all the particles that make up a system

Describe the effect of an increase in temperature on the motion of the particles
→
Use the specific heat capacity equation to calculate the energy required to change the temperature of a certain mass of a substance
→
Use the specific heat capacity equation to calculate mass, specific heat capacity or temperature change

State that when an object changes state there is no change in temperature
→
Describe the latent heats of fusion and of vaporisation
Use the equation $E = mL$
→
Use the particle model to explain why the latent heat of vaporisation is much larger than the latent heat of fusion

State that in the particle model the higher the temperature the faster the molecules move
→
Use the particle model to explain the effect on temperature of increasing the pressure of a gas at constant volume
→
Describe that the temperature of a gas is related to the average kinetic energy of the molecules

Worked example

1 **Alex was heating a beaker of water by the rays of a sunlamp. The energy transferred was 21 000 J. The time taken for the water to increase by 10 °C was 6000 seconds. Calculate the power supplied by the sunlamp.**

3.5

This is the correct numerical answer, but

a You have not given any units to the number. Always give the unit to the quantity.

b You have not shown any working. When working out a calculation write the equation and show step by step how you do the calculation.

2 **Explain how raising the temperature of a gas, keeping the volume constant, increases the pressure exerted by the gas.**

The high temperature makes the molecules vibrate faster so there is a stronger force on the side of the container.

You are on the right lines. It is the force of the molecues hitting the side of the container that creates the pressure. With a gas, the molecules are no longer vibrating but they are free to move around at speed. Heating increases their kinetic energy.

3 **What does it mean to say that the changes of state are reversible?**

It means that the changes go both ways.

Correct, but you should give an example as well. Give an example of a change that goes both ways, e.g. water turns to steam and steam turns back to water.

4 **Explain what heating does to the energy stores of a system.**

Heating raises the total energy inside the system.

Yes it does, but again you should aim to give more specific information about the system. You need to mention the energy transfers that have taken place.

End of chapter questions

Getting started

1 Label these diagrams as solid, liquid and gas. `1 Mark`

2 Describe how these models represent a solid, liquid and gas. `2 Marks`

3 Give the name of the energy needed to change the state of a substance. `1 Mark`

4 Calculate the amount of energy needed to change the temperature of 2 kg of water by 10 °C using the equation $\Delta E = mc\Delta\theta$. (The specific heat capacity of water is 4200 J/kg°C.) `1 Mark`

5 Give the state that a gas turns into when it condenses. `1 Mark`

6 Write the relationship between mass, volume and density. `1 Mark`

7 An object has a mass of 100 g and a volume of 25 cm³. Calculate its density. `1 Mark`

8 The specific latent heat of fusion of water = 340 000 J/kg. Explain carefully what this means. `2 Marks`

Going further

9 Write the name for the type of energy that equals the total kinetic and potential energies of the particles in a substance. `1 Mark`

10 Water in an ice cube tray is put into a freezer. Explain what happens to the energy stored inside the system. `3 Marks`

11 2.0 kg of water was placed in a saucepan and heated to 100 °C.

The water then completely boiled into steam.

Here is some data about water and steam:

density of water = 1000 kg/m³

density of steam = 0.59 kg/m³

latent heat of vaporisation of water = 2 260 000 J/kg.

a Explain why the density of steam is much smaller than the density of the water. `1 Mark`

b Calculate the volume of the steam that was produced once all of the water had boiled. `2 Marks`

c The pressure of the steam was 1.5 × 10⁵ Pa. As the steam rises up, the pressure reduces to 1.0 × 10⁵ Pa. Use your answer to part b to calculate the new volume of the steam. `1 Mark`

d Use the equation $E = mL$ to calculate how much energy was needed to boil the water into steam at 100 °C. `2 Marks`

More challenging

12 When a substance changes state, one energy store increases and the other decreases.

   a What quantity that can be measured of the substance is always conserved? `1 Mark`

   b State what the two possible results are when a substance is heated. `1 Mark`

13 Explain how raising the temperature of a gas, keeping the volume constant, increases the pressure exerted by the gas. `2 Marks`

14 4.50 g of water was frozen to ice at 0 °C. How much energy had to be taken out of the water? The specific latent heat of fusion of ice is 340 000 J/kg. `2 Marks`

15 50 g of steam condensed to water at 100 °C. How much energy was released? Specific latent heat of vaporisation of water = 2260 kJ/kg. `2 Marks`

16 Using the particle model, explain how a gas exerts pressure on the container holding the gas. `2 Marks`

Most demanding

17 A 2 kg block of copper is given 8.88 kJ of energy to raise its temperature by 10 °C. Calculate the specific heat capacity of copper. `2 Marks`

18 Explain why a liquid cools down when it evaporates. `2 Marks`

19 A student investigated the density of cubes of different materials.

The student used a ruler to measure the length of the cube's sides at several different points, and a balance to measure the mass of each cube.

The student's results are shown in the table.

	Length of side (cm)				Mass (g)
	1	2	3	Mean	
aluminium	2.5	2.5	2.4	2.47	44.5
wood	2.4	2.5	2.4	2.43	12.1

   a Calculate the uncertainty in the student's measurements of the length of the sides of the aluminium cube. `2 Marks`

   b Calculate the density of the aluminium cube. Give your answer to 2 significant figures. `3 Marks`

   c The student's value for the density of aluminium was greater than the accepted value. Suggest why. `1 Mark`

`Total: 40 Marks`

ATOMIC STRUCTURE

IDEAS YOU HAVE MET BEFORE:

AN ATOM CONTAINS PROTONS, NEUTRONS AND ELECTRONS

- The atoms of an element have the same number of protons.
- Atoms of different elements have different masses.
- All the atoms of an element have the same chemical properties.
- Atoms are unchanged in a chemical reaction.

Group																		0
1	**2**												**3**	**4**	**5**	**6**	**7**	$^4_2$He helium
			$^1_1$H hydrogen															
$^7_3$Li lithium	$^9_4$Be beryllium												$^{11}_5$B boron	$^{12}_6$C carbon	$^{14}_7$N nitrogen	$^{16}_8$O oxygen	$^{19}_9$F fluorine	$^{20}_{10}$Ne neon
$^{23}_{11}$Na sodium	$^{24}_{12}$Mg magnesium												$^{27}_{13}$Al aluminium	$^{28}_{14}$Si silicon	$^{31}_{15}$P phosphorus	$^{32}_{16}$S sulfur	$^{35}_{17}$Cl chlorine	$^{40}_{18}$Ar argon
$^{39}_{19}$K potassium	$^{40}_{20}$Ca calcium	$^{45}_{21}$Sc scandium	$^{48}_{22}$Ti titanium	$^{51}_{23}$V vanadium	$^{52}_{24}$Cr chromium	$^{55}_{25}$Mn manganese	$^{56}_{26}$Fe iron	$^{59}_{27}$Co cobalt	$^{59}_{28}$Ni nickel	$^{64}_{29}$Cu copper	$^{65}_{30}$Zn zinc	$^{70}_{31}$Ga gallium	$^{73}_{32}$Ge germanium	$^{75}_{33}$As arsenic	$^{79}_{34}$Se selenium	$^{80}_{35}$Br bromine	$^{84}_{36}$Kr krypton
$^{85}_{37}$Rb rubidium	$^{88}_{38}$Sr strontium	$^{89}_{39}$Y yttrium	$^{91}_{40}$Zr zirconium	$^{93}_{41}$Nb niobium	$^{96}_{42}$Mo molybdenum	$^{99}_{43}$Tc technetium	$^{101}_{44}$Ru ruthenium	$^{103}_{45}$Rh rhodium	$^{106}_{46}$Pd palladium	$^{108}_{47}$Ag silver	$^{112}_{48}$Cd cadmium	$^{115}_{49}$In indium	$^{119}_{50}$Sn tin	$^{122}_{51}$Sb antimony	$^{128}_{52}$Te tellurium	$^{127}_{53}$I iodine	$^{131}_{54}$Xe xenon
$^{133}_{55}$Cs caesium	$^{137}_{56}$Ba barium	$^{139}_{57}$La lanthanum	$^{178}_{72}$Hf hafnium	$^{181}_{73}$Ta tantalum	$^{184}_{74}$W tungsten	$^{186}_{75}$Re rhenium	$^{190}_{76}$Os osmium	$^{192}_{77}$Ir iridium	$^{195}_{78}$Pt platinum	$^{197}_{79}$Au gold	$^{201}_{80}$Hg mercury	$^{204}_{81}$Tl thallium	$^{207}_{82}$Pb lead	$^{209}_{83}$Bi bismuth	$^{210}_{84}$Po polonium	$^{210}_{85}$At astatine	$^{222}_{86}$Rn radon
$^{223}_{87}$Fr francium	$^{226}_{88}$Ra radium	$^{227}_{89}$Ac actinium															

ATOMS CANNOT BE CREATED OR DESTROYED

- Atoms obey the law of conservation of matter.
- Atoms cannot be created in a chemical reaction.
- Atoms cannot be destroyed in a chemical reaction.

| ○ sulfur | ● oxygen |

CHEMICAL EQUATIONS SUMMARISE WHAT HAPPENS IN A CHEMICAL REACTION

- The atom is the smallest particle that can take part in a chemical reaction.
- Each element is represented by a symbol of up to 3 letters, starting with a capital letter.
- There is always the same number of atoms before and after a chemical reaction.
- There is always the same number of each type of atom before and after a chemical reaction.

REACTANTS

methane   oxygen

PRODUCTS

carbon dioxide   water

| ● carbon | ○ hydrogen | ● oxygen |

ARE ALL THE ATOMS IN AN ELEMENT EXACTLY THE SAME?

- The number of protons in the nucleus is called the atomic number and this defines an element.
- The number of electrons can change when an atom combines with another element chemically.
- Isotopes are atoms of the same element with different numbers of neutrons and so have a different atomic mass.
- A radioisotope has nuclei that are unstable and undergo radioactive decay.

hydrogen-1 nucleus
(1 proton)

hydrogen-2 (deuterium) nucleus
(1 proton plus 1 neutron)

IS IT POSSIBLE FOR ATOMS TO CHANGE FROM ONE ELEMENT INTO ANOTHER?

- Radioactive decay occurs when an atom emits an alpha or beta particle or a gamma ray.
- If an atom emits an alpha or beta particle, the structure of its nucleus changes and so it changes from one element to another.

carbon-15 β-decay beta particle nitrogen-15

CAN EQUATIONS BE USED TO REPRESENT NUCLEAR REACTIONS?

$$^{238}_{92}\text{U} \rightarrow {}^{234}_{90}\text{Th} + {}^{4}_{2}\text{He}$$

alpha particle

- Atoms can be represented by their atomic symbols with their atomic number and mass number.
- Subatomic particles such as alpha and beta particles are represented by symbols with their atomic number, mass number and charge.
- A nuclear equation summarises what happens in a nuclear reaction.
- There is always the same number of each type of subatomic particle before and after a nuclear reaction.

Atomic structure

Learning objectives:

- describe the structure of the atom
- use symbols to represent particles
- describe ionisation.

KEY WORDS

atomic number
ionise
isotope
mass number
nucleon

Radium is one of the most powerful radioactive substances known. It emits one million times more radiation than uranium.

The structure of the atom

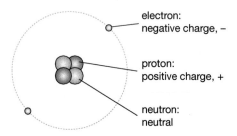

Figure 4.1 An atom contains protons, neutrons and electrons

KEY INFORMATION

The radius of an atom is about 10^{-10} m. It would take around 5 million of them placed side by side to cover the distance of 1 mm. The radius of the nucleus is less than 1/10 000th of the radius of the atom!

An atom contains protons, neutrons and electrons. The protons and neutrons are at the centre of the atom and form the atom's nucleus. Protons and neutrons are also called **nucleons**. The electrons are arranged at different distances from the nucleus (different energy levels).

Neutrons are neutral – they have no charge. Protons have a positive electric charge and electrons have a negative electric charge of the same size. There are the same number of electrons and protons in an atom. This means that atoms have no overall electric charge because the charges cancel out.

1. **A radium atom has 88 protons and 226 neutrons. How many electrons does it have?**

2. **A uranium atom has 92 electrons and 238 nucleons. Determine how many protons and how many neutrons it has.**

The number of protons in the atom determines what element it is. All atoms with six protons, for example, are carbon atoms. Atoms of the same element can have a different number of neutrons though. This means that elements can exist as different **isotopes**. Isotopes of an element have the same number of protons in them but different numbers of neutrons.

3. **Two atoms are from the same element but they form different isotopes. Compare the numbers of electrons, protons and neutrons in the two atoms.**

Using symbols to represent atoms

The number of nucleons in the atom is the **mass number** (A). The number of protons in the atom defines the element and is called the **atomic number** (Figure 4.2).

$$\text{mass number} \longrightarrow {}^{238}_{\ \ 92}U \qquad {}^{234}_{\ \ 90}Th$$
$$\text{atomic number} \longrightarrow$$

Figure 4.2 We represent an atom or a nucleus with the element symbol, mass and atomic number

We use the symbol representation $^A_Z X$, where:

A = mass number (or nucleon number)

Z = atomic number (or proton number)

X = chemical symbol for the element

Z is the number of protons in the nucleus, so the number of neutrons is (A – Z).

For example, $^{14}_6 C$ has a mass number of 14 and an atomic number of 6. So it has 14 nucleons and 6 protons. The number of neutrons in the nucleus is 14 – 6 = 8 neutrons.

When an atom gains or loses one or more outer electrons it becomes **ionised** – it has become charged. The atom has become an ion and can be positively or negatively charged. Ionisation can occur when ionising radiation from radioactive decay knocks one or more outer electrons out of the atoms the radiation passes through.

> **KEY INFORMATION**
>
> You can calculate the number of neutrons by taking the proton number away from the mass number.

Figure 4.3 Absorption and emission and corresponding change in energy levels

4 How many protons and neutrons are in the nucleus of an atom of:

a $^{14}_7 N$

b $^{235}_{92} U$

5 Compare the numbers of protons and neutrons in the uranium atom in Q4 and the uranium atom in Fig 4.2.

6 Explain how ionising radiation can turn some atoms into positive ions and some into negative ions.

Electrons and energy levels

Electrons occupy the space around the nucleus at specific distances or energy levels. An individual electron can change **energy levels** (move closer to or further from the nucleus) only if the atom absorbs or emits electromagnetic radiation, such as light for example (Figure 4.3).

> **DID YOU KNOW?**
>
> The Sun's visible spectrum has dark lines crossing it at certain wavelengths. These are absorption lines caused by atoms in the Sun's gaseous atmosphere absorbing electromagnetic radiation from the Sun's interior. These lines led to the discovery of an unknown element in the Sun's atmosphere in 1870. It was named helium after the Greek sun god, Helios.

Radioactive decay

Learning objectives:

- describe radioactive decay
- describe the types of nuclear radiation
- understand the processes of alpha decay and beta decay.

KEY WORDS

alpha particle
activity
becquerel (Bq)
beta particle
gamma ray
neutron radiation
nuclear radiation
radioisotope
random

Henri Becquerel discovered radioactivity by accident in 1896. When he left some uranium salts next to a wrapped photographic plate he found that the plate had become 'fogged'. He realised that some invisible radiation must be coming from the uranium.

Radioactive decay

Most nuclei are stable but some are not. An unstable nucleus undergoes radioactive decay to become more stable. It emits radiation as it decays. An atom with an unstable nucleus is called a **radioisotope**.

The **activity** of a radioisotope is the number of nuclear decays each second. The activity is measured in **becquerels** (Bq) or counts per second. 1 Bq = 1 count per second.

Radioactivity is a **random** process. It is not possible to predict when a nucleus will decay. If we increase or decrease the temperature of the nucleus, we still cannot predict when it will decay. Radioactive decay is independent of physical changes such as changes in temperature.

KEY INFORMATION

Lead-208 means that the mass number is 208. It is the same as $^{208}_{82}$Pb.

1. **The activity of a radioactive source is 150 Bq. How many counts would be recorded in 20 s?**

2. **What can you say about the nuclei of all elements larger than lead-208?**

3. **Explain what random means with regard to radioactive decay.**

Radioactive decay produces nuclear radiation – radiation emitted from the nucleus. The **nuclear radiation** emitted may be an alpha particle, beta particle, gamma ray or a neutron. **Neutron radiation** is the release of a high-speed neutron from the nucleus, either from the nucleus of a radioactive atom or as the result of nuclear fission.

Alpha decay

In alpha decay, an **alpha particle** is emitted from the nucleus. An alpha particle is a helium nucleus. It has 2 protons and 2 neutrons.

DID YOU KNOW?

The largest stable nucleus is lead-208. When the atoms from larger nuclei decay they often eventually turn into lead. This is why lead is often found near radioactive rocks.

Figure 4.4 Uranium splits into thorium and an alpha particle during alpha decay

When an alpha particle is emitted from a nucleus:

- The nucleus has two fewer protons, so the atomic number (Z, the proton number) decreases by two
- The nucleus also has two fewer neutrons, so the mass number (A, the nucleon number) decreases by four
- A new element is formed.

Beta decay

In beta decay one of the neutrons in the nucleus decays into a proton and an electron. This electron is emitted from the nucleus and is called a **beta particle**.

Figure 4.5 The carbon nucleus emits a beta particle and turns into nitrogen in beta decay

When a beta particle is emitted from a nucleus:

- The nucleus has one more proton, so the atomic number (Z, the proton number) increases by one
- The nucleus has one less neutron, but the mass number (A, the nucleon number) is unchanged
- A new element is formed.

4 **In Figure 4.5, what are the differences between the nitrogen nucleus and the carbon nucleus?**

5 **What happens to a nucleus when:**
   a an alpha particle is emitted?
   b a beta particle is emitted?

Gamma decay

In gamma decay, **gamma rays** are emitted from a nucleus. These are very high-energy electromagnetic waves. They have no charge and no mass.

The emission of a gamma ray does not cause the mass or the charge of the nucleus to change.

6 **When a nucleus undergoes radioactive decay, the mass number is unchanged but the atomic number has increased by 1. What type of decay is it?**

Properties of radiation and its hazards

KEY WORDS

hazard
radioactive contamination

Learning objectives:

- describe how different types of radiation have different ionising power
- describe radioactive contamination
- justify the selection of sources for particular applications.

Different types of radiation have different properties of penetration and ionising power. Many of the servicemen who watched the first nuclear explosion in the Arizona desert then went on to develop cancers. Their bodies were exposed to radiation directly, and also by breathing contaminated air, eating contaminated foods, and drinking affected water.

Radioactive contamination

Radioactive contamination is the unwanted presence of materials containing radioactive atoms. They can be on surfaces or within solids, liquids and gases, including in the human body and on the skin.

Radioactive materials in the environment, whether natural or artificial, can expose people to risks. Radioactive materials are marked with a **hazard** symbol (Figure 4.6).

Contamination occurs when people swallow or breathe in radioactive materials or get them on their skin. Radioactive materials can also enter the body through an open wound or be absorbed through the skin. Some radioisotopes may be absorbed by specific organs, where it is possible they could cause cancer or mutations of genes.

1 What is radioactive contamination?

2 Why is contamination a hazard?

The type and amount of radiation emitted affect the level of hazard.

DID YOU KNOW?

If nuclear radiation enters the body it can cause serious problems if it is absorbed. The severity of the problems depends on the properties of the contamination. This is why it is important to minimise the amount of nuclear radiation getting into the body.

Radiation

Figure 4.6 Radioactive sources are marked with this hazard symbol

Penetration of different types of radiation

The three types of nuclear radiation have different penetrating powers and abilities to ionise particles they hit. Figure 4.7 shows the penetrating power of the three types of ionising radiation. Gamma rays are the most penetrating, able to penetrate through several metres of concrete or several centimetres of lead, but they are the least ionising. Beta particles can travel a few metres in air and can be stopped by aluminium about 3 mm thick. Alpha particles are the least penetrating, and can be stopped by a few centimetres of air or a few sheets of paper, but are the most ionising.

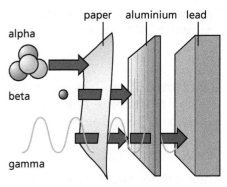

3 Describe the penetrating and ionising powers of beta particles.

4 Which type of radiation can penetrate a few centimetres of aluminium?

Figure 4.7 The three forms of nuclear radiation have very different penetrating powers

How the type of radiation affects the level of hazard

We can use radioactive sources for various applications where their penetrating power is useful. We might not want something that is too penetrating though and we might also want to think about the half-life. Sometimes we need something that ceases to be radioactive fairly quickly.

One example is a smoke alarm; this uses an americium source to ionise air, which can then carry a current. However, smoke prevents the ions from carrying a current and this sets the alarm off.

Another example is the monitoring of the thickness of paper in manufacture. A beta source is used and the particles detected having passed through the paper. Fewer particles mean the paper is too thick; more particles mean it's too thin.

5 Why should the source in the smoke detector have a limited range?

6 Why should the source in the paper thickness monitoring be a beta source?

7 Radioactive tracers may be injected into the body and detected as they escape, forming images of malfunctioning organs. Why should these sources not be alpha sources?

> **REMEMBER!**
>
> Alpha particles cause most ionisation.

Nuclear equations

KEY WORDS

alpha decay
beta decay
nuclear equation

Learning objectives:

- understand nuclear equations
- write balanced nuclear equations.

Uranium-235 undergoes a series of 14 radioactive decays to become lead-206. The series contains both alpha and beta decays.

Nuclear equations

Chemical equations show what happens in a chemical reaction. The number of atoms on each side has to be the same – the equation has to be balanced.

Nuclear equations show what happens when there are changes in the nucleus. They show the number of nucleons and charge. As with chemical equations, they have to be balanced. The number of nucleons and charge has to be the same on both sides of the equation.

1 **What do chemical and nuclear equations have in common?**

2 **What is a key difference between chemical and nuclear equations?**

Nuclear equations for alpha decay

Alpha decay and **beta decay** can be shown as nuclear equations. Figure 4.8 shows the **nuclear equation** for the alpha decay of uranium-238.

$$^{238}_{92}\text{U} \xrightarrow{\alpha\text{-decay}} {}^{4}_{2}\text{He} + {}^{234}_{90}\text{Th}$$

Figure 4.8 The equation for the alpha decay of uranium-238

The mass numbers add up to the same number on both sides of the equation (238 = 234 + 4). This means that mass is conserved.

The atomic numbers also add up to the same on both sides of the equation (92 = 90 + 2), so the number of protons also is conserved. We can also say that the charge has been conserved.

When you write nuclear equations, make sure that the mass numbers and atomic numbers balance on both sides of the equation.

3 **Copy and complete these nuclear equations for alpha decay.**

   a $^{226}_{\underline{}}\text{Ra} \rightarrow {}^{}_{86}\text{Rn} + {}^{4}_{2}\text{He}$

   b $^{219}_{86}\text{Rn} \rightarrow {}^{}_{\underline{}}\text{Po} + {}^{}_{\underline{}}\text{He}$

DID YOU KNOW?

Smoke alarms contain a small amount of americium-241 which decays by emitting an alpha particle. It becomes neptunium-237.

$^{23}_{11}$Na sodium	$^{24}_{12}$Mg magnesium											$^{27}_{13}$Al aluminium	$^{28}_{14}$Si silicon	$^{31}_{15}$P phosphorus	$^{32}_{16}$S sulfur	$^{35}_{17}$Cl chlorine	$^{40}_{18}$Ar argon
$^{39}_{19}$K potassium	$^{40}_{20}$Ca calcium	$^{45}_{21}$Sc scandium	$^{48}_{22}$Ti titanium	$^{51}_{23}$V vanadium	$^{52}_{24}$Cr chromium	$^{55}_{25}$Mn manganese	$^{56}_{26}$Fe iron	$^{59}_{27}$Co cobalt	$^{59}_{28}$Ni nickel	$^{64}_{29}$Cu copper	$^{65}_{30}$Zn zinc	$^{70}_{31}$Ga gallium	$^{73}_{32}$Ge germanium	$^{75}_{33}$As arsenic	$^{79}_{34}$Se selenium	$^{80}_{35}$Br bromine	$^{84}_{36}$Kr krypton
$^{85}_{37}$Rb rubidium	$^{88}_{38}$Sr strontium	$^{89}_{39}$Y yttrium	$^{91}_{40}$Zr zirconium	$^{93}_{41}$Nb niobium	$^{96}_{42}$Mo molybdenum	$^{99}_{43}$Tc technetium	$^{101}_{44}$Ru ruthenium	$^{103}_{45}$Rh rhodium	$^{106}_{46}$Pd palladium	$^{108}_{47}$Ag silver	$^{112}_{48}$Cd cadmium	$^{115}_{49}$In indium	$^{119}_{50}$Sn tin	$^{122}_{51}$Sb antimony	$^{128}_{52}$Te tellurium	$^{127}_{53}$I iodine	$^{131}_{54}$Xe xenon
$^{133}_{55}$Cs caesium	$^{137}_{56}$Ba barium	$^{139}_{57}$La lanthanum	$^{178}_{72}$Hf hafnium	$^{181}_{73}$Ta tantalum	$^{184}_{74}$W tungsten	$^{186}_{75}$Re rhenium	$^{190}_{76}$Os osmium	$^{192}_{77}$Ir iridium	$^{195}_{78}$Pt platinum	$^{197}_{79}$Au gold	$^{201}_{80}$Hg mercury	$^{204}_{81}$Tl thallium	$^{207}_{82}$Pb lead	$^{209}_{83}$Bi bismuth	$^{210}_{84}$Po polonium	$^{210}_{85}$At astatine	$^{222}_{86}$Rn radon
$^{223}_{87}$Fr francium	$^{226}_{88}$Ra radium	$^{227}_{89}$Ac actinium															

Figure 4.9 Part of the periodic table showing the most common isotopes

Nuclear equations for beta decay

In beta decay, a neutron changes into a proton and an electron.

$$^{1}_{0}n \rightarrow ^{1}_{1}p + ^{0}_{-1}e$$

The atomic number can also be thought of as the charge on the particle. This means that the atomic number for an electron is –1. The equation shows that the charge on both sides of the equation is 0, so charge is conserved.

Figure 4.10 demonstrates how the mass number is conserved (15 = 0 + 15) during beta decay. Figure 4.10 also shows that the charge is conserved (6 = 7 – 1) during beta decay.

4 Copy and complete these equations for beta decay.

a $^{90}Sr \rightarrow _{39}Y + ^{0}_{-1}e$ b $_{15}P \rightarrow ^{32}S + ^{0}_{-1}e$

5 When radioactive sodium-24 decays, magnesium-24 is formed. One particle is emitted.

a Copy and complete the equation.

$_{-}Na \rightarrow _{-}Mg + \underline{}$

b What is the name of this particle?

6 This equation represents the decay of thorium-232.

$$^{232}_{90}Th \rightarrow ^{A}_{Z}X + ^{4}_{2}He$$

a What type of radiation is emitted?

b What are the values of A and Z?

7 Write a word equation and symbol equation for each radioactive decay:

a platinum-190, which emits an alpha particle

b rhenium-187, which emits an alpha particle

c copper-66, which emits a beta particle

d nickel-66, which emits a beta particle

e rhodium-105, which decays to palladium-105

f osmium-186, which decays to tungsten-182.

REMEMBER!

Isotopes of the same element can have different mass numbers but they all have the same atomic number.

$$^{15}_{6}C \xrightarrow{\beta\text{-decay}} ^{0}_{-1}e + ^{15}_{7}N$$

15 – 0

6 + 1

Figure 4.10 The equation for the beta decay of carbon-15

KEY INFORMATION

Radioactive decay by emitting a gamma ray causes no change in mass number or atomic number.

Radioactive half-life

KEY WORDS

half-life

Learning objectives:

- explain what is meant by radioactive half-life
- calculate half-life
- calculate the decline in activity after a number of half-lives.

Radioisotopes are often used to monitor a biological process in the body or in the environment. We need to know the half-lives of different radioisotopes so that we can minimise contamination or irradiation.

Half-life

We cannot predict when the nucleus of one particular atom will decay. It could be next week or not for a million years. Radioactive decay is a random process. If there is a very large number of atoms, some of them will decay each second. We plot a graph of activity against time and draw a curve of best fit. We can then use this curve to find when the activity has halved (Figure 4.11). The **half-life** of a radioisotope is the average time it takes for half the nuclei present to decay, or the time it takes for the activity to fall to half its initial level. We use half-life because we cannot predict the time it will take for all the atoms to decay.

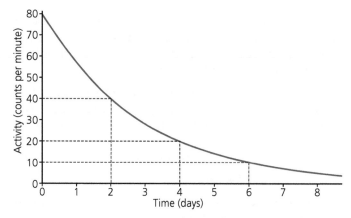

Figure 4.11 The time it takes for the activity to halve is constant

The activity of a radioactive substance gets less and less as time goes on. The graph line in Figure 4.11 gets closer and closer to the time axis but never reaches it because the activity halves each half-life.

1. Explain why you can't predict when a particular atom will decay.

2. Explain what is meant by 'half-life'.

3. What will the activity in Figure 4.11 be after:
   a 2 days? **b** 4 days? **c** 6 days? **d** 8 days?

Calculating half-life

To calculate the half-life of a radioisotope, plot a graph of count rate detected (which is proportional to the total activity) against time, as shown in Figure 4.12. The background count should be subtracted from each reading before the graph is plotted. Plot the points and then draw a smooth curve of best fit through the points. Then find several values for the half-life from the graph by finding the time for the activity in counts per minute to fall from 80 to 40, 40 to 20, 20 to 10 and so on. You should calculate the average of the values you have found. The time for the activity to halve may not be exactly the same each time. Any differences will be due to the random nature of radioactive decay.

KEY INFORMATION

When you draw a curve of best fit on a graph of activity against time for a radioisotope, not all of the points will be on the curve. Some will be above the curve and some will be below the curve because of the random nature of radioactive decay.

4 Calculate the half-life of the radioisotope shown in Figure 4.12.

Figure 4.12

5 The table shows the activity of a radioactive sample over time.

  a Draw a graph of activity against time.

  b Draw a best-fit curve through the points.

  c Calculate the half-life by looking at time for the activity to halve at three different points on your curve. Calculate the average.

6 The activity of a radioactive sample took 4 hours to decrease from 100 Bq to 25 Bq. Calculate its half-life.

Time in minutes	Activity in Bq
0	100
0.5	76
1.0	51
1.5	40
2.0	26
2.5	18
3.0	12
3.5	10
4.0	8

HIGHER TIER ONLY

Calculating decline in activity

For some applications such as a smoke alarm, a radioisotope with a long half-life is most suitable so that the rate of decay does not decrease significantly. Some radioisotopes are used as tracers, using the radiation they emit to trace the path of a substance the radioisope is attached to.

Radioisotopes can be used as environmental tracers (such as detecting a leak in a pipe) or medical tracers. For these applications, a short half-life is best. This means that the activity will decrease to a level similar to the background count fairly quickly because the time taken for half the radioactive nuclei to decay is very short.

DID YOU KNOW?

The half-lives of different radioactive isotopes vary from a fraction of a second to millions of years.

7 Technetium-99m is widely used in medicine. It has a half-life of 6 hours. How much of it remains after 1 day?

8 What fraction of the original sample remains after 80 minutes in Figure 4.12?

9 Caesium-134 has a half-life of 2 years. If its activity was monitored for 6 years, what fraction of the original activity level would it have dropped to after 6 years?

Irradiation

Learning objectives:

- explain what is meant by irradiation
- understand the distinction between contamination and irradiation
- appreciate the importance of communication between scientists.

KEY WORDS

irradiation
mutation
peer review

Some foods are irradiated, which kills microorganisms living on them. The foods can then be kept much longer before they go off.

Irradiation

Irradiation is where an object is exposed to nuclear radiation. The exposure can originate from various sources, including natural sources of background radiation. Figure 4.13 summarises some of the ways we are irradiated each day.

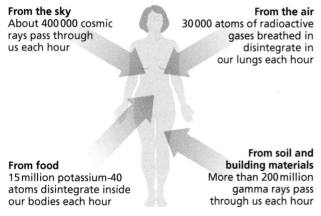

From the sky
About 400 000 cosmic rays pass through us each hour

From the air
30 000 atoms of radioactive gases breathed in disintegrate in our lungs each hour

From food
15 million potassium-40 atoms disintegrate inside our bodies each hour

From soil and building materials
More than 200 million gamma rays pass through us each hour

Figure 4.13 Each day our bodies are irradiated from different sources

DID YOU KNOW?

Low levels of irradiation have little effect on the health of humans. However, if people are exposed to high levels of irradiation it is important to consider the radiation risks for these people and their descendants.

Some things are irradiated with X-rays or gamma rays for therapeutic purposes or to sterilise them. Gamma rays are sometimes used in hospitals to sterilise food for seriously ill patients. Irradiation is also used by some supermarkets to kill bacteria on fresh food so that the food stays fresh for longer.

Nuclear radiation causes ionisation. The cells in our bodies can also be changed by radiation. DNA can be changed by nuclear radiation. This is called **mutation**. Sometimes when a cell mutates it divides in an uncontrollable way. This can lead to cancer.

1. Describe what is meant by irradiation.

2. Compare the level of irradiation we receive from food with the irradiation from the air.

Effects of irradiation

Damage to a person's cells is called damage *by* irradiation. Figure 4.14 shows the effects, which are cell death, accurate repair or misrepair causing mutation of genes.

Suitable precautions must be taken to protect against any hazard the radioactive source used in the process of irradiation may present.

3 **List the three possible effects of irradiation on human body cells in order of increasing harm.**

Natural and artificial sources of radiation include cosmic radiation and nuclear industry wastes respectively. Risks for people who work with nuclear radiation and become irradiated and their descendants must be considered. The calculation of these risks is used to define the tolerance levels of both an irradiation and contamination of drinking water and food products.

Figure 4.14 The three possible effects of irradiation on body cells

4 **Why could irradiation have an effect on somebody's grandchildren?**

5 **Explain the difference between irradiation and contamination.**

KEY INFORMATION

An irradiated object does not become radioactive.

Publishing scientific results

The first scientists to investigate nuclear radiation were unaware of its effects on their health, and many died as a result. When the first atomic bombs were exploded, scientists were not aware of the potential effects on health. They discovered that nuclear radiation can have long-term effects, causing genetic mutations which affect subsequent generations.

It is important for the findings of studies into the effects of radiation on humans to be published. This means that scientists can find out about what other scientists are doing. They can try to repeat experimental results and check the results, which is called **peer review**.

6 **Explain why experimental findings should be checked by peer review.**

7 **Some pigeons were found to be contaminated with caesium-137, a radioisotope of caesium with a half-life of about 30 years. They were almost certainly irradiated too. Suggest why the pigeons were at greater risk from contamination than from irradiation.**

KEY CONCEPT

Developing ideas for the structure of the atom

Learning objectives:

- understand how ideas about the structure of the atom have changed
- understand how evidence is used to test and improve models.

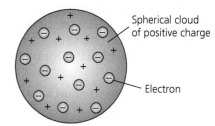

KEY WORDS

alpha particle
atom
electron
neutron
nuclear model
nucleus
plum pudding
  model
proton

The word atom is the Greek for indivisible. Democritus was a Greek philosopher who lived around 400 BC and developed the idea of the atom. For a long time atoms were thought to be the smallest particles.

The atom

Our theories for the structure of the **atom** have changed as new evidence has emerged.

The idea of an indivisible atom existed for over 2000 years. It was only at the start of the 20th century that scientists began to discover our current model of the atom.

At the end of the 19th century, scientists had started to question that the atom is the smallest particle. In the late 1890s, J. J. Thomson discovered the **electron** and that it is very much lighter than an atom. He proposed the **plum pudding model** of the atom where electrons are surrounded by positive charge (Figure 4.15).

Figure 4.15 Thomson's plum pudding model

1. Does this model include protons, neutrons and electrons?

2. Are the positive and negative charges balanced in this model?

Using experimental evidence to test the model

In 1909, Hans Geiger and Ernest Marsden carried out an experiment where they aimed a beam of **alpha particles** at a thin foil of metal. According to Thomson's model, they should all pass straight through. But some of the alpha particles bounced off the foil in all directions (Figure 4.16).

This led Ernest Rutherford to propose a **nuclear model** of the atom in 1911 with a small central **nucleus** that contained most of the mass and was charged with electrons orbiting it (Figure 4.17).

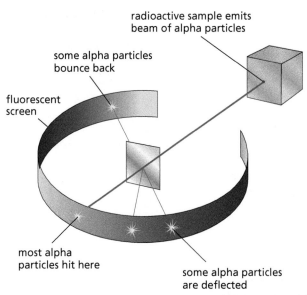

Figure 4.16 Results of the Geiger–Marsden experiment

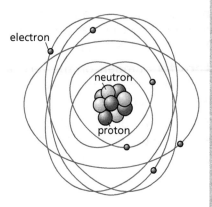

Figure 4.17 Rutherford's model of the atom

There was a problem with this model. Classical mechanics showed that the electrons would not stay in stable orbits and would spiral into the nucleus. So, in 1913, Niels Bohr proposed a refined model in which electrons could only be in certain orbits. This is the model we have today (Figure 4.18).

3 **Explain why it was important for Geiger and Marsden to publish the results of their experiment.**

4 **Explain why the model of the atom had to change.**

Developing the model further

The results of further experiments suggested that the positive charge of the nucleus was made up of charged particles that all had the same charge. This led to the idea of the **proton** which was discovered by Rutherford in 1920. In the same year, he suggested that the nucleus was made up of protons and neutral particles. He thought the neutral particles could be a proton and electron combined in some way. The **neutron** was then discovered in 1932 by James Chadwick.

Figure 4.18 Bohr's model

5 **State what Rutherford's model explained.**

6 **Suggest how a theory becomes accepted.**

MATHS SKILLS

Using ratios and proportional reasoning

KEY WORDS

net decline
ratio

Learning objectives:

- calculate radioactive half-life from a curve of best fit
- calculate the net decline in radioactivity.

When you draw a graph of activity for a radioisotope against time, the points do not fit a straight line – the line of best fit is a curve.

Measuring half-life from a graph

Working out the half-life of a radioisotope usually involves drawing a graph and using the graph to calculate the half-life.

Figure 4.19 shows the activity in counts per minute against time for a certain radioactive isotope. You can use the graph to work out the half-life of the isotope.

Look for numbers on the vertical scale that are easy to halve. For example, you can halve 40 easily to get 20.

From the 40 on the vertical axis, draw a line across to the graph. Then draw a line down to the time axis. So the activity at 2 days is 40 counts/minute.

Now repeat this for 20 counts/minute. The time is 4 days.

It takes 4 – 2 = 2 days for the activity to reduce by half from 40 to 20 counts/minute.

So the half-life is 2 days.

You should always repeat for a second pair of values, just to check. Choose another value that can be halved easily, e.g. 20. Repeating the process for halving the count rate from 20 to 10 gives the same answer, 2 days.

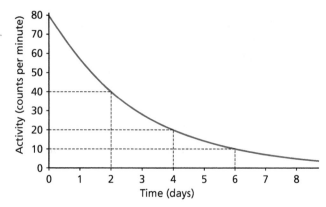

Figure 4.19: Working out the half-life of a radioisotope

Figure 4.20: A line of best fit can be drawn from the data plotted

 a **Calculate the half-life for the source shown in Figure 4.20.**

b **Work out three values for the half-life.**

c **Calculate the average of the values.**

2 **a** **From the data in the table plot a graph of activity against time.**

Time (min)	0	10	20	30	40	50	60	70	80	90
Activity (Bq)	96	78	62	54	40	32	26	21	15	14

b **Calculate the half-life.**

Half-life calculations

Another way of calculating the half-life of a radioactive source is fraction reasoning. After one half-life has passed, the activity decreases by $\frac{1}{2}$. This is always true no matter when you start to measure the activity of the sample. The decrease in activity over several half-lives can be written as a sequence, as shown in the table.

Example: A radioactive source has an initial activity of 1200 counts per minute. If the count rate has fallen to 147 after 6 hours, calculate the half-life.

Starting with 1200 counts per minute at time 0:

- after 1 half-life, the activity should be 600 counts per minute;
- after 2 half-lives, the activity should be 300 counts per minute;
- after 3 half-lives, the activity should be 150 counts per minute. (The actual count rate is 147, showing that radioactivity is a random process.)

After 6 hours, 3 half-lives have passed, so the half-life is 2 hours.

Number of half-lives passed	Fraction of activity remaining
0	$\frac{1}{1}$
1	$\frac{1}{2}$
2	$\frac{1}{4}$
3	$\frac{1}{8}$
4	$\frac{1}{16}$
5	$\frac{1}{32}$
6	$\frac{1}{64}$

3 **A radioactive isotope has an activity of 160 Bq and a half-life of 2 hours. What is the activity after 6 hours?**

4 **The activity of a radioactive source used to sterilise equipment in a hospital is 200 kBq. The activity is measured again in 21 years and is found to be 12.5 kBq. What is the half-life?**

5 **The activity of a sample decreases to $\frac{1}{16}$th of its original value over 24 hours.**

Calculate the half-life of the sample.

HIGHER TIER ONLY

Net decline

In the example above, after 6 hours (3 half-lives) the activity will have reduced to $\frac{1}{8}$th of the original. This can also be expressed as a ratio of the final value to the initial value, 1:8. This ratio is called the **net decline**.

6 **Sodium-24 has a half-life of 15 hours. A sample of sodium-24 has an activity of 640 Bq.**

  a **Calculate the activity after 60 hours.**

  b **Calculate the net decline.**

7 **Iodine-131 has a half-life of 8 days. A sample of iodine-131 has an activity of 1800 counts per second.**

  a **Calculate the count rate after 32 days.**

  b **Calculate the net decline in the activity of the sample.**

8 **A sample of pure polonium-210 decays into lead-206 with a half-life of 138 days. Calculate how long it would take for the sample to contain three times as much lead as polonium.**

Check your progress

You should be able to:

State that the number of protons in an element is the atomic number and the total number of protons and neutrons is the mass number →

Understand that atoms of an element all have the same number of protons but can have different numbers of neutrons, giving different isotopes →

Use nuclear notation to show subatomic particles in an isotope

Recognise that some isotopes called radioisotopes are unstable and decay in a random way →

Explain how the radioactive decay of a radioisotope can be described using a quantity called the half-life →

Calculate the half-life of a radioisotope

List the three types of ionising radiation resulting from nuclear activity →

Describe the structure of each type of ionising radiation →

Explain the properties of each type of radiation

Recognise the symbols used in a nuclear equation →

Write nuclear equations involving alpha and beta decay →

Write balanced nuclear equations for different types of nuclear reaction

Define radioactive contamination and irradiation →

List the hazards of radioactive contamination →

Compare and contrast irradiation and contamination

Worked example

1 **What is an alpha particle?**

A helium atom

2 **Explain what you understand by the half-life of a radioisotope.**

The half-life is the time it takes to lose half its size

3 **What is the difference between irradiation and contamination?**

Contamination is where materials become radioactive. Irradiation is where an object is exposed to nuclear radiation, but it does not become radioactive itself.

4 **An experiment was carried out where the activity of a radioisotope was measured over time. The results are shown on the graph.**

Activity of a radioisotope

a **An adjustment to the readings has not been made. Explain what it is.**

The graph has nearly levelled out above the axis. It looks like the background count has not been subtracted.

b **Explain how you would work out the half-life from the graph once the adjustment had been made**

Pick a value, say 100 Bq and halve it, 50 Bq

Draw a line from 100 Bq on the vertical axis across to the graph, then down to the time axis.

Repeat for 50 Bq. Subtract the first time from the second time to get the half-life.

End of chapter questions

Getting started

1 What type of charge does a neutron have?

  a positive

  b negative

  c neither – it's neutral

  d it has the opposite charge to whichever particle is next to it   `1 Mark`

2 Radioactive decay is when

  a atoms disintegrate   b atoms go rotten

  c atoms merge   d atoms lose electrons   `1 Mark`

3 Which of these is not a type of ionising radiation?

  a alpha   b beta   c gamma   d delta   `1 Mark`

4 The mass number of an element is given by

  a the number of protons

  b the number of neutrons

  c the combined number of protons and neutrons

  d the combined number of protons and electrons   `1 Mark`

5 State one similarity and one difference between an alpha particle and a beta particle.   `2 Marks`

6 State two examples of human activity that cause radioactive emissions.   `2 Marks`

7 Smoke detectors contain a radioactive source. Explain why installing them in a house makes the building safer.   `2 Marks`

Going further

8 DNA can be changed by nuclear radiation. This is referred to as:

  a Isolation

  b Immunisation

  c Mutation

  d Radioactive decay   `1 Mark`

9 Scientists over the years have changed the way they represent the atom in models. This is best explained by them

  a Getting it wrong first time.

  b Not understanding the evidence.

  c Gathering new evidence.

  d Liking to change their minds every so often.   `1 Mark`

10 Draw a diagram to explain how the protons, neutrons and electrons are arranged in an atom.   `2 Marks`

11 Explain what is meant by an isotope.

2 Marks

12 Describe an experiment to demonstrate that different types of ionising radiation have different penetrating properties.

4 Marks

More challenging

13 Explain the difference between irradiation and contamination.

2 Marks

14 Thorium $^{232}_{90}$Th decays to radium $^{228}_{88}$Ra. Use this information to explain why this is an example of alpha decay.

2 Marks

15 The activity of a radioactive sample took 60 minutes to decrease from 400 Bq to 50 Bq. Work out its half-life.

2 Marks

16 The diagram shows an idealised graph of activity against time for a radioisotope. Calculate the half-life for this sample.

4 Marks

Most demanding

17 $^{219}_{86}$Rn decays to $^{x}_{y}$Po by emitting an alpha particle. Write a balanced nuclear equation for the decay.

2 Marks

18 Explain why an alpha particle has the shortest range of any types of radioactive emission but is the most ionising.

2 Marks

19 Write the nuclear equation for the beta decay of carbon-14.

2 Marks

20 Explain how the evidence from Geiger and Marsden's scattering experiment led to the development of the nuclear model of the atom.

4 Marks

Total: 40 Marks

FORCES

IDEAS YOU HAVE MET BEFORE:

SPEED AND CHANGE OF SPEED

- Average speed can be calculated by dividing the distance travelled by the time taken.
- If the speed of a car is changing, it is accelerating.
- A journey can be represented on a distance–time graph.

FORCES CAUSE ACCELERATION

- Forces can speed things up or slow them down.
- The bigger the force, the bigger the change in speed.
- Forces can be contact forces, such as an engine powering a car, or non-contact forces, such as gravity.

FALLING SAFELY

- Falling objects accelerate due to the force of gravity.
- Their acceleration is reduced due to the upward force of air resistance or drag.
- When a parachute opens the drag force increases.

IN THIS CHAPTER YOU WILL FIND OUT ABOUT:

HOW CAN WE DESCRIBE MOTION?

- Acceleration is a useful way of showing how speed is changing.
- When a car changes velocity it is accelerating.
- All moving objects have momentum.

HOW CAN UNDERSTANDING FORCES MAKE DRIVING SAFER?

- Reaction time is the time the brain takes to respond.
- Stopping distances depend upon the driver's reaction time and also on the vehicle and road conditions.

HOW DOES THE MOTION OF A FALLING OBJECT CHANGE AS IT FALLS?

- In the absence of air resistance, all falling objects accelerate at the same rate.
- An object falling through water or the atmosphere reaches a terminal velocity when the resultant force is zero.

Forces

Learning objectives:

- describe a force
- recognise the difference between contact and non-contact forces
- state examples of scalar and vector quantities.

People sometimes use force in a wide range of ways – we talk about someone having a 'forceful personality' or the 'force of their argument'. However, in science we use force in a very particular way. We're interested in direction, size and contact.

What is a force?

A force is a push or a pull that is applied by one object on another.

Force is measured in **newtons (N)**. The force needed to pick up a bag of sugar is 20 N. The force needed to support an apple is around 1 N.

Figure 5.1 The aeroplane's engines give it a forward force or thrust. Air resistance is a frictional force that resists movement in air.

Contact and non-contact forces

All forces between objects are either contact or non-contact forces.

Contact forces – the objects are physically touching, such as a parachute in contact with air (Figure 5.2).

Non-contact forces – the objects are physically separated (Figure 5.3).

Figure 5.2 Air resistance – a contact force

Contact forces	Non-contact forces
friction	gravitational force
air resistance	electrostatic force
tension	magnetic force
normal contact force	

Figure 5.3 Attraction and repulsion between magnetic objects is an example of a non-contact force

1 **Give an example of a contact force (other than the one in Figure 5.2).**

2 **Give an example of a non-contact force (other than the one in Figure 5.3).**

Scalar and vector quantities

A **scalar** quantity has magnitude (size) only.

A **vector** quantity has magnitude and direction.

A vector quantity can be represented by an arrow. The length of the arrow represents the magnitude, and the direction of the arrow shows its direction (as in Figures 5.1 and 5.2).

Force is an example of a vector quantity.

Scalar	speed, distance
Vector	velocity, displacement

For example: speed = 10 m/s but velocity = 10 m/s due north.

Distance is a measure of how far an object moves but doesn't indicate the direction it has moved in; it is therefore a scalar quantity. **Displacement** is sometimes used instead. It includes both the distance moved and the direction so it is a vector quantity. It is measured as a straight line from the start point to the end point.

> **KEY INFORMATION**
>
> **Velocity** is speed in a particular direction.

3 a **Which of the following are vector quantities?**

   mass   **acceleration**   **force**

   temperature   **energy**   **momentum**

   b **Explain your answers.**

4 **Draw two arrows to represent vectors of 20 N due south and 10 N due north.**

5 **A runner runs a 400 m race around a track. If he finishes at the same place as he started, what is his final distance and displacement?**

Speed

KEY WORDS

average speed
distance–time
 graph
gradient
speed
tangent

Learning objectives:

- calculate speed using distance travelled divided by time taken
- calculate speed from a distance–time graph
- measure the gradient of a distance–time graph at any point.

The astronauts who landed on the Moon travelled at an average speed of 8000 km/h to get there.

Speed and average speed

Speed tells us how fast something is moving.

If a car has a speed of 50 km/h, it means it travels 50 km in 1 hour.

$$\text{speed } (v) = \frac{\text{distance} (s)}{\text{time} (t)} = \frac{s}{t}$$

You can convert a speed in km/h to m/s.

$$50 \text{ km/h} = \frac{50\ 000 \text{ m}}{3600 \text{ s}} = 13.9 \text{ m/s}$$

We usually calculate its **average speed** because speed changes during a journey. It is rarely constant.

$$\text{average speed} = \frac{\text{total distance}}{\text{total time}}$$

Example: A Formula One racing car driver completes a 520 km race in 2 hours. Calculate the average speed.

$$\text{average speed} = \frac{\text{total distance}}{\text{total time}} = \frac{520 \text{ km}}{2 \text{ h}} = 260 \text{ km/h}$$

The distance travelled in a specific time can be calculated using the equation:

distance travelled = speed × time $s = v\,t$

Distance–time graphs

Drawing a graph of distance against time shows how the distance moved by a car from its starting point changes over time. It is easier to interpret than simply looking at a table of results. Look at the graphs shown in Figures 5.4a–c.

The **gradient** of a **distance–time graph** is equal to the speed of the object.

The gradient of the graph in Figure 5.4a = $\dfrac{AC}{BC}$

$$= \frac{(30 \text{ m} - 15 \text{ m})}{(6 \text{ s} - 0\text{s})}$$

$$= \frac{15 \text{ m}}{6 \text{ s}}$$

$$= 2.5 \text{ m/s}$$

So the speed is 2.5 m/s.

MATHS

To change a speed in km/h to m/s multiply by 1000/3600.
To change a speed in m/s to km/h multiply by 3600/1000.

1. **Explain why it is usually impossible to maintain a constant (steady) speed during a car journey.**

2. **Abi swam 50 m in $2\frac{1}{2}$ minutes. Calculate her average speed in m/s.**

3. **Farah walks 10 km in $1\frac{3}{4}$ hours. What is her average speed in m/s?**

4. **A snail travels at an average speed of 0.5 mm/s. How far does it travel in 1 hour?**

KEY INFORMATION

Typical speeds are:
• 1.5 m/s walking
• 3 m/s running
• 6 m/s cycling.

(a) Object travelling at a constant speed

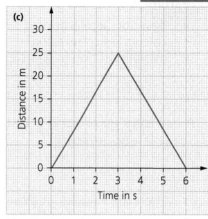

(b) Object stationary

(c) Object travelling and returning to its original place

Figure 5.4 Distance–time graphs

5 **How would the graph change if the object went faster?**

- A straight line indicates the speed is constant. A curved line shows the speed is changing.
- When the gradient increases the speed increases.
- When the gradient decreases the speed decreases.

6 **a** **Sketch a distance–time graph for a car that is slowing down.**

    b **Describe how the speed changes for the car in Figure 5.5.**

Figure 5.5 A distance–time graph for a car

HIGHER TIER ONLY

Tangents to a distance–time graph

If an object is travelling at a steady speed, its distance–time graph will be a straight line (Figure 5.4a). However, if its speed is changing, the line of the graph will be curved (Figure 5.5). We can find the speed at any particular point by drawing a **tangent** to the line and working out the gradient of the tangent.

For example, if we wanted to know the speed of this object after it had travelled 80 m, we would draw a tangent to the line at the point for 80 m and find its gradient.

The gradient of the tangent to the curve

$$= \frac{(140\,\text{m} - 20\,\text{m})}{(9\,\text{s} - 4\,\text{s})} = \frac{120\,\text{m}}{5\,\text{s}}$$

$$= 24\,\text{m/s}$$

So the speed at this time is 24 m/s.

KEY INFORMATION

If the speed is changing, we say the motion is non-uniform.

7 **For the distance–time graph in Figure 5.6, describe how the gradient of the graph changes from 0 to 10 s. What does this tell you about how the speed changes?**

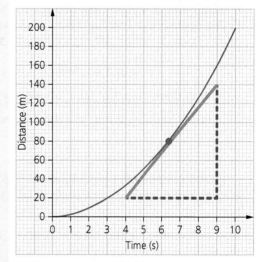

Figure 5.6 Finding the speed from a curved distance–time graph

Acceleration

Learning objectives:

- describe acceleration
- calculate acceleration
- explain motion in a circle.

KEY WORDS

acceleration
air resistance
(or drag)
deceleration

A car may go around a roundabout at a constant speed but it is accelerating.

Acceleration

- When the velocity of a car is increasing it is **accelerating**.
- When the velocity of a car is decreasing it is **decelerating**. Its acceleration is negative.

The faster the velocity changes, the greater the acceleration. A car which has a high acceleration reaches a high speed in a short time.

1 Car A accelerates from 10 m/s to 40 m/s in 6 s. Car B accelerates from 20 m/s to 30 m/s in 5 s. Determine which car has the greater acceleration.

There is a story that a famous scientist called Galileo dropped two cannon balls – one large and one small – at the same time from the top of the Leaning Tower of Pisa (Figure 5.7). The balls reached the ground at the same time. This showed that both objects accelerated at the same rate and so the acceleration due to gravity does not depend on size. From this experiment, scientists deduced that all objects accelerate at the same rate under gravity (about 9.8 m/s^2).

If an object is dropped, its speed increases as it falls. It accelerates because it is pulled towards the centre of the Earth due to the force of gravity.

If a ball and a feather are dropped, the ball reaches the ground first because the feather has a large surface area. This slowing down force is called **air resistance** or **drag**.

2 Explain why a ball accelerates when you drop it.

3 Why does a feather fall more slowly than a ball?

4 What happens when you throw a ball upwards?

Calculating acceleration

A sports car speeds up to 40 km/h in 5 s and a van speeds up to 40 km/h in 10 s. The acceleration of the car is twice as big as the acceleration of the van.

You can work out the acceleration of the car or van using the equation:

$$\text{acceleration} = \frac{\text{change in velocity}}{\text{time taken}}$$

Figure 5.7 The Leaning Tower of Pisa

DID YOU KNOW?

On the surface of the Moon, the acceleration of free fall is only 1.6 m/s^2. As there is no atmosphere a feather would fall with the same acceleration as a lump of lead.

$$a = \frac{\Delta v}{t}$$

If change of velocity Δv is in m/s and time t is in s, acceleration a is in m/s^2.

Example: A car accelerates from 10 m/s to 30 m/s in 8 s. Calculate its acceleration.

$$\text{Acceleration} = \frac{\text{change in velocity}}{\text{time taken}}$$
$$= \frac{(30 \text{ m/s} - 10 \text{ m/s})}{8 \text{ s}}$$
$$= 2.5 \text{ m/s}^2$$

MATHS

The symbol Δ means the difference or change in a quantity. Δv means a change in velocity.

(5) A car takes 10 s to increase its velocity from 20 m/s to 40 m/s. What is its average acceleration?

(6) A car has an acceleration of +2 m/s^2

   a What does this tell you about the velocity of the car?

   b What is meant by an acceleration of −2 m/s^2?

MATHS

Remember – to change a speed in km/h to m/s: $\times \frac{1000}{3600}$.

E.g. 180 km/h
$$= \frac{(180 \times 1000)}{3600}$$
$$= 50 \text{ m/s}.$$

(7) Kevin is driving his car at 24 m/s. He brakes and stops in 3 s. Find his acceleration.

(8) Jane is driving at a speed of 72 km/h. She accelerates to 108 km/h in 5 s. Find her acceleration in m/s.

(9) A glacier is accelerating at 4 mm/s/year. Explain carefully what this means.

HIGHER TIER ONLY

Motion in a circle

When a vehicle goes round a roundabout at a constant speed its direction of movement is changing. This means that its velocity is changing because velocity is a vector. When the velocity of an object is changing, it is accelerating. There is a force towards the centre of the roundabout in the same direction as the acceleration which causes the change in velocity.

Figure 5.8 These vehicles are changing direction and so are accelerating

(10) Dan and Karen are riding on a carousel at a fairground. They are moving at a constant speed. Why are they accelerating?

Velocity–time graphs

Learning objectives:

- draw velocity–time graphs
- calculate acceleration using a velocity–time graph
- calculate displacement using a velocity–time graph.

KEY WORDS

displacement
gradient
rate of change
sketch graph
velocity–time graph

Constant acceleration does not mean constant velocity.

Velocity–time graphs

A **velocity–time graph** shows how the velocity of a moving object changes over time.

① **The table gives some velocities of a racing car at different times from the start of a race. Draw a velocity–time graph for the racing car.**

Time (s)	0	1	2	3	4	6	8	10	12
Velocity (m/s)	0	10	20	29	36	50	59	64	64

A graph is easier to interpret than a table of results.

When drawing velocity–time graphs remember that the velocity scale will have positive and negative values if there is a change in direction.

A **sketch graph** does not have plotted points, just the shape of the graph and the parts of the journey where the velocity is positive or negative (Figure 5.9). A sketch graph does not usually need numbers or units on the axes.

Figure 5.9a is a velocity-time graph for an object travelling at a constant velocity. Figure 5.9b shows velocity increasing steadily. Figure 5.9c shows velocity decreasing steadily to zero, then the velocity still continuing to decrease. The negative velocity shows that there is a change in direction. This could be for a car braking to a halt, then accelerating (increasing speed) in the opposite direction.

② **A tube train travels between two stations, A and B. Sketch a velocity–time graph for a journey from A to B and back to A.**

Acceleration

The **gradient** of a velocity–time graph (Figure 5.10) shows how velocity changes with time. This is the **rate of change** of velocity or acceleration. A steep gradient means the acceleration is large. The object's velocity is changing rapidly.

Acceleration = $\dfrac{\text{change in velocity}}{\text{time taken}}$ or $a = \Delta\dfrac{v}{t}$

= gradient of a velocity–time graph.

REMEMBER!

Don't confuse distance–time and velocity–time graphs. Look at the axis labels carefully.

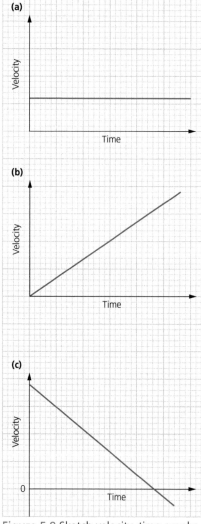

Figure 5.9 Sketch velocity–time graphs

3. Calculate the acceleration in each of the graphs in Figure 5.10.

4. A motor cycle travelling at 20 m/s takes 5 s to stop. What is its average acceleration?

5. A truck travelling at 25 m/s puts on its brakes for 4 s. This produces an acceleration of –2 m/s². What is the truck's velocity after braking?

HIGHER TIER ONLY

Displacement

Displacement is equal to the area under a velocity–time graph.

If we have a velocity–time graph and want to know the distance the object travelled, we can find this out by working out the area under the line.

Figure 5.11

Example: For the journey shown in Figure 5.11 we can divide the area under the line into three simple shapes.

The area of the triangle on the left represents $\frac{1}{2}$ × 5 s × 50 m/s = 125 m, the area of the rectangle represents 2 s × 50 m/s = 100 m and the area of the second triangle represents $\frac{1}{2}$ × 1 s × 50 m/s = 25 m. So the total distance travelled by the object is 250 m.

6. a Describe the motion of a train that has the graph shown in Figure 5.12.

   b How far did the train travel?

7. Amy is cycling through a town.
   - For the first 10 s she travelled at a constant velocity.
   - She started to climb a hill so she slowed down.
   - At the top of the hill she had to stop for some traffic lights.
   - When the lights turned green she accelerated away.
   Sketch a velocity–time graph for Amy's journey.

8. A stone was thrown upwards. Which of the graphs in Figure 5.10 could represent the motion of the stone? Describe how the graph could be extended to show the motion of the stone as it fell back down.

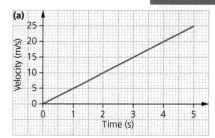

(a)

Object moving with constant acceleration from rest

(b)

Object with constant negative acceleration slowing down to rest

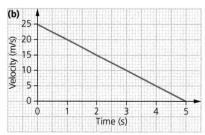

(c)

Object moving at a steady speed

Figure 5.10 Velocity–time graphs

Figure 5.12 Velocity–time graph for a train

DID YOU KNOW?

Acceleration is a change in velocity over time. But we often use change of speed over time when calculating acceleration in situations where the direction is not important.

Calculations of motion

KEY WORDS

uniform motion

Learning objectives:

- describe uniform motion
- use an equation for uniform motion
- apply this equation to vertical motion.

- -

On 15 October 1997 Thrust SSC (Figure 5.13), driven by Andy Green, broke the land speed record, reaching a speed of 763 mph, measured over a distance of 1 mile.

Describing motion

In **uniform motion** the acceleration is constant.

We use these symbols when we are describing motion:

s = displacement in m
u = initial velocity in m/s
v = final velocity in m/s
a = acceleration in m/s^2

Figure 5.13 Andy Green was required to do two 1 mile runs in opposite directions.

ADVICE

Remember that s means displacement. Make sure you don't confuse this with speed.

1. **What is meant by:**
   a **initial velocity?**
   b **final velocity?**

2. **Why are the units for acceleration different from those for velocity?**

An equation for uniform motion

When an object accelerates uniformly you can use this equation to link initial and final velocities, acceleration and distance:

(final velocity)^2 − (initial velocity)^2 = 2 × acceleration × distance

$v^2 - u^2 = 2as$

Example: A car accelerates from 8.0 m/s at 2.5 m/s^2 for the next 11 m. What is its final velocity?

u = initial velocity = 8.0 m/s
a = acceleration = 2.5 m/s^2
s = displacement = 11 m

Substitute the values into the equation:

$$v^2 - 8^2 = (2 \times 2.5 \times 11)$$
$$= 64 + 55$$
$$= 119$$

Therefore $v = \sqrt{119}$
$ = 11$ m/s (to 2 significant figures)

Example: A train approaching a red signal has a speed of 10 m/s. The signal then changes to green and the train accelerates.

KEY INFORMATION

To use this equation, we need to substitute values into it. We need to know three values and from these we can work out the fourth.

MATHS

Notice that it is only u that is squared and that the multiplication has to be done before the addition; you must then take the square root to get v. Also notice that the answer is rounded to 2 significant figures, because the data is to 2 significant figures.

By the time it has travelled another 1000 m it is now travelling at 20 m/s. What is its acceleration?

Rearrange $v^2 - u^2 = 2as$ by dividing both sides by $2s$

$$a = \frac{(v^2 - u^2)}{2s}$$

Substituting values:

$$a = \frac{(20^2 - 10^2)}{2 \times 1000}$$

$$= \frac{(400 - 100)}{2000}$$

$$= \frac{300}{2000} = 0.15 \text{ m/s}^2$$

3 An aircraft accelerates from rest at 2.5 m/s². Its take-off speed is 60 m/s. What length of runway does it need to take off?

4 A car accelerates from rest at 3 m/s² along a straight road. How far has the car travelled after 4 s?

5 A train is travelling at 40 m/s when its brakes are applied. This produces a deceleration of 2 m/s². Determine the distance the train travels before stopping.

> **REMEMBER!**
>
> When the object is slowing down, v will have a smaller value than u.

Applying the equation to vertical motion

Useful points to remember:

- If there is no air resistance, gravity gives a falling object an acceleration of approximately 9.8 m/s² downwards. When a ball is thrown upwards it decelerates. Acceleration is then equal to −9.8 m/s². Acceleration is negative.
- When the ball falls back to the ground it accelerates. Acceleration = +9.8 m/s².
- The equation can only be used when an object travels with constant uniform acceleration in a straight line.

Example: A ball is thrown vertically upwards at 16 m/s. Ignoring air resistance and taking $g = 9.8$ m/s² calculate how high it goes.

We know that when it reaches the highest point it will be (momentarily) stationary, so velocity, $v = 0$.

$u = 16$ m/s
$v = 0$ m/s
$a = -9.8$ m/s²
$v^2 - u^2 = 2as$
$0 - (16)^2 = (2 \times -9.8 \times s)$
$0 - 256 = -19.6s$
$19.6s = 256$, so $s = 13$ m (to 2 significant figures)

6 A ball is thrown upwards with a velocity of 11 m/s. How high does it go? Assume $g = 9.8$ m/s².

7 An apple drops from a tree and falls 2.5 m to the ground. What is its speed when it hits the ground? Assume $g = 9.8$ m/s² and ignore air resistance.

Heavy or massive?

Learning objectives:

- identify the correct units for mass and weight
- explain the difference between mass and weight
- understand how weight is an effect of gravitational fields.

Everyone knows that most things fall to the ground and that it's gravity that causes this to happen. This doesn't mean that gravity only acts downwards. It's a force of attraction between any two objects, such as you and the person you're sitting next to. However, you only notice it if at least one of the objects is massive.

Weight or mass?

Some people say they want to lose weight and they may keep weighing themselves. The scales are probably marked in kilograms (kg). Even if you never use scales, you'll know that you buy food such as sugar and flour by weight. The bags are marked in kilograms. In these examples weight is being confused with mass.

It's important, in science, to understand that mass and weight are not the same thing.

Mass is the amount of substance that is present in an object. It is measured in kilograms. **Weight** is the force acting on that mass, if it is in a gravitational field. As weight is a force, it is measured in newtons (N).

1 **An astronaut on the Moon feels much lighter than on Earth. Have they lost weight?**

2 **Denzil says that a weighing scale is actually a forcemeter. Is he right? Explain.**

newtonmeter

Figure 5.14 The weight of an object can be measured using a **newtonmeter**

Weight is a force

Gravity is a non-contact force. It is useful to think of it as a force field; anything in a gravitational field will experience a force of attraction. We are all in the Earth's gravitational field; it is attracting us towards the Earth.

Weight is the force acting on an object due to gravity. The weight of an object depends on the **gravitational field strength** at the point where the object is, and on the mass of the object. The weight of an object can be calculated using the equation:

weight = mass × gravitational field strength

$$W = mg$$

KEY INFORMATION

Remember that in science we measure mass in kilograms and weight in newtons. We use different units because they are different things, but there is a relationship between them.

Weight W is measured in newtons N (Figure 5.14), mass m in kg and gravitational field strength g in N/kg. On Earth g is taken to be 9.8 N/kg. g is also given as 9.8 m/s^2. The units are equivalent.

Example: Calculate the weight on Earth of a 5 kg mass. Assume g = 9.8 N/kg.

$W = mg$

$\quad$ = 5 kg × 9.8 N/kg

$\quad$ = 49 N

3 Write down the weight on Earth of objects having a mass of:

$\quad$ a 7 kg

$\quad$ b 0.5 kg

$\quad$ c 400 g

4 A steel block weighs 30 N on Earth.

$\quad$ a What is its mass?

$\quad$ b The steel block is taken to Mars where it weighs 11.1 N. Calculate the gravitational field strength on Mars.

Losing weight in space

Mass is a property of an object and is constant wherever you are. Weight, however, depends not only on the mass but also on the gravitational field strength. On the Moon, gravity (at the surface) is around a sixth of that on Earth, so everything weighs one sixth of what it does on Earth. Scales are forcemeters where the scale is given in kilograms. Standing on the scales in a lunar space station would give a reading one sixth of that on the Earth. Your mass is a constant but your weight is much less.

In deep space, well away from any stars or planets, you would be weightless. You would still have mass though, and if you wanted to move from one end of your spacecraft to the other, you would still need to apply a force.

5 Alex says that weighing scales should all carry a label saying 'calibrated for use on planet Earth only'. Is he right?

6 An astronaut in deep space (where there is no gravity) is at one end of her craft and wants to move to the other. She pushes against the inside of the craft with a force of 25 N and this causes her to accelerate at 0.5 m/s^2. What is her weight?

7 Describe a measuring instrument that could give a correct measurement of mass on the Earth and on the Moon without having to change any settings.

KEY INFORMATION

The weight of an object can be considered to act at a single point. We call this point the object's centre of mass.

Weight▼

The weight is shown as a force vector passing through the object's centre of mass, X

Forces and motion

Learning objectives:

- understand what a force does
- explain what happens to an object if all the forces acting on it cancel each other out
- analyse how this applies to everyday situations.

KEY WORDS

balanced forces
equilibrium
Newton's first law
resultant force

ABS (anti-lock braking system) brakes stop a car more quickly by rapidly pumping the brakes and preventing skidding.

Thinking about forces

If we think about an object, we can usually identify the forces that are acting on it. For example, an apple growing on a tree (Figure 5.15) has the force of gravity acting downwards; this is its weight. There is another force acting, vertically upwards, through the stalk. These two forces are equal and opposite. They cancel out and the apple doesn't move.

Let's think of another situation: that of a parachutist. The parachutist jumps out of an aircraft and is falling. After a while, the parachutist reaches a steady speed called the terminal velocity. There is a downwards force weight, and an upwards force, which is called drag, or air resistance (Figure 5.16). When these two forces are equal and opposite, they cancel out.

Figure 5.15 **Balanced forces** on an apple hanging from a stalk

Figure 5.16 Balanced forces on a parachutist falling at a steady speed

1. **The weight of the apple in Figure 5.15 is 1 N. What is the force upwards in the stalk?**

2. **When the parachutist in Figure 5.16 opens the parachute:**

   a **What will happen to the size of the drag force?**

   b **Will the two forces still be in balance immediately after the parachute opens?**

3. **Is it *always* true that when all the forces on an object balance out it will be stationary?**

DID YOU KNOW?

For a parachutist in free fall, before the parachute is released, the terminal velocity is around 50 m/s (180 km/h). However, by assuming a diving position this can increase to twice as much.

Newton's first law

Figure 5.17 If the forces cancel out, the resultant force is zero

An object may have several forces acting on it (Figure 5.17). A number of forces acting on an object may be replaced by a single force that has the same effect as all the original forces acting together. This single force is called the **resultant force**. If the forces are in balance, they cancel each other out and the resultant force is zero. The object behaves as if there is no force on it at all. The object will be in **equilibrium**; it will not accelerate.

Newton's first law says that if the resultant force acting on an object is zero, it will:

- if stationary, remain stationary
- if moving, keep moving at a steady speed in a straight line.

4. **If the resultant of two forces is zero, what must be true about:**

   a their size?

   b their direction?

5. **Look at the three forces shown in Figure 5.17. If the resultant of the three forces is zero, what must be true about the sizes of those forces?**

6. **In addition to the forces shown in Figure 5.17, there will also be weight, acting downwards, and a reaction force, acting upwards. How do these also obey Newton's first law?**

Applying Newton's first law

One of the most important questions to ask about a situation in which forces are acting on an object is whether the resultant force in a certain direction is zero. In this case Newton's first law applies and a stationary object will remain at rest and if the object is moving it will continue to move in a straight line and at constant velocity. Examples of this are a boulder resting on the ground and a bicycle being pedalled along a level road at steady speed in a straight line.

7. **Explain why there is a zero resultant force for a boulder on the ground.**

8. **Explain why there is a zero resultant force in the horizontal direction for a bicycle being pedalled along a level road at steady speed in a straight line.**

9. **Explain why, in the example of the bicycle, if the cyclist gets tired, the resultant force may no longer be zero.**

10. **Describe the motion of the Earth if the Sun suddenly vanished.**

DID YOU KNOW?

Deep in space, with no drag or gravitational forces to affect it, a spacecraft moving with its rockets off will keep moving forever without slowing down or speeding up.

REMEMBER!

A normal contact force is exerted on an object by, for example, the surface of a floor or wall it is in **contact** with. The force is at right angles to the surface. In physics, 'normal to' means 'at right angles to'.

Resultant forces

KEY WORDS

balanced forces
components of a force
free-body diagram
resolving a force
resultant force
unbalanced forces

Learning objectives:

- calculate the resultant of a number of forces
- draw free-body diagrams to find resultant forces
- understand that a force can be resolved into two components acting at right angles to each other.

There's always more than one force acting in a situation. For example, when you pull a box across the floor the friction force acts in the opposite direction to the pulling force on the box.

Combining forces

When there are several forces acting on an object, we can work out what their combined effect is. If one child is behind a sledge, pushing it along, and another is in front, pulling it, we can combine these forces by adding them. In a tug-of-war, two teams are pulling in opposite directions. The force applied by one team should be subtracted from that applied by the other team to find out what the combined force is. The combined force is called the **resultant force**.

Figure 5.18 The forces are **balanced**. The resultant force is zero.

Figure 5.19 The forces are **unbalanced**. The resultant force is not zero.

1. Gemma and Alan are pushing a packing case across the floor, each applying a force of 40 N. The friction opposing the motion is 50 N. What is the resultant force?

2. Jo is driving her car along a level road. The engine is providing 1500 N of force. Air resistance is opposing the motion with a value of 1000 N and friction accounts for another 500 N. What is the resultant force?

HIGHER TIER ONLY

Free-body diagrams

A **free-body diagram** shows the magnitude and direction of the forces acting on an object. This saves us from having to spend a lot of time drawing the exact shape. The object (such as the aircraft shown in Figure 5.20) is represented by a point. The force arrows all start from the centre of the point.

Figure 5.20 Forces on an aircraft

A free-body diagram for the jet aircraft is shown in Figure 5.21. It shows all the forces acting. The direction of the forces is shown by the direction of the arrows, and the size of the forces by the length of the arrows.

3. Draw a free-body diagram for a stationary car.

4. Draw a free-body diagram for an aeroplane flying horizontally with positive acceleration.

Figure 5.21 The free-body diagram for the jet aeroplane

Finding forces from a vector diagram

You can determine the magnitude and direction of a resultant force by drawing a scale diagram.

To work out the resultant of the forces in Figure 5.22, draw the 3 N force as shown in Figure 5.23. Then draw the 4 N force with its tail joining on to the head of the 3 N force. The lengths of the arrows represent the magnitudes of the forces. Choose a suitable scale, such as 1 cm = 1 N.

The resultant force is the imaginary line that goes from A to B in Figure 5.23. The magnitude of the resultant force is found by measuring the length of the line and the direction of the resultant force is found by measuring the angle θ. In this case you should find that the resultant force is 5 N at an angle of 37° above the horizontal.

Figure 5.22 Free-body diagram for two forces acting at right angles

Figure 5.23 A scale diagram to calculate the resultant force

5 Two forces act on an object. One force is 5 N to the right and the other force is 12 N upwards. Draw a scale diagram to find the magnitude and direction of the resultant force.

6 A 12 N force is pulling an object to the right and a 16 N force is pulling it downwards. Determine the size of the third force, required to keep the object still, by drawing a scale diagram.

Looking at this the other way round, if you take a single force you can find two forces which, when combined, will produce a resultant force with the same magnitude and direction as the original. This is called **resolving the force** into **components**. It is useful to resolve a force into two perpendicular components, such as the horizontal and vertical components of the force. For example the 5 N force in Figure 5.23 has the same effect as the 3 N and 4 N forces acting together at right angles. You can use a scale diagram to determine the size of the components.

Example:

A force of magnitude 100 N acts in a direction of 40° to the horizontal. Resolve this force into horizontal and vertical components.

Draw a scale diagram with the 100 N force at 40° to the horizontal. Choose a scale that will give a large triangle. At 5 N:1 cm the force arrow is 20 cm long.

Draw a straight line down to the *y*-axis and measure the length of the line. This is the horizontal component of the force.

Length = 15.4 cm so horizontal component = 77 N

Draw a straight line down to the *x*-axis and measure its length. This is the vertical component of the force.

Length = 12.8 cm so vertical component = 64 N

Figure 5.24 Scale diagram for example

7 A 14.1 N force acts at 45° above the horizontal to the right. Determine the vertical and horizontal components of this force.

8 The 14.1 N force in question 7 acts together with a 14.1 N force which points at 45° below the horizontal. Determine the resultant force produced by these two forces.

Forces and acceleration

Learning objectives:

- explain what happens to the motion of an object when the resultant force is not zero
- analyse situations in which a non-zero resultant force is acting
- explain what inertia is.

The record for the fastest object made by humans is held by the Helios 2 spacecraft, which reached over 246 000 km/h. It has a very elliptical orbit around the Sun which means it accelerates as a result of the Sun's massive gravitational field.

What does a force do?

When the driver presses on the accelerator pedal, it increases the forward **force** of the engine. This makes the car accelerate.

The force of the engine acts forwards and there will be other forces opposing this: friction and air resistance. However, at this point the force from the engine is greater than the opposing forces and so the car accelerates (Figure 5.25). It speeds up.

Figure 5.25 The car accelerates

(a)

(b)

Figure 5.26 Forces on a car

① In which direction are the resultant forces acting in Figures 5.25 and 5.26?

② The driver of the car in Figure 5.26 presses the accelerator harder so that the speed increases. What will happen to the resultant force?

Newton's second law

Force, mass and acceleration are linked by the equation:

resultant force = mass × acceleration

$F = ma$

where F is the **resultant force** in N, m is the mass in kg and a is the acceleration in m/s². This is **Newton's second law**.

The resultant force is a single force that has the same effect as all the original forces acting together.

Example: A car has a mass of 1000 kg. What force is needed to give it an acceleration of 5 m/s²?

$F = ma$

$= 1000$ kg $× 5$ m/s²

$= 5000$ N

3 A car of mass 1200 kg has a resultant forward force acting on it of 4200 N. Calculate its acceleration.

4 The weight of an apple is 1 N and it accelerates downwards at 10 m/s². What is its mass?

5 What force is needed to accelerate a 4000 kg rocket upwards at 2 m/s²? (g = 9.8 N/kg)

HIGHER TIER ONLY

Inertia

Figure 5.27 Once a massive tanker is moving it is difficult to stop

Massive objects are hard to start to move and also very difficult to stop (Figure 5.27). They have an inbuilt reluctance to start or stop moving. This is called **inertia** (from the Latin for laziness). Inertia is the natural tendency of objects to resist changes in their velocity.

Inertial mass is a measure of how difficult it is to change the velocity of an object.

Inertial mass is defined by the ratio of force over acceleration:

$$\text{inertial mass} = \frac{\text{force}}{\text{acceleration}}$$

DID YOU KNOW?

Some large ships can take 10 km to stop from a cruising speed of 12 km/h.

6 What is inertia?

7 How do you calculate inertial mass?

8 Another form of mass is **gravitational mass**. Suggest what the difference is between gravitational mass and inertial mass.

9 An object has a mass of 2 kg. What are its inertial mass and its gravitational mass?

REQUIRED PRACTICAL

Investigating the acceleration of an object

Learning objectives:

- plan an investigation to explore an idea
- analyse results to identify patterns and draw conclusions
- compare results with scientific theory.

There is a very important relationship between force, mass and acceleration. This is a fundamental idea in physics, yet it is possible to demonstrate it using fairly straightforward apparatus and analysing the results with care.

Planning your investigation

The relationship being explored here is the one between force, mass and acceleration. The acceleration can be determined in several ways; for example, light and a data logger or a ticker timer could be used. The effects of varying either force or acceleration can then be investigated.

Figure 5.28 A smartphone accelerometer chip measures acceleration. This enables the auto-rotate function to turn the screen display vertical or horizontal when the phone is moved.

Figure 5.29

Look at Figure 5.29. The falling mass is attached to the trolley by a thread. If the trolley moves to the right it will pull the tape through the timer so the speed can be measured.

1. **Describe the motion of the trolley when the mass hanging on the string is released.**

2. **What force makes the trolley move? What is true about the size of this force during this experiment?**

3. **How could the force on the trolley be altered?**

KEY INFORMATION

With both the ticker timer and light gate apparatus, the acceleration of the trolley is calculated by measuring its speed at two points and the time taken to go between the two points. A data logger can be set up to measure speed directly, from the time it takes a card attached to the trolley to pass through the light gate. With a ticker timer, the separation in time between dots on the ticker tape is 1/50th of a second (0.02 s). Measuring the distance between each dot and dividing this by the time (0.02 s) gives the velocity of the trolley at one point.

4 When we are altering the force, what can we do with the remaining masses to make sure the mass of the system doesn't change?

5 Explain how the mass of the trolley could be altered.

Analysing the results

When analysing results we look for patterns or similarities and draw these together in a conclusion. Adam's group are seeing if their data confirmed that the acceleration of the trolley was proportional to the force acting on it. They used the equipment in Figure 5.29, altering the force on the trolley but keeping the mass on the trolley constant. The table shows their results.

6 What would you expect Adam to find happened to the acceleration when he increased the force acting on the trolley and kept the mass of the system constant?

7 Do his group's results show this?

8 Plot a graph of force against acceleration. What shape is it?

9 What does this show?

10 What is happening to the acceleration of the trolley as its mass is increased?

11 What shape would the graph of mass against acceleration have?

Amy's group were doing a different investigation. They kept the force acting on the trolley constant but altered the mass of the trolley. Their results are shown in the table below.

> These pages are designed **❶** to help you think about aspects of the investigation rather than to guide you through it step by step.

Force (N)	Acceleration (m/s^2)
1	0.5
2	0.9
3	1.4
4	2.1
5	2.5
6	3.0
7	3.6
8	4.1

> **REMEMBER!**
>
> We can show relationships of direct or inverse proportionality both by calculation and by graphing.

Mass of trolley (g)	Acceleration (m/s^2)
20	5.0
30	3.3
40	2.5
50	2.0
60	1.7
70	1.4
80	1.2

Exploring the connection with accepted theory

Newton's second law of motion says that if a force accelerates an object, the acceleration is directly proportional to the force and inversely proportional to the mass of the object. We should be able to analyse the results to see whether they show this relationship.

12 Explain how Adam's and Amy's results support this.

13 If the force is tripled and the mass is doubled, what happens to the acceleration?

Newton's third law

KEY WORDS

Newton's third law

Learning objectives:

- identify force pairs
- understand and be able to apply Newton's third law.

Soldiers firing a large gun never stand behind the gun because the gun moves backwards when it is fired (Figure 5.30).

Force pairs

When two objects, A and B, interact and A exerts a force on B, there is always another force: B exerts a force on A. The forces are equal in size but act in opposite directions and on different objects.

Some examples of force pairs:

- When you walk, your foot pushes the ground backwards; the ground pushes your foot forwards.
- If you stand on a skateboard next to a wall and push on the wall, the wall pushes back on you.
- In a small boat, if you push on the quayside, it pushes back on you, and you and the boat move away.

Figure 5.30 A cannon being fired

1 **What can you say about each pair of forces?**

2 **The tyres of a car push on the road. Name the other force in the force pair.**

Newton's third law

Newton's third law states that whenever two objects interact, the forces they exert on each other are equal and opposite. When two cars collide, the forces on each are of equal size but in opposite directions (Figure 5.31):

$F_1 = F_2$

Figure 5.31 Forces in a collision

The forces in the pair:

- are the same size
- act in opposite directions
- act on *different* objects.

COMMON MISCONCEPTION

When a pair of objects produce a force on each other we draw the forces as vectors. But, unlike the forces in a free-body diagram, the forces in a Newton's third law pair act on *different* objects.

3. Imagine two people, each sitting on an office chair with wheels. One pushes against the other.

    a Describe what happens next.

    b Explain how this illustrates Newton's third law.

4. Kim and Ben are standing on ice. Kim pushes Ben with a force of 50 N. What force acts on Kim? Describe what happens next.

5. A lorry collides head on with a small car. Compare:

    a the resultant forces acting on the lorry and the car

    b the decelerations of the lorry and the car.

6. An astronaut is floating in space and has become detached from her spaceship. She is wearing a backpack that she is able to remove from her suit. Suggest what she could do to get back to the ship.

Further ideas about force pairs

It is often useful to realise that the pair of forces in Newton's third law are between two objects only. If object A exerts a force on object B, then object B exerts a force of equal size but in the opposite direction on object A. The two forces must be the same type of force.

7. A cat is falling to the ground having jumped out of a tree. Ignoring air resistance, the only force acting on the cat is its weight.

    a Complete the sentence by selecting the correct word.

    The force on the cat is due to the Earth pulling on the cat. This type of force is a **magnetic / electrostatic / gravitational** force.

    b Describe the other force in the force pair in this situation.

8. The cat is now sitting on a table.

    a What is the other force in the force pair to the cat's weight?

    b State the other pair of forces which involve the cat.

9. The cat jumps off the table and falls to the ground. Describe how the cat affects the motion of the Earth as it is falling.

10. Describe all of the forces that occur between your body and the Earth when you jump upwards, reach a maximum height and land again.

KEY INFORMATION

The normal contact force when two surfaces are in contact is one of a force pair. But Newton's third law also applies to non-contact forces, for example due to gravitational attraction.

Figure 5.32 By Newton's third law, the boy exerts a gravitational force upwards on the Earth of the same size as the gravitational force downwards on the boy (**weight**)

Momentum

KEY WORDS

conservation of
momentum
momentum

Learning objectives:

- explain what is meant by momentum
- total momentum is always conserved in collisions.

Understanding momentum explains what happens to both vehicles in a car crash.

HIGHER TIER ONLY

Understanding momentum

A moving object has **momentum**. The amount of momentum an object has depends on its mass and its velocity:

momentum = mass × velocity

$p = mv$

where p is the momentum in kg m/s, m is the mass in kg and v is the velocity in m/s.

Example: Evie has a mass of 60 kg. Her momentum is 120 kg m/s. How fast is she moving?

momentum = mass × velocity

$$\text{velocity} = \frac{\text{momentum}}{\text{mass}} = \frac{120 \text{ kg m/s}}{60 \text{ kg}} = 2 \text{ m/s.}$$

KEY INFORMATION

Velocity is a vector, so momentum is also a vector.

1. Calculate the momentum of a car with a mass of 1000 kg travelling at 20 m/s.

2. Tom has a mass of 60 kg. His momentum is 240 kg m/s. How fast is he moving?

3. Calculate the momentum of:

    a a football of mass 420 g, velocity 35 m/s

    b a football player of mass 65 kg, velocity 3.0 m/s.

4. What velocity must a 50 kg football player have to have the same momentum as the player in question 3b?

Conservation of momentum

The principle of **conservation of momentum** states that the total momentum of a closed system does not change. This means that the total momentum before an event, such as a collision or explosion, is equal to the total momentum after the event. For example, think about two moving objects that collide then move apart. If one object gains momentum from the collision, the other object must lose the same amount of momentum so that the total momentum remains the same.

KEY INFORMATION

A closed system means that no external forces act on the objects involved in the event.

Example: A skater is standing still on ice in the middle of a frozen lake. The skater takes off her shoulder bag and throws it forwards. Explain why the skater moves backwards.

momentum before = momentum after

Before throwing the bag, nothing is moving. The total momentum of the skater and bag is zero. After throwing the bag, the bag has forwards momentum, so the skater has equal backwards momentum.

5 Consider yourself and the Earth as one system. Imagine jumping in the air. While you are in the air, what has happened to:

    a your momentum

    b the Earth's momentum

    c the system's momentum?

6 Two toy cars of equal mass are clamped together with a compressed spring. Describe the motion of the two cars when the clamp is released.

7 A man stands in a boat in the middle of a lake. He kicks a football into the water. Explain what happens to the motion of the man and the boat.

DID YOU KNOW?

If everyone in the world got together in one place and jumped up at the same time, while all the people were in the air, the Earth would gain momentum in the opposite direction. However, due to the extremely large mass of the Earth, the speed would be tiny – of the order of 10^{-13} m/s.

Transfer of momentum in collisions

When two objects travelling on the same straight line collide, momentum can be transferred between them, although the total momentum does not change. For example, when a snooker ball strikes another snooker ball, some or all of the first ball's momentum is transferred to the second ball, making it move. If the second ball is stationary, it is possible for *all* of the first ball's momentum to be transferred to the second ball.

8 A car runs into the back of a stationary lorry. After colliding, the car and lorry move off together. How does the final speed of the joined car and lorry compare with the initial speed of the moving car before the collision?

9 Tom slides a penny towards another penny that is not moving. Explain why it is possible for the penny that was stationary to move away with about the same speed of the original moving penny.

10 If Tom slides a pound coin towards a penny that is not moving, what will happen to the penny?

Keeping safe on the road

Learning objectives:

- explain the factors that affect stopping distance
- explain the dangers caused by large deceleration.

Road safety campaigns use slogans such as 'Kill your speed not a child!' What difference does reducing speed make in the case of an accident?

Driving safely

A car driver cannot begin to stop a car immediately. It takes time for the driver to react to a stimulus. This is called **reaction time**. The greater the speed of the car, the further it travels while the driver thinks (Figure 5.33).

Thinking distance is the distance travelled during the reaction time. It is the distance travelled between the driver seeing a danger and taking action to avoid it, such as braking.

Braking distance is the distance travelled before a car stops after the brakes have been applied. It increases as the speed of the car increases.

Stopping distance = thinking distance + braking distance (Figure 5.34)

Figure 5.33 How speed affects stopping distance, for a typical car in good conditions

Figure 5.34 Stopping distance

> **REMEMBER!**
>
> Don't confuse thinking distance and braking distance.

1. Laura's thinking distance is 12 m. Use Figure 5.33 to determine:
   a her speed
   b her braking distance
   c her stopping distance
2. Joe is driving at 80 km/h (22 m/s). Use Figure 5.33 to find out what his stopping distance is in m.

Factors that affect stopping distance

Reaction time varies between 0.2 s and 0.9 s, but is typically about 0.7 s. Reaction time and hence thinking distance may increase if a driver is:

- tired
- under the influence of alcohol or other drugs
- distracted or lacks concentration.

The braking distance may increase when:
- the road is wet or icy
- the car has poor brakes or bald tyres
- the speed of the car is greater.

Figure 5.34 shows how important it is to keep a suitable braking distance to avoid accidents.

The dangers caused by large deceleration

Kinetic energy is transferred away from a vehicle that is slowing down. Work done by the friction force between the brakes and the rotating wheel reduces the kinetic energy of the vehicle. Energy is transferred to the brake pads, which heat up.

Many journeys involve slowing down to rest from a high speed and do so without discomfort or injury. However, it is when the vehicle needs to stop from a very high speed in a short time (a large deceleration) that problems can arise.

If deceleration is very rapid, it means a large braking force is being applied. This can result in the brake pads overheating or the driver losing control of the direction of the vehicle.

HIGHER TIER ONLY

To estimate the force needed to stop a vehicle, you could either calculate the deceleration and then find the force from $F = ma$, or calculate how much kinetic energy ($\frac{1}{2}mv^2$) must be transferred away from the car and equate this to the work done (Fs) by the braking force.

Example: A lorry is travelling on the motorway. Estimate the braking force needed to stop the lorry in a distance of 100 m.

We need to estimate the following values: mass of lorry (40 000 kg), initial speed of lorry (25 m/s) and braking distance of lorry (100 m).

$v^2 - u^2 = 2as$

$0 - 25^2 = 2 \times a \times 100$

$\quad a = -625/200 = -3.125 \text{ m/s}^2$

force $= \text{mass} \times \text{acceleration}$

$\quad = 40\ 000 \text{ kg} - 3.125 \text{ m/s}^2$

$\quad = -125\ 000 \text{ N or} -125 \text{ kN}$

3 A car is travelling on the motorway. Use the idea of work done to estimate the braking force needed to stop the car safely. Give your answer to three significant figures.

Forces and energy in springs

Learning objectives:

- explain why you need two forces to stretch a spring
- describe the difference between elastic and inelastic deformation
- calculate extension, compression and elastic potential energy.

KEY WORDS
....

compression
elastic deformation
elastic potential energy
extension
inelastic deformation
limit of proportionality
linear
nonlinear
spring constant

Some skyscrapers are mounted on springs. This prevents the building from shaking too much in an earthquake. The builders need to make sure that the springs are strong enough to withstand the weight of the building.

Forces on a spring

The spring in Figure 5.35 is being stretched by two forces. The weight of the mass is pulling the spring downwards. However, if this was the only force acting on the spring then it would accelerate towards the ground. The spring is in equilibrium. The other force is from the bar, which is pulling the top of the spring upwards.

1. **What is the resultant force on the spring if it is at rest?**

2. **Determine the force at the top of the spring when the weight of the mass is 3 N.**

Forces can stretch and squash a spring elastically or inelastically. **Elastic deformation** occurs when the spring returns back to its original length when the forces are removed. A spring that is permanently altered has undergone **inelastic deformation**.

3. **What would happen to a bed mattress if its springs had been inelastically deformed?**

The **extension** or **compression** of the spring is how much its length changes when the forces are applied. You measure extension when the spring is being stretched, and compression when it is being squashed.

4. **A spring has an original length of 6.0 cm. It is then squashed to a length of 4.8 cm. Determine the compression of the spring.**

Figure 5.35 Forces stretching a spring

The relationship between force and extension

You can see that the graph in Figure 5.36 is a straight line up to a point which is called the **limit of proportionality**. This shows that there is a **linear** relationship between the force and extension when the force applied is small.

DID YOU KNOW?
....

Scientists have developed a material that can elastically deform to 20 times its original length without breaking.

Since the straight line goes through the origin, we can also say that the force is directly proportional to the extension.

You can calculate the force or the extension using the equation:

force = **spring constant** × extension

$F = ke$

where k, the spring constant, is measured in N/m and depends on the spring; e can be the extension or the compression and is measured in m.

Since $F = ke$, $k = F/e$ and the spring constant for an elastic material can be found from the gradient of the straight part of a force–extension graph. Note, however, that the graph in Figure 5.36 is plotted for extension against force, so the gradient of this graph is $1/k$.

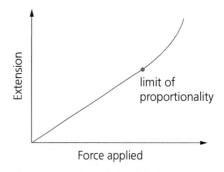

Figure 5.36 The relationship between force and extension for an elastic object, such as a spring

5 **A spring has an extension of 0.08 m when it is stretched by a force of 4 N. What is its spring constant?**

6 **A spring has a spring constant of 2000 N/m and is 10 cm long. What force is needed to compress the spring to a length of 4 cm?**

Beyond the limit of proportionality, the line in Figure 5.36 begins to curve. The relationship between force and extension is now **nonlinear**.

Elastic potential energy

Doing work on the spring transfers energy into the **elastic potential energy** store of the spring. The amount of work done equals the amount of elastic potential energy stored. This energy can be transferred to other energy stores when the spring returns to its original length.

If the limit of proportionality is not exceeded, you can calculate the elastic potential energy from the equation:

elastic potential energy
= 0.5 × spring constant × (extension or compression)²

$E_e = \frac{1}{2} ke^2$

Example: A block is attached to a spring. The spring constant is 28 N/m and the total mass of the block and spring is 50 g. What is the maximum vertical height the block can reach after the spring is compressed by 5 cm then released? (g = 9.8 N/kg)

$E_e = \frac{1}{2} ke^2 = \frac{1}{2} \times 28 \times (0.05)^2 = 0.035$ J

Provided no energy is dissipated, the decrease in the elastic potential energy store equals the increase in the gravitational potential energy store:

$E_p = mgh = 0.035$ J

$h = \dfrac{0.035}{(0.05 \times 9.8)} = 0.07$ m

7 **Calculate the elastic potential energy stored by a spring that has been stretched by 2 cm. The spring constant is 30 N/m.**

8 **A 10 g spring is stretched by 10 cm. It is then released and flies 1 m upwards before it starts to fall down again. Assuming all of the elastic potential energy transfers to gravitational potential energy, estimate the spring constant of the spring. What else have you assumed in your calculation? (g = 9.8 N/kg)**

REQUIRED PRACTICAL

Investigate the relationship between force and the extension of a spring

KEY WORDS

anomaly
extension
mean
spring constant

Learning objectives:

- interpret readings to show patterns and trends
- interpret graphs to form conclusions
- apply the equation for a straight line to the graph.

A class of students have been making and testing springs. They have then investigated how these springs behave when loaded with a weight. They have carried out the experiment and gathered the data. Their next job is to see what it shows.

> These pages are designed to help you think about aspects of the investigation rather than to guide you through it step by step.

Analysing the results

When analysing results look for patterns or similarities and see whether these can be used to draw a conclusion.

Ellie investigated three springs and recorded her data in a table. The table shows the readings and the calculations.

Force (N)	Spring 1 extension (mm)				Spring 2 extension (mm)				Spring 3 extension (mm)			
	1st reading	2nd reading	3rd reading	Mean	1st reading	2nd reading	3rd reading	Mean	1st reading	2nd reading	3rd reading	Mean
10	8	9	7	8	3	3	4	3	4	4	4	4
20	20	13	12	15	6	7	6	6	8	9	10	9
30	20	19	30	23	10	10	11	10	14	13	12	13
40	34	30	32	32	13	13	13	13	16	16	16	16
50	35	45	40	40	16	17	17	17	22	22	20	21

1. What apparatus should be used to measure the force applied to the spring?

2. How should the **extension** of the spring be measured?

3. How did Ellie calculate the **mean** values?

4. Are there any **anomalies**?

5. Suggest whether these calculations are a good way of getting close to the true values of the extension.

DID YOU KNOW?

The relationship between the force on a spring and the extension it produces was first put forward by Robert Hooke in 1660. He was an inventor, a scientist and an architect. He invented the universal joint now used in the transmission systems of motor cars, the iris diaphragm used in cameras, and he was first to coin the word 'cell' in biology. He designed many of the new buildings after the Great Fire of London.

Making sense of the graph

Darren's group have drawn a graph showing extension against the weight hung from the spring for one of their springs (Figure 5.37). They are now looking at the graph to see what conclusion they can draw.

6 What does the straight part of the graph show?

7 What happened in the curved part of the graph?

8 What conclusion could Darren draw from this graph?

Using the equation of a straight line on a graph

Katie's group have plotted the graphs from the results of their experiments for three springs on a graph (Figure 5.38). They know that any straight line graph can be described using the general formula $y = mx + c$ and they are applying it to these lines.

With the first of these (A) they can see that:

- x is the force, which changes from 0 N to 8 N
- y is the extension, which changes from 0 cm to 16 cm
- c is the y-intercept, which is 0 as the line crosses the y-axis at (0,0)

Therefore $16 = (m \times 8) + 0$, so the gradient $m = 2$.

Since the intercept on Figure 5.38 is zero, the extension is directly proportional to the force. Since:

force applied to a spring = **spring constant** × extension

extension = force applied to a spring/spring constant

so the gradient of the graph is 1/spring constant.

The spring constant can be found from 1/gradient, or $1/m$.

9 Calculate the value of m for springs B and C.

10 Use the formula $k = F/e$ to calculate the spring constant for springs B and C. Explain which of the springs was the stiffest.

11 The spring constant can also be found by redrawing the graph so that extension is on the horizontal axis and force on the vertical axis. The spring constant is then the gradient of the line for each of the springs.

Try doing this and then check your answers against those for the previous question.

12 a Determine the area under line A in Figure 5.38. (Make sure the extension is in metres.)

b Calculate the elastic potential energy stored in spring A when a force of 8 N is applied. ($E_e = \frac{1}{2} ke^2$.)

c Compare your answers to parts (a) and (b) and explain why this is the case.

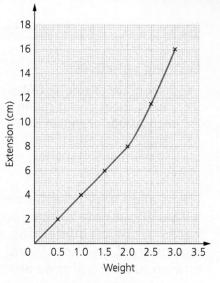

Figure 5.37 Results from Darren's group

Figure 5.38 Results from Katie's group

REMEMBER!

The spring constant is always measured in N/m, so it is important to make sure extension is measured in metres.

KEY CONCEPT

Forces and acceleration

Learning objectives:

- recognise examples of balanced and unbalanced forces
- apply ideas about speed and acceleration to explain sensations of movement
- apply ideas about inertia and circular motion to explain braking and cornering.

KEY WORDS

acceleration
balanced
force
inertia
speed
velocity

The reason why scientists study forces is that they tell us about how things move. If you know all the forces acting on something, you can predict very accurately if and how it will move. Newton's laws of motion are very simple but the situations you can apply them to can be complex. The laws were first suggested by Isaac Newton and published in 1686. NASA used these simple laws to get men safely to the Moon and back, and theme parks use them to thrill us on their rides.

Figure 5.39 Isaac Newton

Balanced and unbalanced forces

People who design rides for theme parks understand what will make a ride exciting. It's not just **speed**. Stealth, at Thorpe Park, is the UK's fastest roller coaster and reaches 128 km/h, which is not much faster than a car on a motorway, but is much more exciting. You need high **acceleration** for a good ride and that requires **force**, or, to be precise, unbalanced force.

Newton explained that if all the forces on an object balance out, its speed will be constant and its direction will not change, or it will not move if it is at rest. If the forces are not **balanced**, the object's speed or direction will change.

It is the acceleration that makes roller coasters (Figure 5.40) such fun. Newton's first law of motion states that a moving object tends to stay moving. This resistance to change is called **inertia**. When the roller coaster speeds up, the back of the seat pushes you forward, accelerating you. When the roller coaster slows down, your body tries to keep going at its original speed. The harness in front of you pushes your body backwards. These pushes and pulls on your body give you the thrills you enjoy.

Figure 5.40 A roller coaster

1 **What happens to the acceleration of the roller coaster if the force propelling it forwards increases?**

Figure 5.41 Going around a loop

2. **Explain what would happen if the roller coaster had a negative acceleration and the passengers weren't wearing restraints.**

Looping the loop

Curves and loops on the ride (Figure 5.41) cause the direction you are travelling in to change, so your **velocity** changes. Remember that a change in velocity is acceleration even if the speed remains constant. To change direction, there needs to be a force towards the centre of the circle that the curve is part of. This is an example of Newton's second law.

3. **You feel the seat pushing you as you go round the loop. Suggest what would happen if there was no seat.**

4. **Why do we say that a train going round a loop is accelerating, even when its speed is constant?**

5. **Use your answer to question 4 to explain the difference between speed and velocity.**

6. **Newton said that unless there is an unbalanced force, an object will continue in a straight line at a steady speed. Describe how this force is applied to the riders in the roller coaster.**

Drop towers

Zumanjaro: Drop of Doom in America is the world's tallest drop tower at 125 m. After a brief pause at the top, you are released and fall under the pull of gravity. You are in free-fall for over 10 s, reaching speeds of over 140 km/h. The force is unbalanced and causes acceleration; the same thing happens (but much more gently) when you descend in a lift.

To slow the ride down and stop it, another unbalanced force is needed. This is provided by giant permanent magnets which provide an upward force.

7. **If a free-fall ride accelerates at 10 m/s² and the loaded car has a mass of 2500 kg, what force is acting?**

8. **If the braking force at the end of the ride was half the size of the force of gravitational attraction, what acceleration would the riders experience?**

9. **A passenger on Zumanjaro was holding an open bottle of water. As the ride accelerated downwards he decided to tip the bottle upside down to make the water fall out. Explain what happened to the water.**

Figure 5.42 A drop tower

DID YOU KNOW?

g-force is a way of comparing forces by measuring the acceleration they produce. A force of $1g$ causes acceleration the same as that of gravity (around 9.8 m/s²). Humans can tolerate greater g-forces horizontally than vertically; accelerating downwards rapidly forces blood into the brain and eyes; any more than $2g$ is dangerous.

MATHS SKILLS

Making estimates of calculations

Learning objectives:

- estimate the results of simple calculations
- round numbers to make an estimate
- calculate order of magnitude.

KEY WORDS

estimate
order of
   magnitude
round

In 1945 the nuclear physicist Enrico Fermi estimated the energy released by the first atomic bomb test by dropping small pieces of paper from his hand. He based his estimate only on the displacement of the scraps of paper (about 2.5 m) while the blast wave was passing and his distance from the site of the explosion (about 15 km).

Making sensible estimates

It is often useful to **estimate** a quantity. To make an estimate, make a sensible approximation. The symbol ~ means 'approximately equal to'.

Example: Estimate the average acceleration of a typical family car that accelerates from rest to a velocity of 100 km/h (about 30 m/s).

Make a sensible approximation of the time taken to accelerate of around 6 s:

The initial velocity is zero.

$$\text{acceleration} = \frac{\text{change in velocity}}{\text{time taken}}$$
$$\sim \frac{(30 \text{ m/s} - 0 \text{ m/s})}{6 \text{ s}}$$
$$\sim 5 \text{ m/s}^2$$

Example: Estimate the sprinting speed for a typical adult.

Make a sensible approximation of the time he or she takes to sprint 100 m: around 15 s.

$$\text{speed} = \frac{\text{distance}}{\text{time}}$$
$$= \frac{100 \text{ m}}{15 \text{ s}}$$
$$= 6.67 \text{ m/s}$$

Write estimates to one significant figure.

speed ~ 7 m/s

1 **Estimate the volume of this book. Show your working and assumptions.**

② **Estimate the running speed for a typical adult over a distance of 500 m. Show your working and assumptions.**

Estimating the result of a calculation by rounding

It is often useful to estimate the result of a calculation without using a calculator. Do this by **rounding** quantities up or down to one significant figure.

Example: Without using a calculator, estimate the deceleration of a van that makes an emergency stop from a speed of 33 m/s. The time taken to brake to a stop is 13 seconds.

$$a = \frac{(v - u)}{t}$$

Substituting rounded values:

$$a \sim \frac{(0 - 30)}{10}$$
$$\sim -3 \text{ m/s}^2$$

③ **Without using a calculator, estimate the deceleration of a car that makes an emergency stop from a speed of 21 m/s. The time taken to brake to a stop is 3.5 seconds.**

④ **For the car whose deceleration you estimated in question 3, use the equation $v^2 = u^2 + 2as$ to estimate the car's braking distance. Then calculate the overall stopping distance using an estimate for a typical value for the reaction time.**

⑤ **Estimate the braking force required to stop the car in question 3. Make a sensible approximation of the mass of the car.**

Orders of magnitude

In question 1, two students estimated the volume of this book. Their estimates were 400 cm³ and 600 cm³.

Both estimates are of the same order of magnitude. An **order of magnitude** is a factor of 10. When two numbers are the same order of magnitude, this means that one of the numbers is less than 10 times larger than the other.

Example: Make an order of magnitude estimate for the time taken by light to travel across our galaxy, the Milky Way. The diameter of the Milky Way is about 7×10^{17} km to 9×10^{17} km. The speed of light is 3.0×10^8 m/s.

$$\text{time} = \frac{\text{distance}}{\text{speed}}$$

Using the nearest order of magnitude:

$$\text{time} = \frac{10^{17} \times 10^3 \text{ m}}{10^8 \text{ m/s}}$$
$$= \frac{10^{20}}{10^8} \text{ s}$$
$$= 10^{12} \text{ s}$$

⑥ **Make an order of magnitude estimate for the mass of air in this room. The density of air at ordinary atmospheric pressure and room temperature is 1.2 kg/m³.**

⑦ **Make an order of magnitude estimate for the time taken by light to travel across the length of the UK.**

> **KEY INFORMATION**
>
> Using rounded values to make an estimate allows you to check that the result you find using your calculator is correct. If your estimate and your calculated answer are not similar, then you may have made a mistake in your calculation, for example when typing in the numbers.

> **KEY INFORMATION**
>
> Use an order of magnitude when the precise value of a quantity is unknown. Make an estimate rounded to the nearest power of 10 and use that in your calculation.

Check your progress

You should be able to:

Know that forces are vectors and have magnitude and direction → Explain the difference between contact and non-contact forces → Represent vector quantities by arrows

Understand that average speed = distance/time → Know that acceleration is the rate at which speed changes → Calculate acceleration from change in velocity/time taken

Explain the significance of the gradient of a distance–time graph → Interpret a journey represented on a distance–time graph → Determine the instantaneous speed from the tangent to a distance–time graph of an accelerating object

Explain the significance of the gradient of a velocity–time graph → Interpret a journey represented on a velocity–time graph → Determine total distance travelled from a velocity–time graph

Recall the equation for uniform motion → Apply the equation for uniform motion → Rearrange the equation for uniform motion

Draw a free-body diagram to represent forces acting on an object → Calculate the resultant force acting on an object → Determine the components of a force

Apply Newton's first law to a stationary object and an object moving in a straight line at a constant speed → Link Newton's first law to the idea of a zero resultant force → Explain what is meant by inertia

State Newton's second law and recall the equation $F = ma$ → Use $F = ma$ to determine force, mass or acceleration → Explain what is meant by inertial mass

Recognise that weight and mass are not the same → Explain the difference between weight and mass → Relate the ideas of weight and mass to Newton's second law

State Newton's third law → Apply Newton's third law to simple equilibrium situations → Explain how Newton's third law applies

State that vehicle speed and reaction time affect the stopping distance of a vehicle → Describe factors that affect a driver's reaction time and a vehicle's braking distance
Explain why the temperature of a vehicle's brakes increases during braking → Calculate braking forces using ideas of stopping distance and energy transfer

Identify measures to increase road safety
Explain what is meant by momentum → Relate measures to increase road safety to ideas about forces and kinetic energy → Describe how the principle of conservation of momentum applies to collisions

Worked example

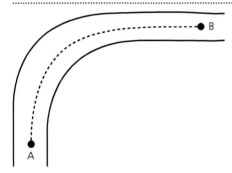

The diagram shows a car travelling round a bend at a constant speed. It took the car 4.5 s to move 90 m from point A to B.

1 Explain why the distance travelled by the car from A to B is greater than the car's displacement at B.

The car's displacement is the distance from A to B in a straight line. The car travelled a further distance as it was going round the curve.

> This is correct. You should also note that distance is a scalar quantity but displacement is a vector quantity with size and direction.

2 Calculate the distance the car travelled from A to B.

$s = v t$ so $v = s t$

$v = 90 \times 4.5$

$= 405 \text{ m/s}$

> The student correctly remembered the equation $s = v t$ but failed to rearrange it correctly as $v = \frac{s}{t}$ to give the answer 20 m/s.

3 Explain why the car is accelerating as it travels round the bend at a constant speed.

Acceleration is a change in velocity and the car's velocity is changing as it goes round the bend.

> Velocity is speed in a given direction. As the car goes round the corner, its speed stays the same but the direction is constantly changing, so its velocity is constantly changing, which is acceleration.

4 Explain what is meant by stopping distance for a car and what factors might affect this.

Stopping distance is the distance the car takes while braking and the distance travelled while thinking to apply the brakes. Ice on the road will cause the brakes not to work and increase the stopping distance.

> You should aim to give at least two factors that affect thinking distance and two factors that affect braking distance. Thinking distance can be affected by tiredness, drugs and alcohol. Braking distance can be affected by adverse road conditions such as rain or ice, and worn tyres or brakes.

End of chapter questions

Getting started

1. In what units are forces measured? `1 Mark`

2. Which one of these is not a force? `1 Mark`

   a weight   b air resistance   c mass   d upthrust

3. Give an example of a contact force and a non-contact force. `2 Marks`

4. A diver has jumped off a diving board and is accelerating vertically downwards towards the water, due to gravity. Draw and label a diagram to show the forces acting on the diver, indicating their relative sizes. `2 Marks`

5. Calculate the average speed of a car when it travels 100 m in 5 s. `2 Marks`

6. On Earth, what is the weight of a 50 kg boy? (g = 9.8 N/kg) `2 Marks`

Going further

7. Look at this distance–time graph for an object.

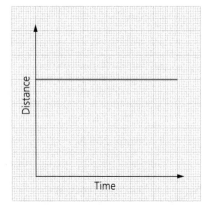

   a Sketch what a velocity–time graph would look like for the same motion. `2 Marks`

   b Explain your answer. `1 Mark`

8. On a distance–time graph, what is represented by a straight line sloping upwards? `1 Mark`

9. A car of mass 1500 kg is travelling at 30 m/s. The driver brakes and the car stops 6s later. Calculate:

   a the initial momentum of the car

   b the deceleration the braking produced

   c the force applied by the brakes to stop the car. `3 Marks`

10. Describe **two** factors that affect the stopping distance of a car. `2 Marks`

More challenging

11 The forces on a car are unbalanced; the resultant force acting on it is not zero. Which *one* of the following statements *cannot* be true?

a It is accelerating

b It is decelerating

c It is travelling in a straight line at a steady speed

d It is travelling in a circular path at a steady speed

`1 Mark`

12 A car is travelling at a constant speed of 20 m/s. Its mass is 1000 kg and the force of friction opposing the motion of the car is 1500 N.

Determine the size of the force that the engine is providing to drive the car.

`1 Mark`

13 Explain the meaning of **limit of proportionality** for a spring.

`2 Marks`

14 Three girls are standing on a wobbly platform, which is on a spring. The spring constant of the spring is 8000 N. The weight of the platform is 100 N. The girls weigh 300 N, 300 N and 500 N.

Calculate the compression of the spring and explain what you have assumed in the calculation.

`3 Marks`

15 The school minibus has a mass of 10000kg and is travelling at 20m/s. The driver then brakes to stop at a red traffic light, taking 10s to do so.

Calculate:

a The acceleration

b The force needed to bring the vehicle to rest.

`4 Marks`

Most demanding

16 What is Newton's third law?

`2 Marks`

17 A car of mass 1500 kg is travelling along a motorway at 25 m/s. Calculate the braking distance of the car if the brakes exert a force of 3000 N.

`2 Marks`

18 A snooker player hit a white ball with her cue. The white ball then collided with a stationary red ball. The player noticed that the white ball stopped after the collision. She also noticed that the red ball moved with the same velocity as the white ball had before the collision.

Explain the physics behind these observations and make a conclusion about the mass of the balls. Assume no friction acts during the collision.

`6 Marks`

`Total: 40 Marks`

WAVES

IDEAS YOU HAVE MET BEFORE:

LIGHT WAVES AND WATER WAVES HAVE SOME THINGS IN COMMON

- All waves carry energy from one place to another.
- When waves hit an object they may be absorbed by it, transmitted or reflected back.
- Waves may change direction (refract) at the point where two different materials meet.

DESCRIBING WAVES

- Frequencies of waves are measured in hertz (Hz).
- Waves travel at different speeds in different materials.
- Sound waves are longitudinal.
- Ripples on the surface of water are transverse.

VISIBLE LIGHT

- Sunlight (white light) is made up of a mixture of many different colours.
- Each colour of light has a different frequency.
- Different colours are absorbed or reflected by different surfaces.
- Light waves can travel through a vacuum.

IN THIS CHAPTER YOU WILL FIND OUT ABOUT:

IN WHAT WAYS DO OTHER ELECTROMAGNETIC WAVES BEHAVE LIKE LIGHT?

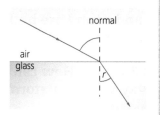

- All electromagnetic waves are transverse waves that transfer energy.
- All electromagnetic waves can be reflected and refracted at a boundary between two different media.

WHAT CHARACTERISTICS OF WAVES CAN BE MEASURED?

- We can measure the speed, wavelength and frequency of waves.
- We can calculate one of these three properties using the other two.
- The amplitude of a wave is its maximum displacement from its rest position.

ARE THERE ANY WAVES BEYOND THE VISIBLE SPECTRUM?

- The visible spectrum is only a small part of a much wider spectrum called the electromagnetic spectrum.
- The invisible waves beyond red are called infrared and those beyond violet are called ultraviolet.
- Gamma rays, X-rays and ultraviolet rays have the highest frequencies (smallest wavelengths) and transfer the most energy.

Describing waves

Learning objectives:

- describe wave motion
- define wavelength and frequency
- apply the relationship between wavelength, frequency and wave velocity.

Light and sound are both waves, but in a thunderstorm, you see lightning before you hear thunder. Light is almost instantaneous on Earth but sound travels at about 330 m/s. How can you use this to estimate how far away a thunderstorm is?

Wavelength, amplitude and frequency

Wavelength (λ) is the distance from a point on one wave to the equivalent point on the adjacent wave. Wavelength is measured in metres (m).

The **amplitude** of a wave is the maximum displacement of a point on a wave away from its undisturbed position.

Frequency (**f**) is the number of complete waves passing a point in 1 second. It is measured in **hertz (Hz)**. A frequency of 5 Hz means there are five complete waves passing a point in 1 second. Frequencies are also given in kilohertz (kHz) and megahertz (MHz).

1000 Hz = 1 kHz

1000 kHz = 1 MHz

Time period (**T**) is the time to complete one wavelength.

Time period is the reciprocal or inverse of frequency.

$$\text{period} = \frac{1}{\text{frequency}} \qquad T = \frac{1}{f}.$$

For example: When the frequency of a wave is 5 Hz there are 5 waves passing a point each second. Calculate the time period of the wave.

The period is the time for one wave to pass a point.

$$T = \frac{1}{f}$$
$$= \frac{1}{5}$$
$$= 0.2 \text{ s}$$

> **REMEMBER!**
>
> Displacement includes both the distance an object moves and the direction.

Figure 6.1 Amplitude and wavelength of a wave

> **DID YOU KNOW?**
>
> Sea waves carry a lot of kinetic energy (Figure 6.2). In 2014 severe storms destroyed part of the sea wall and the railway line at Dawlish in Devon.

Figure 6.2 These waves carry a lot of kinetic energy

1 A wave has a frequency of 2 Hz. How many waves pass a point in 1 second?

2 Suggest how the amount of energy transferred by a wave changes as the amplitude increases.

3 Work out the frequencies of waves with time periods of

  a 0.1 s

  b 0.25 s.

The wave equation

A wave transfers energy. The wave speed is the speed that the wave transfers energy across a distance, or the speed the wave moves at, in metres per second.

All waves obey the wave equation:

wave speed = frequency × wavelength

$v = f\lambda$

where the wave speed v is in metres per second (m/s), the frequency f is in hertz (Hz) and the wavelength λ is in metres (m).

If we know two of these three variables we can calculate the third using the wave equation.

Example:

A radio station produces waves of frequency 200 kHz and wavelength 1500 m.

a Calculate the speed of radio waves.

b Another station produces radio waves with a frequency of 600 kHz. What is their wavelength? Assume that the speed of the wave does not change.

  a $v = f\lambda$ = 200 000 Hz × 1500 m

      = 300 000 000 m/s

      = 3×10^8 m/s

  b wavelength, $\lambda = \dfrac{v}{f}$

      $= \dfrac{300\ 000\ 000 \text{ m/s}}{600\ 000 \text{ Hz}}$

      = 500 m

REMEMBER!

Always check that you put values into the wave equation using SI units (e.g. wavelengths in metres, frequency in hertz). If the values in the question are **not** in SI units, you first have to convert them.

DID YOU KNOW?

The light that we can see has a wavelength of about $\dfrac{1}{2000}$ of a millimetre!

4 A wave has a frequency of 2 Hz and a wavelength of 10 cm. What is the speed of the wave?

5 When the frequency of a wave doubles, what happens to its wavelength?

6 The frequency of a wave triples and its wavelength doubles. What has happened to its speed?

Transverse and longitudinal waves

Learning objectives:

- compare the motion of transverse and longitudinal waves
- explain why water waves are transverse waves
- explain why sound waves are longitudinal waves.

Why wouldn't anyone hear you if you screamed in space?

Transverse and longitudinal waves

Transverse and **longitudinal waves** can be produced on a Slinky spring.

In a transverse wave on a spring, the vibrations of the particles are at right angles to the direction of the energy transfer (Figure 6.3). If the particles move up and down, the energy carried in the wave is transferred horizontally, away from the energy source creating the wave. The wave moves but the spring oscillates about a fixed position.

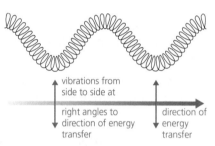

vibrations from side to side at

right angles to direction of energy transfer

direction of energy transfer

Figure 6.3 A transverse wave on a Slinky spring

1. **Make a sketch of a transverse wave to explain what is meant by the terms (a) amplitude and (b) wavelength.**

Ripples on water are transverse waves (Figure 6.4). The wave looks as if it is moving outwards but the water particles actually move up and down.

A cork floating in water bobs up and down on a water wave. It only has vertical motion and it is not carried along by the wave.

2. **What evidence do you have that suggests water waves are transverse waves?**

3. **Alex says, 'The particles in a transverse wave do move because waves carry items over the sea.' Suggest reasons why he is wrong.**

In a longitudinal wave the vibrations of the particles are parallel to the direction of energy transfer (Figure 6.5). Longitudinal waves show areas of **compression** and **rarefaction**. A compression is when the particles are closer together. A rarefaction is when they spread out. If the particles move from side to side horizontally, the energy carried in the wave moves parallel to the vibrations of the particles, away from the energy source.

Sound waves in air are longitudinal waves.

Figure 6.4 If the water moved outwards it would leave a hole in the centre

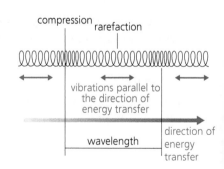

compression rarefaction

vibrations parallel to the direction of energy transfer

wavelength

direction of energy transfer

Figure 6.5 A longitudinal wave on a Slinky spring

4. When the oscillations are at right angles to the direction of energy transfer, the wave is a _____ wave.

   A longitudinal   **B** sound   **C** standing   **D** transverse

5. Describe a method you could use to measure the amplitude of a longitudinal wave on a Slinky spring.

Sound waves

All sound is produced by vibrating particles. The vibrations are parallel to the direction of the energy transfer. The particles bunch up and spread out. This sets up a pressure wave with compressions and rarefactions.

Sound waves are longitudinal. However, a microphone connected to a cathode ray oscilloscope can be used to display sound waves on graphs of potential difference against time, so they look like transverse waves. It makes it easier for us to see and measure the frequency of sound waves.

Figure 6.7 shows two sound waves. They have the same amplitude but one wave has twice the frequency of the other wave. The frequency is found from the time for one complete cycle of the wave.

Figure 6.6 A sound wave reaching a microphone makes the diaphragm vibrate

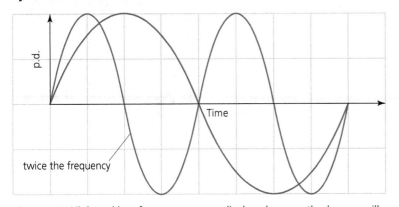

Figure 6.7 High and low frequency waves displayed on a cathode ray oscilloscope

6. Which wave in Figure 6.7 has the highest frequency?

KEY INFORMATION

A medium (plural media) is a material through which a wave travels. The medium itself does not travel.

KEY INFORMATION

Sound waves cannot travel in a vacuum because longitudinal waves travel by passing the vibrations from one particle to another.

DID YOU KNOW?

Mice can sing like birds but usually at such high frequencies (up to 70 000 Hz) we don't hear them.

KEY CONCEPT

Transferring energy or information by waves

Learning objectives:

- understand that all waves have common properties
- understand how waves can be used to carry information
- understand various applications of energy transfer by different types of electromagnetic waves

KEY WORDS

absorb
amplitude
energy
 transfer
vibration

All waves transfer energy or information from one place to another. Water waves at the seaside transfer energy when they hit the shore to move sand and shingle up the beach. Radio waves transfer picture and sound information from the transmitter to your television set at home.

A wave is a regular vibration that carries energy. Ripples on the surface of a pond, sound in air, ultrasound, visible light, X-rays and infrared rays are all types of wave. In water, the surface just moves up and down, but the energy is carried outwards from the source. A Mexican wave in a stadium is caused by spectators just standing up and sitting down but the wave travels all round the stadium (Figure 6.8).

Why not look on YouTube at the world record of a Mexican wave?

Figure 6.8 A Mexican wave

Common properties of waves

No matter what their speed, wavelength or frequency, waves **transfer energy**. When we watch a firework display, sound waves travel slowly compared with light waves but they still transfer energy from the explosion to our eardrums. We see the flash of the explosion when light waves transfer energy to sensors in our eyes.

Amplitude measures the height of the wave above or below its rest point. The larger the amplitude of a water wave, the more energy it can transfer. An underwater earthquake can create a tsunami with a wave 30 m high near the shore. This huge amplitude wave could transfer enough energy to power the whole of the UK for a year.

1 Why do you hear the sound of thunder after you see the flash of lightning?

2 Draw a diagram to show two transverse waves with different amplitudes.

3 What would you notice if the amplitude of a sound wave increased?

Using waves to transmit information

Since waves can carry energy, we use them to transmit information by varying the amount of energy carried by the wave. This can be done by simply switching the wave source on and off to create a pulsed code, as in Morse code by light, or by varying the frequency or amplitude of the wave.

Visible and infrared light is used to send internet data and telephone calls down fibre optic cables. Information that has been transformed into binary code is sent as pulses of light to be converted into digital signals read by computers or converted into vibrations in the air by telephones. The use of fibre optic cables and light waves enables vast amounts of information to be sent over far greater distances than with copper wires.

4 **What are the advantages of fibre optic cables over copper wires?**

Electromagnetic waves

Each different part of the electromagnetic spectrum is used to transfer energy.

- Microwaves can transfer data to mobile phones.
- An electric fire transfers energy to our bodies by infrared waves warming us up.
- Some energy from the Sun is transferred by ultraviolet rays.
- Not all energy from an X-ray machine is transferred. Some is **absorbed** by the body when an X-ray image is produced.
- Energy from radioactive sources can be transferred by gamma rays.

Mobile phones use microwaves that are similar to the waves that are used in microwave ovens (Figure 6.10). However, strict limits are applied to the amount of energy a mobile phone can transfer. In the UK it is illegal to sell phones that transfer more than 2 J of energy per second (2 W). This energy is transmitted in all directions not just into your brain. Typically your phone transfers about 5000 times less energy to your brain than a microwave oven would.

5 **For each of the examples of electromagnetic waves in the list above, suggest one piece of evidence that shows the energy transferred by the wave can be either absorbed or reflected.**

6 **If energy is being transmitted away from the Sun, why isn't the Sun continually cooling down?**

Figure 6.9 Light is transmitted along fibre optic cables

Figure 6.10 Do mobile phones cook your brain?

Measuring wave speeds

Learning objectives:

- explain how the speed of sound in air can be measured
- explain how the speed of water ripples can be measured.

KEY WORD

....

echo

Sound travels pretty quickly but slow enough for us to measure using school laboratory equipment.

Measuring the speed of sound in air

Zoe and Darren measured the speed of sound in air. Sound reflects off a wall in a similar way to light reflecting off a mirror. The reflected sound is called an **echo**.

Zoe stood 50 m away from a large wall. She clapped and listened to the echo (Figure 6.11).

Zoe tried to clap each time she heard an echo, while Darren timed 100 of her claps with a stop clock. He timed 100 claps in 40 s.

The time between claps is $\frac{40}{100} = 0.4$ s

During the time from one clap to the next the sound had time to go to the wall and back, a distance of 100 m.

$$\text{Speed} = \frac{\text{distance}}{\text{time}}$$

$$= \frac{100 \text{ m}}{0.4 \text{ s}}$$

$$= 250 \text{ m/s}$$

1 Javid and Sam also measured the speed of sound in air using the same method. They counted 50 claps in 23 s. Javid also stood 50 m from the wall.
   What value did they get for the speed of sound?

2 Suggest why this method is not likely to produce an accurate value for the speed of sound in air.

DID YOU KNOW?

....

For ripples on a water surface or sound waves in air, it is the wave and *not* the water or air itself that travels.

Figure 6.11 Zoe tried to clap each time she heard an echo (not to scale)

The speed of water waves

The speed of a water wave can be found by measuring the time it takes for a water wave to travel a measured distance. For example, make a splash at one end of a 25 m swimming pool and measure, with a stop clock, the time it takes the wave to travel to the other end.

3   **a**   **Is the swimming pool method an accurate way of measuring the wave speed? Explain why.**

    b   **Explain how you could improve the accuracy.**

4   **The crest of an ocean wave moves a distance of 20 m in 10 s. Calculate the speed of the ocean wave.**

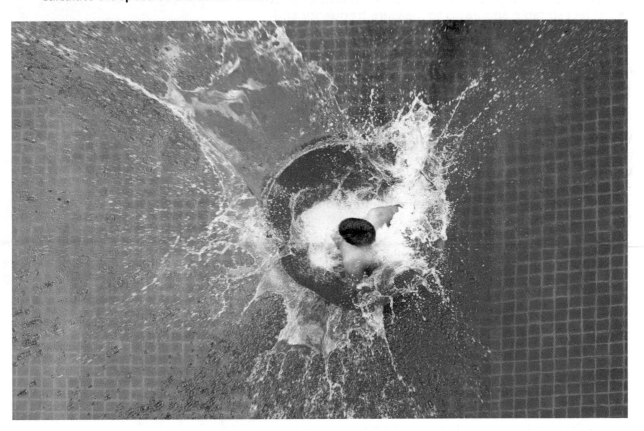

REQUIRED PRACTICAL

Measuring the wavelength, frequency and speed of waves in a ripple tank and waves in a solid

KEY WORDS

frequency
speed
wavelength

Learning objectives:

- develop techniques for making observations of waves
- select suitable apparatus to measure frequency and wavelength
- use data to answer questions.

These pages are designed to help you think about aspects of the investigation rather than to guide you through it step by step.

Frequency and wavelength of waves in a ripple tank

We can use a set of equipment called a ripple tank to explore waves. By careful observation and measurement we can measure and calculate the **wavelength** and **frequency** of the waves and then work out their **speed**. A strobe light can be used to 'freeze' the movement of the waves for making certain measurements.

1. A motor is attached to the wooden rod. What does this do?
2. What are the units of
   a wavelength?
   b frequency?
3. Suggest what equipment you could use to measure the wavelength, and how you should set it up.
4. When measuring the wavelength, you might measure the length of ten waves on the screen or table and then divide by ten. Explain why this is done.
5. Louise is looking at a certain point on the screen and counting how many waves pass that point in ten seconds. How can she then calculate the frequency of the waves?

Speed of waves in a ripple tank

Sahil's group are comparing two ways of working out the speed of the waves as they travel through the water. One of these is by using speed equals distance/time and the other is by using speed equals frequency times wavelength.

6. Explain how the group could measure the speed of the waves using the equation speed = distance/time.

Figure 6.12 Ripple tank used for observing waves in water

Figure 6.13 Shadows of waves travelling across a ripple tank. The wavelength is the distance between two dark patches, which are the peaks (crests) of the waves.

7 Now explain how the group could calculate the speed of the waves using the equation speed = frequency × wavelength.

8 Why do scientists sometimes try to use two different methods to answer a question?

Speed of sound on a stretched string

We can use a mechanical vibrator to vibrate a stretched string or elastic cord (Figure 6.16). It transfers energy continuously to the string. This produces transverse waves that travel along the string, just like when you shake a rope up and down. Changing the vibration frequency changes the wavelength of the waves. The speed of the wave travelling along the string stays the same – it depends on how heavy the string is and how tightly it is stretched.

By changing the frequency of vibration, it is possible to produce a stable wave pattern. You can then count the number of wavelengths along the string and work out their speed. The frequency will be the frequency of the signal generator.

REMEMBER!

If you have a set of readings, don't simply average all the results but look at them first to see whether there are any anomalies. These should be eliminated before finding the average or they will influence the outcome.

Figure 6.14 Setting up waves on a stretching string

9 Suggest what equipment you could use to measure the wavelength, and how you should set it up.

10 What difficulties are there in measuring the wavelength accurately in this experiment?

11 By changing the frequency of the vibration generator or changing the length of string allowed to vibrate (moving the wooden bridge in Figure 6.14) it is possible to increase the number of 'loops' seen in the vibrating string.

How could you use this effect to verify the speed of the waves on the string?

DID YOU KNOW?

It may seem strange that you are calculating a wave speed along the string when the string is moving up and down and has some points that don't move at all. In this special situation there are two waves travelling in opposite directions along the string (the wave created at the vibrating end and a wave reflected at the other end). These two waves meet and actually pass through each other!

Reflection and refraction of waves

Learning objectives:

- describe reflection, transmission, refraction and absorption of waves
- interpret ray diagrams.

KEY WORDS

absorption
normal
ray diagram
reflection
refraction
transmission

When sunlight enters sea water, most of the visible light is absorbed within 10 m of the surface. Some is absorbed by phytoplankton, the producers in the marine food web. The rest of the energy that is absorbed increases the thermal energy store of the oceans, which helps drive ocean currents.

Reflection, absorption and transmission

Waves travel out from a point source in all directions. A **ray diagram** is a model that shows a number of lines (rays) travelling in a straight line between the wave source and an object or surface. The arrow on a ray diagram shows the direction that the wave travels. The incident ray is the ray coming in from the wave source to the surface. The reflected ray is the ray coming away from the surface.

When a wave meets the boundary between two materials, some of its energy is **reflected**, some is **absorbed** and some is **transmitted** (Figure 6.15). For example, in a thick piece of glass like a shop window you can see your reflection and see through it at the same time. In the case of a perfect reflector, no energy is transmitted or absorbed.

The dashed line in Figure 6.16 is called the **normal**. It is at 90° to the boundary and is the line from which all angles are measured.

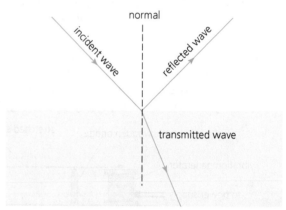

Figure 6.15 Reflection and transmission at a boundary between two materials

1. **Describe what you would observe if the following waves were reflected: light, sound and water waves.**

2. **Describe what you would observe if a sound wave crossed from air into a material where it was**
   a **completely absorbed**
   b **partly absorbed and partly transmitted.**

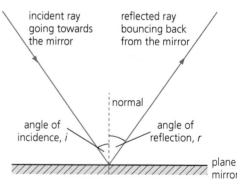

Figure 6.16 The reflection of light from a plane mirror

Refraction

A wave changes direction when it enters a different medium, unless it is incident along the normal. This is called **refraction**. In Figure 6.15 the transmitted wave is refracted.

Figure 6.17 shows a ray of light in air, entering a glass block. The glass is denser than air, so the light slows down and bends towards the normal. The angle the refracted ray makes with the normal to the refracting surface is called the angle of refraction. You can see that when the light ray enters the glass block the angle of refraction (*r*) is smaller than the angle of incidence (*i*).

When the light ray exits the glass block, the light speeds up again and the ray refracts again, this time away from the normal. The angle of refraction is greater than the angle of incidence.

This effect can also be seen with water waves moving between deep and shallow water.

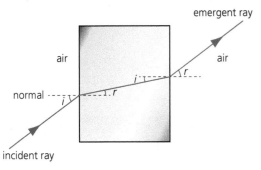

Figure 6.17 Ray of light going through a glass block

Figure 6.18 Fibre optic lamp

3. **When is the angle of refraction bigger than the angle of incidence?**

HIGHER TIER ONLY

Wavelength dependence

The proportion of a wave's energy that is reflected, transmitted or absorbed depends on its wavelength and on the medium it enters. For example, while some radio waves from stars pass through the atmosphere and can be detected on Earth, some radio wavelengths are reflected back into space from the Earth's upper atmosphere (the ionosphere). At other wavelengths, gas molecules in the air absorb incoming radio waves.

4. **Long wavelength radio waves are reflected by upper layers of the atmosphere. Draw a diagram to suggest how this can be used in long distance communications.**

5. **Suggest why beams of waves being transmitted to satellites in orbit around the Earth use microwave frequencies.**

The electromagnetic spectrum

Learning objectives:

- recognise that electromagnetic waves are transverse waves
- describe the main groupings and wavelength ranges of the electromagnetic spectrum.

All electromagnetic radiation from the Sun (including visible light) travels the 149 million kilometres to the Earth in about 8 minutes.

Electromagnetic waves

We know light is a wave because it has the same properties as other waves: it can be reflected and refracted.

White light is a mixture of waves with different wavelengths which we see as different colours. These colours can be separated into what we call the **visible spectrum**. When scientists investigate the visible spectrum they can detect invisible waves on both sides, showing that the visible spectrum is really part of a much wider spectrum, which we call the **electromagnetic spectrum**.

All the waves in the electromagnetic spectrum are **transverse waves** with many properties in common with visible light.

Just like other waves, all **electromagnetic waves** transfer energy from one point to another. In electromagnetic waves, electromagnetic fluctuations occur at right angles to the direction in which energy is being transferred by the wave.

Some waves have to travel through a material. Sound waves can travel through air, liquids and solids but not a vacuum. Water ripples travel along the surface of water.

Electromagnetic waves are different from other waves because they do not need a material. They can travel through a vacuum. This is a special property of electromagnetic waves, which enables light and infrared waves to reach us from the Sun. All electromagnetic waves travel at the same speed in a vacuum, 3.0×10^8 m/s.

1. What are the similarities and differences between transverse and longitudinal waves?

2. Explain how waves in the electromagnetic spectrum are different from other waves.

3. What properties do all electromagnetic waves have in common?

The electromagnetic spectrum

Figure 6.19 shows that electromagnetic waves span a wide, continuous range of wavelengths and frequencies.

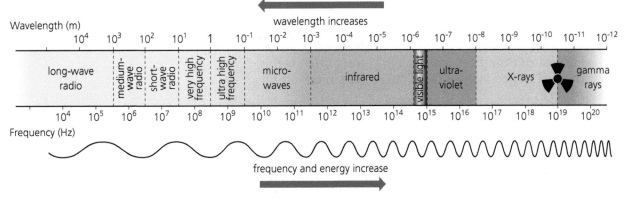

Figure 6.19 The wavelengths and frequencies of waves in the electromagnetic spectrum

The wavelength ranges of the groups of waves in the electromagnetic spectrum are (from long to short):

- radio, TV and microwaves
- infrared
- visible (red to violet)
- ultraviolet
- X-ray
- gamma ray

> **REMEMBER!**
>
> Remember the order of electromagnetic wave groupings.

The shorter the wavelength of the electromagnetic wave, the further it can travel through other materials. The higher the frequency of a wave, the more energy it can transfer to another object when the radiation is absorbed.

4. Which grouping in the electromagnetic spectrum has the highest frequency?

5. Ultraviolet light used in a sunbed has a wavelength of 3.5×10^{-7} m. Calculate the frequency of this light.

6. Calculate the frequency of an electromagnetic wave with a wavelength of 20 cm. Use standard form for your answer.

7. Suggest why ultraviolet waves are more dangerous than radio waves.

> **KEY INFORMATION**
>
> All electromagnetic waves travel at the same speed in a vacuum, 3.0×10^8 m/s.

Waves as energy carriers

Waves can transfer energy from one place to another. Heat lamps keep newly hatched chicks warm, bulbs transfer energy as light throughout a room and sunbathers receive energy directly from the Sun by UV waves. The energy becomes dissipated however; the waves often spread out as they travel, meaning that the energy is spread over a larger area.

8. Explain how a microwave oven demonstrates the idea of waves carrying energy.

9. Why might it be difficult to use a mobile phone if the nearest phone mast is a long distance away?

Refraction, wave velocity and wavefronts

Learning objectives:

- explain refraction and how it may vary with wavelength
- construct ray diagrams to illustrate refraction
- use wavefront diagrams to explain refraction in terms of the difference in velocity of the waves in different substances.

A rainbow is caused by the refraction of sunlight by raindrops. When entering a raindrop, blue light in sunlight is slowed down more than red light, so is refracted by a greater angle.

Refraction of electromagnetic waves

We saw earlier that when light waves travel from one medium into another, they change speed and may change direction (Figure 6.20). This is called **refraction**.

1 Copy and complete the **ray diagram** in Figure 6.21 to show a ray of light travelling from air to water.

Figure 6.21

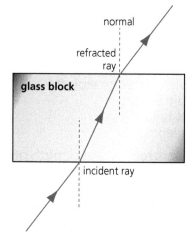

Figure 6.20 Light is refracted towards the normal when it travels from air to glass, and away from the normal when it travels from glass to air

---

HIGHER TIER ONLY

All electromagnetic waves can be refracted when they enter a medium in which the wave velocity is different. The shorter the wavelength, the more the wave is refracted.

Different substances refract the same wavelength in different ways. For example, radio waves travel in a straight line from the transmitter, but are refracted in the lower layer of the atmosphere. The amount of refraction can be affected by differences in atmospheric temperature and pressure.

2 Suggest why radio signals can sometimes travel further between two points on the Earth as atmospheric conditions change.

Explaining refraction

A **wavefront** is a line that joins all the points on a wave which are moving up and down together at the same time. The wavefront is at right angles to the direction the wave is travelling. We can see what happens when waves are refracted by looking at plane (straight) water waves in a ripple tank (Figure 6.22).

When a wave strikes a boundary at an angle, one part of the wave reaches the boundary before the rest of the wave. This part changes speed first. In Figure 6.22 the left-hand parts of the wavefronts get closer together, because waves travel slower in shallower water. The wavefront changes direction. The wave is refracted towards the normal.

Figure 6.22 The way that waves refract when going from a higher-speed medium to a lower-speed medium is similar to what happens when a car drives at an angle into mud. The wheels that reach the mud first slow down first so the car changes direction.

> **KEY INFORMATION**
>
> The wavefronts get closer together because speed = frequency × wavelength and the frequency of the waves (which depends on the source of the waves) is constant. If the speed decreases, the wavelength must also decrease.

3 Water waves are affected by the depth of the water they travel through.

   a What happens to the wavefronts in Figure 6.23 when the water waves move from deep to shallow water?

   b Do the waves travel faster in deep or shallow water? Explain your answer.

Figure 6.23 Water waves with a plane (straight) wavefront travelling from deep to shallow water

Gamma rays and X-rays

Learning objectives:

- list the properties of gamma rays and X-rays
- compare gamma rays and X-rays.

KEY WORDS

gamma ray
radiation dose
tracer
X-ray

X-ray machines called pedoscopes were introduced in the 1930s in shoe shops in the UK. They enabled parents and children to see how well shoes fitted. They were very popular with children, who loved to watch their bones move as they wriggled their toes. Unfortunately, people using these machines did not realise how dangerous X-rays can be, and some shoe shop assistants might have developed cancer because of using them.

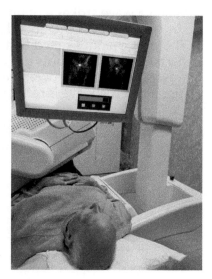

Figure 6.24 This patient is having a scan using a gamma tracer and gamma camera

Gamma rays

Gamma rays have the shortest wavelengths and transfer the most energy of all the waves in the electromagnetic spectrum. This means they can be harmful to living cells. Gamma rays are used to kill cancer cells or reduce the size of a tumour (radiotherapy). However, the **radiation dose** from a single treatment is usually low in comparison with the level of background radiation. Radiation dose is measured in sieverts (Sv) and millisieverts (mSv).

Gamma rays are also used in medical imaging. Technetium-99m is a radioactive isotope that emits gamma rays. It is used as a radioactive **tracer**. A gamma camera monitors where gamma rays are emitted from in the body, to produce a moving image that shows how organs are functioning (Figure 6.24). Technetium-99m has a half-life (the average time it takes for half the nuclei present to decay) of 6 hours, so it stays in the body long enough for diagnosis but not long enough to cause lasting damage to cells.

1. Why is a half-life of 6 hours good for diagnostic scans?

2. Name other properties that a radioisotope should have used for medical diagnosis.

X-rays

X-rays pass through soft tissues in the body but will be absorbed by bone. X-ray images can be used to check for broken bones (Figure 6.25).

Figure 6.25 This X-ray shows a broken ulna in the wrist

X-rays are also used in computerised tomography (CT) scans. Multiple images are taken at many different angles to build up a detailed picture of inside a patient's body (Figure 6.26).

In addition to medical imaging for diagnosis, X-rays are used in radiotherapy to treat cancer.

3 Should X-rays used in radiotherapy have longer or shorter wavelengths than those used for medical diagnosis? Explain your answer.

4 Suggest why gamma rays are not used for medical imaging in the same way as X-rays.

Figure 6.26 A CT scan can give good pictures of soft tissue regions but exposes a patient to a much higher radiation dose than a single X-ray

Comparing gamma rays and X-rays

Gamma rays and X-rays have very similar ranges of wavelengths and frequencies, and so have very similar effects. Their high frequencies mean they carry the most energy and are the most penetrating forms of electromagnetic radiation, so therefore they can also be the most dangerous to human body tissue when the radiation is absorbed.

Both gamma rays and X-rays are highly ionising radiation. This is how they damage and destroy cancer cells. Large doses of ionising radiation can cause the mutation of genes in cells, which can cause cells to become cancerous.

The key difference between gamma rays and X-rays is how they are produced. Gamma rays are emitted from the nucleus of an unstable atom during radioactive decay. This is a random process. X-rays are generated by an X-ray machine when high-speed electrons collide with metals and lose energy.

> **KEY INFORMATION**
>
> Like all electromagnetic waves, gamma rays and X-rays travel at the same velocity in both a vacuum and air, but at slower speeds when they travel in a material.

5 Describe the similarities and differences between gamma rays and X-rays.

6 Explain why an X-ray source needs an electric power supply but a gamma source does not.

7 Why must great care be taken when using X-rays and gamma rays?

8 Suggest how X-rays are used to detect faults in welds.

9 The radiation dose from a chest X-ray is 0.014 mSv. The dose from a CT scan of the head 1.4 mSv. The average annual dose a person in the UK receives from natural sources is 2.7 mSv, although the typical exposure for radiation workers is 5 mSv per year.
Evaluate the risks of undergoing these medical imaging tests.

Ultraviolet and infrared radiation

Learning objectives:

- describe the properties of ultraviolet and infrared radiation
- describe some uses and hazards of ultraviolet radiation
- describe some uses of infrared radiation.

KEY WORDS

infrared radiation
ultraviolet radiation

Some of the dyes in inks are only visible under ultraviolet light. These are used in security pens used to mark valuable equipment such as computers and bicycles. Many banknotes have a special feature which is only visible under ultraviolet light.

Figure 6.27 Some of the ink used in euro banknotes is only visible in UV light

Ultraviolet radiation and its uses

Ultraviolet rays have shorter wavelengths than violet light. They are emitted from very hot objects (4000°C or more) such as the Sun.

One use of ultraviolet radiation is in fluorescent lighting. This type of light is more energy efficient than traditional filament light bulbs and this technology is used in compact fluorescent light bulbs. Fluorescent lights have a white phosphor coating inside the glass. When the UV rays strike this, it glows and emits visible light.

Our skin absorbs ultraviolet radiation from sunlight. Small doses of ultraviolet rays are good for us, as this produces vitamin D in our skin. A suntan (from sunlight or a sunbed) is a natural darkening of the skin to protect itself from too much ultraviolet radiation.

1. State three uses of ultraviolet radiation.

2. Describe how ultraviolet radiation can be used to mark a TV.

3. Suggest why many shops have an ultraviolet lamp by the till.

4. John says that ultraviolet light has a purple colour. Explain whether John is correct.

The hazards of ultraviolet radiation

Ultraviolet radiation has a higher frequency than visible light and transfers more energy when it is absorbed by skin. Too much sunlight or use of sunbeds causes premature ageing of the skin, such as wrinkles and dark pigmentation spots. Large doses of ultraviolet radiation can be harmful to our eyes and may also cause skin cancer, especially in people with fair skin.

Sunscreens can reduce the risks of getting sunburn and skin cancer (Figure 6.28).

Figure 6.28 Sunscreens contain substances that absorb or reflect some of the Sun's ultraviolet radiation

5. Explain why small doses of ultraviolet rays can be good for you but large doses can be harmful.

6. Suggest why skiers might be at a greater risk of sunburn than people on the beach.

Infrared radiation

Infrared radiation is next to red light on the electromagnetic spectrum, and has longer wavelengths than red light. Anything that is warmer than its surroundings emits energy by giving out infrared radiation. You cannot see infrared radiation but you can feel the infrared radiation given out by hot things such as a fire, a heater or an oven.

The traditional way of cooking is by using infrared radiation. However, infrared radiation only heats the surface of food. The radiation is not transmitted very far into food. Meat that appears to be cooked may be raw on the inside (Figure 6.29).

Energy from infrared radiation is absorbed by the particles on the surface of the food. They vibrate more and energy can then be transferred slowly by conduction to the food below the surface.

7. Why is the chicken in Figure 6.29 still undercooked in the middle when it appears to be fully cooked on the outside?

8. What energy transfer process heats the centre of the food?

Remote controls for electronic devices such as TVs and radios work by emitting infrared radiation. The remotely controlled device won't work if an object is between it and the control because the infrared radiation is absorbed. Infrared beams can also be used for security alarms.

Thermal imaging cameras (Figure 6.30) detect low levels of infrared radiation from warm objects.

9. Suggest two ways that infrared sensors can be used in a burglar alarm.

10. Suggest one way a TV remote control could still work when not pointed directly at the TV set.

Figure 6.29 This chicken is undercooked in the middle

Figure 6.30 A thermal imaging camera detects infrared radiation given off by an object or person

REQUIRED PRACTICAL

Investigate how the amount of infrared radiation absorbed or radiated by a surface depends on the nature of that surface

KEY WORDS
....
absorption
infrared
  radiation
radiation

Learning objectives:

- explain reasons for the equipment used to carry out an investigation
- explain the rationale for carrying out an investigation
- apply ideas from an investigation to a range of practical contexts.

Anything that is warm gives off infrared radiation and the warmer it is, the better an emitter it is. However, the colour of an object also affects how much radiation it emits. If we want a radiator to work as well as possible, the colour matters.

Colour also makes a difference to absorbing infrared radiation. If you want to make sure you stay cool on a hot day, choose the right clothing. You'll cook in the wrong colour!

> These pages are designed to help you think about aspects of the investigation rather than to guide you through it step by step.

Investigating absorption

Alex's teacher is showing the class how to compare different surfaces to see which is better at absorbing **infrared radiation**. She has set up two metal plates, one on either side of a heater. One plate has a shiny surface and the other has been blackened. On the back of each plate a glass stopper has been stuck on with wax. The heater is turned on. After a few minutes one of the stoppers drops off and the other follows several minutes later.

1. What does this experiment show?

2. With what you have learnt about absorbers of infrared radiation, which stopper would drop off first?

3. What needs to be done to make sure the experiment is a fair test?

Figure 6.31 Experiment to compare **absorption** of infrared radiation by different surfaces

Commenting on the design of an experiment

Experiments have to be designed well if the results are to be meaningful. The experiment shown in Figure 6.32 has been designed to compare how good different surfaces are at emitting infrared radiation (radiating thermal energy). The cube is filled with very hot water and an infrared detector is held opposite each of the various faces in turn. The different faces have different finishes on them and it is possible to compare the readings from each.

Figure 6.32 Experiment to compare infrared radiation emitted by different surfaces. The matt black surface produces the highest reading and the shiny, silvered surface produces the lowest reading.

4 Why does the experiment use one can with four different surfaces rather than four cans, each a different type of surface?

5 Why is it designed so that each face has the same width?

6 What needs to be true about the positioning of the infrared detector?

An alternative way of investigating the amount of infrared radiation emitted by different surfaces is to replace the infrared detector with a thermometer with a blackened bulb.

7 Explain why a thermometer with a blackened bulb is used.

8 Which apparatus would give the greatest resolution for temperature readings – the infrared sensor or the thermometer?

Applying the ideas

Some ideas in science have an immediate application and ones about infrared radiation affect our everyday lives. We can use the results of these experiments to inform us about the way that various objects should be designed.

Think about the investigation into absorbing infrared radiation.

9 What does this suggest about the best colour for:
  a a firefighter's suit?
  b solar panels on the roof of a house, absorbing thermal energy into water to use inside?

Now think about the experiment on emitting infrared radiation.

10 What does this suggest about the best colour for:
  a a teapot?
  b the pipes on the back of a refrigerator, which need to radiate thermal energy from the inside of the fridge to its surroundings?

11 Explain what you would see if you touched a thermometer to each side of the cube in Figure 6.32.

> **DID YOU KNOW?**
>
> Firefighters use infrared cameras to locate unconscious bodies in smoke-filled buildings. Even though visible light can't penetrate the smoke to enable the body to be seen, the infrared radiation from the body can.

> **REMEMBER!**
>
> Make sure you understand about the main features of the design of an experiment. The equipment has been developed in a particular way for good reasons and you need to know what they are.

Microwaves

Learning objectives:

- list some properties of microwaves
- describe how microwaves are used for cooking food and in radar.

KEY WORD

microwaves

Mobile phones use microwaves. A mobile phone today can have more computing power than the first computers used to land humans on the Moon.

Properties of microwaves

Microwaves are radio waves with short wavelengths. The wavelengths of microwaves vary between 1 mm and 30 cm. Microwaves used for communication have a longer wavelength than those used for cooking. This means that there is less energy associated with mobile phones than with microwave ovens.

1. List two uses of microwaves.

2. Suggest what use is likely to be made of microwaves with a wavelength of 25 cm.

> **REMEMBER**
>
> The higher the frequency of electromagnetic waves, the more energy associated with the radiation.

Cooking with microwaves

Microwave ovens do not use a flame or heated metal to cook food. They use microwaves instead. Microwave ovens cook food faster and are less expensive to run than conventional ovens.

Microwaves penetrate about 1 cm into the outer layers of food before being absorbed. The energy transferred by the microwaves makes water or fat molecules in the outer layers of food vibrate more (Figure 6.33). Energy is then transferred from the vibrating water or fat molecules to the centre of the food by conduction.

microwaves produced
in microwave oven

cold water   hot water

Figure 6.33 Microwaves cook food by making the water or fat molecules vibrate more

> **DID YOU KNOW?**
>
> The inside walls of microwave ovens must be made of metal. Metal reflects microwaves so the microwaves are trapped inside. This is important to make sure we do not cook ourselves. The door of a microwave oven is made from special glass that also reflects microwave radiation.

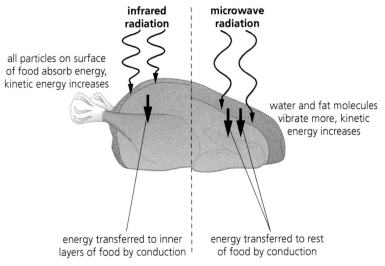

infrared radiation

microwave radiation

all particles on surface of food absorb energy, kinetic energy increases

water and fat molecules vibrate more, kinetic energy increases

energy transferred to inner layers of food by conduction

energy transferred to rest of food by conduction

Figure 6.34 Microwaves are transmitted further into the food than infrared radiation before being absorbed

3 **Explain the differences between the ways a microwave oven and a conventional oven cook food.**

4 **Suggest two advantages of using a microwave oven instead of an infrared oven.**

5 **Explain what would happen if you tried to make toast in a microwave oven.**

Radar

Radar was developed during the Second World War to detect aircraft outside the normal range of sight and hearing. Radar uses microwaves, which pass through the atmosphere even when visible light is blocked by clouds or dust.

Radar works by sending out microwave pulses from a transmitter mounted on the aircraft. Microwaves reflect from a metal target in a similar way to light reflecting off a mirror. The reflected microwaves are detected by the radar system's receiving antenna.

Example: An aircraft sends out a very brief microwave pulse and receives an echo after 10.8 µs. If the speed of microwaves in air is 3.0×10^8 m/s, how far away is the target?

$$speed = \frac{distance}{time}$$

distance = speed × time = $(3.0 \times 10^8$ m/s$) \times 10.8$ µs = 3240 m

The distance to the target is half this, 1620 m.

6 **If a radar echo takes 64 µs to return, how far away is the target?**

7 **Suggest why there is a maximum range at which targets can be detected using radar.**

KEY INFORMATION

'Micro' is a standard prefix when showing quantities. It means one millionth and is represented by the symbol µ. One microsecond is written 1µs and is 1×10^{-6} seconds.

Radio and microwave communication

KEY WORDS

microwaves
radio wave
receiver
satellite
transmitter

Learning objectives:

- describe how radio waves are used for television and radio communications
- describe how microwaves are used in satellite communications
- describe how radio waves are produced and received
- describe the reflection and refraction of radio waves.

Bluetooth is a wireless technology for exchanging data over short distances using microwaves.

Using radio waves for communication

A system using electromagnetic waves to communicate must contain a **transmitter** to send a signal and a **receiver** to receive it. Terrestrial radio and TV signals are sent by **radio waves**. The radio waves travel through the air at the speed of light. The path between transmitter and receiver usually has to be a straight line with no large obstructions such as hills and large buildings, so the transmitters are placed on towers that may be hundreds of metres tall.

1 Describe the properties that make radio waves useful for communication.

2 A radio wave has a wavelength of 100 m. What is its frequency?

HIGHER TIER ONLY

Radio waves can be produced by oscillations in electrical circuits. When a current flows through a wire it creates an electric field around the wire. When the current changes, the electric field changes. The changing current produces radio waves. This is how radio transmitters work.

Radio waves can induce oscillations in an electrical circuit, with the same frequency as the radio wave itself.

3 Suggest how a radio receiver works.

4 Some radios do not need a power supply (even a clockwork one). Suggest where they might get the energy from that they need to produce the sound.

Using microwaves for communication

Microwaves are used to transmit mobile phone signals. Microwave transmitters or base stations are placed on high buildings or masts to give better line of sight communication over large distances. Although most microwave signals are sent directly, some are sent from a transmitter to a receiver via a **satellite** (Figure 6.35). Microwave satellite communications are used for satellite phones and for satellite TV.

5 Suggest why satellite dishes are placed on the walls or roofs of houses.

6 Suggest why aerials for mobile phone signals are placed close together in towns and cities.

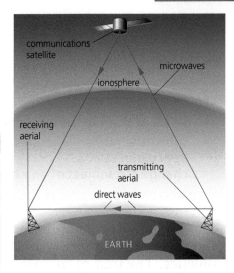

Figure 6.35 Direct and satellite microwave communication

HIGHER TIER ONLY

Reflection and refraction of radio signals

Like all other electromagnetic waves, radio waves can be reflected and refracted. Radio waves are refracted in the upper layers of the atmosphere, called the ionosphere. The amount of refraction depends on the frequency of the wave.

Waves with a long wavelength and low frequency undergo most refraction in the ionosphere. Figure 6.36 shows how radio waves are refracted in the ionosphere so the wave returns to the Earth's surface. Microwaves with shorter wavelengths are not refracted or reflected and pass straight through the ionosphere. This is why microwaves, not radio waves, are used for satellite communication.

7 State what happens to some radio waves in the ionosphere.

8 A radio station broadcasts with a frequency of 103.4 MHz from the transmitter in Figure 6.36. Explain why a radio at point X will not receive the signal.

DID YOU KNOW?

....

Using a satellite for communication delays a signal by less than 0.3 s.

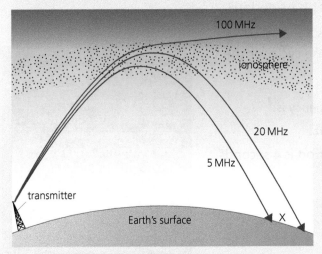

Figure 6.36 Waves of different frequencies are refracted by different amounts when entering the ionosphere

MATHS SKILLS

Using and rearranging equations

Learning objectives:

- select and apply the equations $T = \frac{1}{f}$ and $v = f\lambda$
- substitute numerical values into equations using appropriate units
- change the subject of an equation.

The names of units are often taken from the name of the scientist who first worked in that particular field of physics. The unit of frequency is the hertz (Hz) after the German physicist Heinrich Hertz.

Period and frequency

Remember, frequency, f, is the number of waves passing a point each second. The unit of frequency is the hertz (Hz), which means cycles per second. The time period, T, is measured in seconds (s).

Period and frequency are linked by the equation:

period, $T = \dfrac{1}{\text{frequency, } f}$

Example: A wave has a frequency of 5 Hz. What is its period?

Substituting 5 Hz into the equation $T = \frac{1}{f}$ gives $T = \frac{1}{5}$ s. When there are 5 cycles of a wave in 1 second, then one cycle, or the period T, is $\dfrac{1}{5\text{Hz}}$ or 0.2 s.

① **Work out the period of a wave when the frequency is:**

    a 100 Hz   b 1000 Hz   c 15 000 Hz.

Example: Calculate the frequency when the period is 4 seconds.

Use the equation $T = \frac{1}{f}$.

Rearrange it to make f the **subject of the equation**.

Multiply both sides by f: $Tf = 1$

Divide both sides by T: $f = \dfrac{1}{T}$

Substitute $T = 4$ s into the rearranged equation.

$f = \dfrac{1}{4s} = 0.25$ Hz

② **Work out the frequency of a wave with period:**

    a 5 s   b 10 s   c 150 s.

Speed, frequency and wavelength

You can calculate the speed at which a wave moves using the equation:

$$\text{speed} = \frac{\text{distance}}{\text{time}}$$

The unit of distance is the metre (m). The unit of time is the second (s). So the unit of wave speed is metres per second (m/s).

Wavelength is the distance from a point on one wave to the equivalent point on the adjacent wave, such as between two adjacent crests. The symbol for wavelength is λ and the unit is the metre (m).

Figure 6.37 Wavelength of a transverse wave

The wave equation links wave speed, frequency and wavelength:

wave speed = frequency × wavelength

$v = f\lambda$

3 Use the equation $v = f\lambda$ to calculate the speed of a wave with:

   a frequency 100 Hz and wavelength 2 m

   b frequency 100 Hz and wavelength 2 cm

   c frequency 100 Hz and wavelength 2 mm.

4 Rearrange the wave equation to make frequency the subject.

5 Calculate the frequency of a wave with

   a wavelength 0.5 m and speed 25 m/s

   b wavelength 0.05 m and speed 250 m/s

   c wavelength 0.005 m and speed 2500 m/s.

6 a Rearrange the wave equation to calculate the wavelength given the speed and the frequency.

   b Calculate the wavelength of a sound wave in air with frequency 500 Hz and speed 330 m/s.

> **MATHS**
>
> When you rearrange an equation, always do the same operation (such as multiplication or division) to both sides. For example, if you divide one side of the equation by the variable λ, you must divide the other side of the equation by λ.

Changes in velocity, frequency and wavelength

Sound travels at different speeds through different media. The denser the material, the closer the molecules and the quicker the vibrations will travel through that substance.

If speed increases when a sound wave is transmitted from one medium to another, what effect does that have on the wave's frequency and wavelength?

If speed increases then either frequency or wavelength must also increase. This is because in the wave equation, wave speed is **proportional** to frequency and wavelength.

7 Red light has a wavelength of 6.5×10^{-7} m and moves a distance of 3.0 m in 1.0×10^{-8} s. Calculate the frequency of red light.

Material	Speed of sound (m/s)
Air	330
Water	1500
Wood	3300
Titanium	6100

8 A sound wave has a wavelength of 25 cm in air.

Use the data in the table to calculate its wavelength in titanium. Assume that the frequency of the wave does not change.

Check your progress

You should be able to:

Describe the amplitude, wavelength, frequency and period of a wave → Use the wave equation $v = f\lambda$ to calculate wave speed → Rearrange and apply the wave equation

Realise that waves can be transverse or longitudinal → Give examples of longitudinal and transverse waves → Explain the difference between transverse and longitudinal waves

Describe how sound waves travel through air or solids → Describe how to measure the speed of sound waves in air → Explain how to measure the speed of ripples on a water surface, and relate this to more general wave behaviour

Understand that waves transfer energy or information → Give examples of energy transfer by waves (including electromagnetic waves) → Describe evidence that, for e.g. ripples on a water surface, it is the wave and not the water itself that travels

Understand that waves can be absorbed, transmitted or reflected at a surface → Describe examples of reflection, transmission and absorption of waves (including electromagnetic waves) at material interfaces → Describe how different substances may absorb, transmit, refract or reflect electromagnetic waves in ways that vary with wavelength

Explain what happens to a ray that is refracted → Construct ray diagrams to illustrate refraction at a boundary → Use wavefront diagrams to explain refraction in terms of a change in wave velocity

Name the main groupings of the electromagnetic spectrum → Compare the groupings of the electromagnetic spectrum in terms of wavelength and frequency → Describe how radio waves are produced

Describe the hazardous effects of gamma rays, X-rays and ultraviolet radiation → Explain the risks associated with the use of ionising and ultraviolet radiation → Evaluate the risks and consequences of exposure to radiation

Give examples of the uses of the main groupings of the electromagnetic spectrum → Describe examples of energy transfer by electromagnetic waves → Explain why each type of electromagnetic wave is suitable for the application

Worked example

The table below shows the electromagnetic spectrum.

A	microwave	infrared	visible light	B	X-rays	gamma rays

1 **State the names of the waves labelled A and B.**

A = radio waves   B = ultraviolet waves

> Both answers are correct. Use a mnemonic to remember the correct order.

2 **X-rays are dangerous to humans. Explain how they can also be used in medical therapy without lasting harm.**

We can use them for X-rays to see our bones and for treating cancer by killing the cancer cells.

> This answer is a good start but is incomplete. It doesn't give a full explanation. The answer should also say that we can use them by controlling the exposure dose.

3 **Complete the wavefront diagram to show the refraction of light from air to water.**

> This correctly shows the wavelength being less but as the waves are entering a denser medium they will be refracted towards the normal. The wavefronts change direction but they still match up (see Fig 6.37).

End of chapter questions

Getting started

1 Which of the following is a longitudinal wave?   `1 Mark`
   a sound wave   b water wave   c light wave   d radio wave

2 Name the type of wave which has compressions and rarefactions.   `1 Mark`

3 Which is a correct unit of frequency?   `1 Mark`
   a metres   b watts   c hertz   d metres per second

4 Explain what is meant by the **amplitude** of a wave.   `2 Marks`

5 Which electromagnetic wave has the shortest wavelength?   `1 Mark`

6 A water wave in a ripple tank has a frequency of 4 Hz. Calculate the time period (T) of the wave using the formula $T = 1/f$.   `1 Mark`

7 A microwave has a wavelength of 1 cm. What type of wave, other than a microwave, might have a wavelength of 1 m?   `1 Mark`

8 A ray of light travels from one medium to another and, as it does so, is refracted towards the normal. What does this indicate about the second medium?   `2 Marks`

Going further

9 Name the missing parts of the electromagnetic spectrum labelled A and B in the diagram.   `2 Marks`

| radio waves | microwave | A | visible light | ultraviolet | B | gamma rays |

10 Name the two types of electromagnetic radiation that are used to cook food.   `2 Marks`

11 Describe two practical applications for

   a microwaves   `1 Mark`

   b gamma rays.   `1 Mark`

12 A student investigates how a wavelength of a wave on a piece of string varies with the frequency.

   Suggest what apparatus the student could use.   `2 Marks`

13 What is the speed of a water wave if it has a wavelength of 8 cm and a frequency of 2 Hz?   `2 Marks`

More challenging

14 Suggest why microwaves are not reflected by upper layers of the atmosphere.   `1 Mark`

15 Give one way in which ultraviolet waves can harm the body.   `1 Mark`

16 Explain why houses would benefit in both hot and cold countries if they had a white roof.   `2 Marks`

17 a Explain what refraction means.   `1 Mark`

   b Draw a diagram using wavefronts to explain how refraction works.   `4 Marks`

   c Describe what happens to the wavelength of a wave when it refracts.   `1 Mark`

Most demanding

18 Jemima comments that the electromagnetic waves that are hazardous all seem to be in one part of the electromagnetic spectrum. Suggest why this might be.

`2 Marks`

19 A group of students set up a ripple tank and use the oscillating motor beam to make straight waves travel across the surface of the water.

   a Suggest how they could measure the wavelength of these waves.

   b Suggest how they could measure the frequency of these waves.

   c Identify the potential sources of error in each of those values, referring to the method used.

`4 Marks`

20 Explain how you could use a pendulum to demonstrate that the period of its oscillation was inversely proportional to the frequency of its oscillation.

`4 Marks`

`Total: 40 Marks`

ELECTROMAGNETISM

IDEAS YOU HAVE MET BEFORE:

PERMANENT MAGNETS

- Permanent magnets are made from nickel, cobalt and most steels.
- Iron is a magnetic material but loses its magnetism when the magnetising force is removed.
- Like poles repel and unlike poles attract.

EARTH'S MAGNETISM

- The Earth's magnetic field is very similar to the magnetic field due to a bar magnet.
- A compass uses the Earth's magnetic field to indicate magnetic north.
- The Earth behaves as if there is a gigantic bar magnet inside it.

MAGNETIC EFFECT OF A CURRENT

- The wires carrying an electric current produce a magnetic field.
- The magnetic field made by the current in a wire is a circular shape around the wire.
- The magnetic field is increased if more turns are wound on the coil and/or the current in the wire is increased.

direction of current

circular magnetic field around wire

ELECTROMAGNETS

- A coil of wire with an iron rod in it makes an electromagnet.
- The iron rod becomes magnetised when a current flows in the coil.
- The iron rod loses its magnetism as soon as the current is switched off.

IN THIS CHAPTER YOU WILL FIND OUT ABOUT:

WHAT ARE PERMANENT AND INDUCED MAGNETS?

- Permanent magnets can be used to test for a magnet.
- The difference between permanent and induced magnets is that the latter has a field that can be turned off by switching the current flow off.

HOW DOES A MAGNETIC FIELD VARY?

- The strength and direction of a magnetic field varies according to distance and direction of current flowing in the coils of an electromagnet.
- The behaviour of a magnetic compass is indicates that the core of the Earth is magnetic.

WHAT ARE THE EFFECTS OF CURRENT AND MAGNETISM?

- The direction of the magnetic field can be worked out from the direction of the current.
- The force on a current-carrying wire in a magnetic field can be calculated.
- Fleming's left-hand rule can be used to work out the direction of force or motion on a current-carrying wire in a magnetic field.

WHAT IS A MOTOR AND HOW DOES IT WORK?

- Describe some uses of motors.
- Explain how a motor works.
- Explain how a commutator is used.

Magnetism and magnetic forces

Learning objectives:

* explain what is meant by the poles of a magnet
* plot the magnetic field around a bar magnet
* describe magnetic materials and induced magnetism.

KEY WORDS

attract
induced magnet
magnetic field
permanent magnet
poles
repel

A maglev (magnetic levitation) train has no wheels. It uses the fact that like poles repel so that it hovers above its track. The maglev train in Shanghai can carry passengers 30 km to the airport in 7 minutes and 20 seconds (Figure 7.1).

The poles of a magnet

The **poles** of a magnet are the places where the magnetic forces are strongest. When a bar magnet is suspended by a thread, it will settle with one end pointing north. This end is called the north-seeking pole, or north pole.

When the ends of two bar magnets are brought near each other, two north poles or two south poles **repel** each other but a south pole and a north pole **attract** each other (Figure 7.2). These are examples of non-contact forces.

Figure 7.1 A maglev train in Shanghai

KEY INFORMATION

Magnetic field lines always start at a north pole and finish at a south pole. The lines show the direction of the magnetic field.

Figure 7.2 Like poles repel, unlike poles attract

1 What happens when the south poles of two magnets are brought together?

Magnetic fields

A **magnetic field** is the region around a magnet where a force acts on another magnet or on a magnetic material. The direction of a magnetic field is the direction of the force on a north pole placed at a point in the field.

You can use a plotting compass to reveal the magnetic field of a magnet. Put the magnet on a piece of paper and draw round it. Place the plotting compass near the north pole of the magnet. Draw a dot by the head of the arrow on the compass. Move the compass so that the tail of the pointer is by the dot you have just drawn. Draw another dot by the head of the arrow.

Repeat moving the compass and drawing a dot by the head of the arrow until you have gone all the way round to the south pole. Draw a smooth curve to join all your points.

Repeat for slightly different starting points near to the north pole of the magnet.

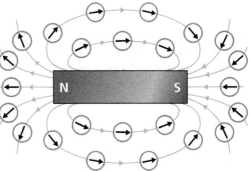

2 **Explain why you need to put the plotting compass in several different places near the north pole of the magnet when using it to plot the magnetic field.**

Figure 7.3 The needle of a plotting compass can be used to show the direction of the magnetic field around a bar magnet

Induced magnetism and magnetic materials

Iron, some steels, nickel and cobalt are magnetic materials. They can all be magnetised. Iron only makes a temporary magnet. It loses its magnetism as soon as the magnetising force is removed.

A permanent magnet produces its own magnetic field. An **induced magnet** is a material that becomes a magnet when it is placed in a magnetic field. When removed from the magnetic field it loses most or all of its magnetism quickly. Iron is an example of this type of magnetic material. **Permanent magnets** are made from nickel, cobalt and some types of steel.

The force between a magnet and a magnetic material is always attractive.

Steel pins or iron tacks are attracted to a magnet (Figure 7.4). Each pin or tack becomes a small magnet because of induced magnetism. If you carefully separate the magnet from the steel pins and tacks, the steel pins remain magnetised but the iron tacks lose their magnetism and are no longer attracted to each other.

You can test whether a material is a magnet by bringing another magnet close to it.

> **KEY INFORMATION**
>
> Magnetic field lines never meet or cross.

3 **Explain why the pins and tacks behave as described.**

4 **Explain what forces of attraction and repulsion can take place between the pins and tacks once they have been removed from the magnet (Figure 7.4).**

5 **Suggest how you know whether an object is a magnet when you bring another magnet close to it.**

6 **Suggest how the behaviour of a magnetic compass is related to evidence that the core of the Earth must be magnetic.**

Figure 7.4 Magnets attract some metals such as iron and steel

Compasses and magnetic fields

KEY WORDS

magnetic field

Learning objectives:

- describe the Earth's magnetic field
- describe the magnetic effect of a current.

Objects like steel girders in bridges are often found to be slightly magnetised by induction from the Earth's magnetism, particularly if the structure is hammered or shaken by vibrations.

Magnetic compass

A compass contains a small bar magnet. One end is a north pole and the other end is a south pole. The south pole of a compass needle is attracted to a magnetic north pole. This is how we use a compass to plot the magnetic field of another magnet (Figure 7.3 in topic 7.1).

1 **Draw a labelled diagram to show how a compass needle will behave when placed near:**

   a a north pole

   b a south pole.

The Earth's magnetic field

The fact that a compass needle points north is evidence that the Earth has a magnetic field. The Earth behaves as if there is a bar magnet inside it. (Such a magnet cannot really exist because the centre of the Earth is too hot.) The odd thing is that the south pole of this imaginary magnet is in the northern hemisphere near the Earth's geographic north pole (Figure 7.5). The geographic north pole is a magnetic south pole. The end of the compass that points towards geographic north is called a north-seeking pole.

DID YOU KNOW?

At the Earth's centre is a solid inner core surrounded by a fluid outer core, which is hottest next to the inner core. Hot molten iron rises within the outer core, then cools and sinks. These movements create an electric current, which, combined with the rotation of the Earth, are thought to produce the Earth's magnetic field.

DID YOU KNOW?

The magnetic poles move around over time, and the Earth's magnetic field has reversed direction many times in the Earth's history. These flips are becoming more frequent. Many millions of years ago, the field reversed direction every 5 million years, but now it reverses approximately every 200 000 years.

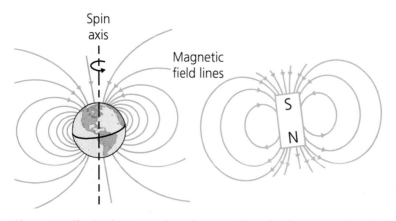

Figure 7.5 The Earth's magnetic and geographic poles do not exactly coincide

The closer the field lines are together, the greater the strength of the magnetic field. Figure 7.5 shows that the Earth's magnetic field is strongest at the poles.

2 What is the polarity of the end of the imaginary bar magnet inside the Earth that is nearest the geographic south pole?

3 Explain why the north pole of a compass is often called the north-seeking pole.

The magnetic effect of a current

When a current flows in a wire, the current creates a magnetic field around the wire. This effect can be investigated using a plotting compass placed at different points around the wire (Figure 7.6).

Figure 7.6 The magnetic field around a current-carrying wire is circular

The strength of the magnetic field decreases with distance from the wire. Further from the wire, the field lines would get further apart. The strength of the magnetic field also depends on the current through the wire. The higher the current, the stronger the magnetic field.

If the current direction is reversed, the direction of the magnetic field is reversed. The direction of the magnetic field is given by the right-hand grip rule (Figure 7.7).

To work out the direction of the magnetic field, grip the wire in your right-hand so that your thumb points in the direction of the conventional flow of current (from positive to negative). Then your fingers point around the wire in the direction of the magnetic field.

Figure 7.7 The right-hand grip rule

4 A wire goes into the plane of a page. Draw a diagram to show the magnetic field and its direction around the wire.

5 Copy Figure 7.6 and sketch a diagram to show how the magnetic field pattern would change if the current in the wire was increased.

6 Explain why a compass placed towards the edge of the card in Figure 7.6 might not point along the field line as expected.

The magnetic effect of a solenoid

Learning objectives:

- draw the magnetic field around a conducting wire and a solenoid
- describe the force on a wire in a magnetic field.
- apply the left-hand rule to work out the direction of a magnetic field, a current or a force around a wire.

Electricity and magnetism are very closely connected. By combining the two, we can create much more powerful magnets or electromagnets.

Magnetic field of a loop of wire

You have seen how a current flowing through a wire creates a magnetic field around it. The magnetic field becomes more complicated when the wire becomes a loop. The field lines are squashed together in the middle of the loop.

plotting compasses

Figure 7.8 The magnetic field in the centre of a loop is stronger than outside the loop

plotting compasses

Figure 7.9 The magnetic field around a solenoid is similar to that of a bar magnet

1 The direction of the current in the wire in Figure 7.8 is reversed. What is the direction of the magnetic field now?

The magnetic field in a solenoid

A **solenoid** is a long straight coil of wire. When a current is passed through a solenoid the magnetic field of all the coils combines to produce a magnetic field like that of a bar magnet. Adding an iron core increases the strength of the magnetic field of a solenoid, to make an **electromagnet**.

The polarity of the solenoid can be worked out by looking at the end of the solenoid and seeing which way the current passes (Figure 7.10).

2 Sadie looks at the end of a solenoid and notes that the current is in a clockwise direction. What is the magnetic pole at that end of the solenoid?

north pole   south pole

end view

anticlockwise   clockwise

Figure 7.10 North and south poles of a coil of wire

3 Suggest two things that you can do to make the magnetic field stronger.

The kicking wire

When a straight wire with a current passing through it is placed between the poles of a magnet, the two magnetic fields combine, making the resultant magnetic field stronger in one area and weaker in another area. This produces a force on the wire which makes the wire move (Figure 7.11). This is called the **motor effect**. The direction of the force and the motion is perpendicular to both the magnetic field and the current.

Fleming's left-hand rule (Figure 7.12) allows us to work out the relative directions of the current, magnetic field and motion of the wire.

> **REMEMBER!**
>
> The right-hand grip rule and Fleming's left-hand rule use different hands. Be careful not to muddle them up.

> **KEY INFORMATION**
>
> Conventional current is from the positive to negative terminal of a battery. This is the *opposite* direction to the direction of electron flow.

Figure 7.11

Figure 7.12 Fleming's left-hand rule

Hold your thumb and first two fingers of your left hand at right angles to each other.

Point your first finger in the direction of the magnetic field (from north to south).

Point your second finger in the direction of the current. This is what is known as conventional current – flowing from positive to negative.

Your thumb then shows the direction of motion of the wire.

You can increase the force on the wire by increasing:

- the size of the magnetic field
- the current passing through the wire
- the length of the wire that is in the magnetic field.

4 A wire is placed between the poles of a magnet. When the current is switched on the wire moves to the left.

   a Which way does the wire move when the current direction is reversed?

   b Which way does the wire move when the poles of the magnet are reversed?

5 Explain how you could decrease the force on the wire.

6 Which way will the wire move when the switch is pressed in Figure 7.11?

Calculating the force on a conductor

KEY WORDS

magnetic flux
   density
tesla (T)

Learning objectives:

- explain the meaning of magnetic flux density, B
- calculate the force on a current-carrying conductor in a magnetic field.

A conducting wire in a magnetic field experiences a force – the motor effect. The application of this effect is the basis for all electric motors.

HIGHER TIER ONLY

Magnetic flux density, B

The spacing of the magnetic field lines in Figure 7.13 tells us how strong the magnetic field is. Where the lines are closer together, the field is stronger. The magnetic field inside the coil is much stronger than the magnetic field outside the coil.

The strength of a magnetic field is called the **magnetic flux density**, denoted by B and measured in **tesla** (T).

1 **Explain how the strength of the magnetic field varies inside the solenoid.**

coil carrying
electric current

the magnetic field around a
solenoid resembles that
around a bar magnet

Figure 7.13 Magnetic flux density tells us about the strength of a magnetic field

Force on a wire

The size of the force, F, in N on a wire carrying a current at right angles to a magnetic field is proportional to:

- the current, I, in A
- the length of wire in the field, l, in m.

So *F* is proportional to *Il*. The force is given by the equation

F = BIl

where *B* is the magnetic flux density, in **tesla** (T).

Example:

A wire carrying a current of 10 A passes at right angles through a magnetic field of 0.15 T. Calculate the force acting on a wire of length 0.2 m.

F = BIl

B = 0.15 T, *I* = 10 A, *l* = 0.20 m

F = 0.15 × 10 × 0.20 = 0.30 N

2 What happens to the force on a wire carrying a current when:

  a the current in the wire doubles?

  b the current in the wire and the length of wire in the magnetic field both double?

3 Calculate the force on each wire. The wire is perpendicular to the magnetic field.

  a Length of wire is 2 m, current is 0.5 A and the magnetic flux density is 0.05 T.

  b Current in the wire is 2 A, length of the wire is 50 cm and the magnetic flux density is 0.1 T.

4 A wire lies at right angles to a uniform magnetic field of magnetic flux density 0.02 T. 0.3 m of the wire is inside the length of the magnetic field. If the force on this length of wire due to the current in it is 0.03 N downwards, what are the magnitude and direction of the current in the wire?

5 A wire is perpendicular to a magnetic field and has a force on it of 0.05 N. 0.25 m of wire is inside the magnetic field. Calculate the magnetic flux density when the current in the wire is 3 A.

> **REMEMBER!**
> ....
> Make sure you use the correct units when substituting in the equation *F = BIL*. If the values in the question are not in tesla, amps and metres, you have to change the values to the correct units before starting the calculation.

Forces and magnetic fields

6 Will there be a force acting on a wire carrying a current of 2 A running parallel to a magnetic field? Explain your answer.

7 A metal wire is lying near the equator perpendicular to the Earth's magnetic field. Length of the wire = 2.0 m, weight of wire = 0.30 N, Earth's magnetic flux density *B* = 0.00003 T.

  a Calculate the current needed to lift the wire off the ground.

  b Explain whether the wire could be lifted if it was placed near one of Earth's magnetic poles.

Electric motors

Learning objectives:

- list equipment that uses motors
- describe how motors work
- describe how to change the speed and direction of rotation of a motor.

KEY WORDS

Fleming's
 left-hand rule
split-ring
 commutator

Every part of a car where you press a button to move something requires a motor.

HIGHER TIER ONLY

Using motors

Electric motors have many uses around the home. Any electrical machine that has moving parts is likely to have a motor. For example, an electric lawn mower, a food processor and an electric drill (Figure 7.14) all contain electric motors.

1 Give three more examples of equipment that contains an electric motor.

Figure 7.14 Electric motors are used in many appliances such as this drill

How motors work

When a current passes through a coil placed between the poles of a magnet there is a force on each side of the coil. **Fleming's left-hand rule** shows that the forces on each side of the coil are in opposite directions, so the coil will move. One side of the coil moves up and the other side moves down. This makes the coil start to spin.

A direct current (dc) motor has a **split-ring commutator** that rotates with the coil between two carbon brushes (Figure 7.15). The commutator allows the motor to continue to spin without reversing direction every time it gets to the vertical position.

Figure 7.15 The circuit for a d.c. motor

You can use Fleming's left-hand rule to work out the direction of the force. On the left-hand side of the coil in Figure 7.15, the direction of the current is towards the commutator and the field is to the right. So the force is upwards. On the right-hand side of the coil, as the current is in the opposite direction, away from the commutator, the force will also be in the opposite direction, which is downwards. So the coil spins clockwise. When the coil is vertical, the circuit is broken and no current flows. Since the coil is moving, there is enough momentum for the coil to carry on rotating a little further. The side of the coil that was on the left is now on the right, and in contact with the other carbon brush. The direction of the current in the coil then reverses and the force on the other side of the coil is now upwards, so the motor continues to spin in the same direction.

Practical motors have curved pole pieces. This produces a radial field (Figure 7.16).

The coil is always at right angles to the magnetic field. This increases the force and keeps it constant as the coil turns.

The direction the motor turns can be reversed by reversing the current or reversing the direction of the magnetic field.

2. Why does the coil start to spin in Figure 7.15?

3. Explain how a split-ring commutator works.

4. For the rectangular coil in Figure 7.15, only two of the sides experience a force. Why does no force act on the other two sides?

Ac motors

Motors also work with alternating current (ac). Ac motors have slip rings instead of a split-ring commutator (Figure 7.17). As the coil rotates, the direction of the current passing through the coil reverses direction. When the coil has gone through half a turn, the direction of the current has reversed. Look at the left-hand side of the coil. The current flows in the direction AB. The force is downwards and the coil moves anticlockwise. By the time this part of the coil has rotated through half a turn, the direction of the current has reversed and is in the direction CD. The force is upwards so it continues rotating anticlockwise.

Figure 7.16 A radial field in a motor

Figure 7.17 An a.c. electric motor

5. What would be the effect if both the current and magnetic field were reversed?

6. Give two things that could be done to make the motor turn more slowly.

7. Suggest why you could not use wires to connect the coil of the motor without a commutator.

8. In practical motors, the coil is often wound round some iron. Explain what advantage this gives.

KEY CONCEPT

The link between electricity and magnetism

Learning objectives:

- describe simple uses of electromagnets
- explore how electricity and magnetism are connected.

In 1820, Hans Christian Oersted was demonstrating an experiment with batteries and electric current in a circuit. He noticed that every time he switched the batteries on and off, the needle in a compass that was lying on the bench beside his work deflected from magnetic north. This was when he realised that there was a direct relationship between electricity and magnetism.

Simple electromagnets

In a simple **electromagnet** (Figure 7.18) a coil of copper wire (solenoid) is wound round an iron core. This magnetises the core, creating an electromagnet about 1000 times stronger than the coil by itself. An electromagnet can be switched on and off because the iron core is a temporary magnet. It loses its induced magnetism when the current is switched off, because there is no longer a magnetic field caused by the current in the wire.

① Why is the core of an electromagnet made of iron?

② Explain what would happen if the core was made from steel.

DID YOU KNOW?

An electromagnet used in a scrapyard can lift up to 15 tonnes of metal.

Figure 7.18 An electromagnet can be switched on and off

KEY INFORMATION

The strength of an electromagnet is increased by adding an iron core. The strength also depends on the current through the coil, the material in the core, and the number of turns on the coil.

Electricity and magnetism

Electricity has to do with the properties and movement of electrically charged particles. Magnetism involves the properties of magnets and magnetic materials.

Electricity and magnetism are interrelated. Movement of electrical charges creates **magnetic fields**.

Current flowing through a circuit creates a magnetic field around the wire.

3 Name a device where an electric current is used to produce a magnetic field.

4 Name a device where an electric current and a magnetic field produce motion.

Figure 7.19 A modern electric motor in a disc drive

Explaining the motor effect

Imagine you put a current-carrying conductor, which has a magnetic field around it, into a magnetic field. The magnetic field around the conductor interacts with the magnetic field of the magnet. The combination of the magnetic fields creates an instantaneous force between the magnet and the conductor. This is the underlying principle behind the electric motor.

5 Describe in your own words the underlying principle of the electric motor.

6 A wire carrying a current is placed between the poles of a U-shaped magnet (Figure 7.20). Describe how the direction of the resulting magnetic force on the wire can be found.

conventional
current direction

Figure 7.20

MATHS SKILLS

Rearranging equations

Learning objectives:

- change the subject of a equation.

KEY WORDS

rearrange an
  equation
subject of an
  equation
substitute

Equations are used throughout physics. Calculating the value of *a* from the equation $a = b \times c$ when you know *b* and *c* is straightforward. It becomes more difficult when you want to work out the values of *b* or *c*. You need to rearrange the equation.

HIGHER TIER ONLY

Force on a conductor

The force on a conductor carrying a current is $F = BIL$ where the force (*F*) is in newtons, N, *B* is the magnetic flux density in tesla, T, the current (*I*) flowing through the conductor is in amps, A, and the length (*L*) of the conductor is in metres, m.

To work out the force when you know *B*, *I* and *L*, **substitute** the values into the equation.

To work out one of *B*, *I* or *L* you need to **rearrange** the **equation**. You can rearrange the equation and substitute the values or substitute the values and rearrange the equation.

Example:

A conductor 50 m long carrying a current of 5 A is placed in a magnetic field. Calculate the magnetic flux density when a force of 0.02 N is produced on the conductor.

Method 1: substitute the values and rearrange the equation to make *B* the **subject of the equation**:

$F = BIl$

$0.02 \text{ N} = B \times 5 \text{ A} \times 50 \text{ m}$

Rearrange the equation: divide both sides by 5 A × 50 m:

$B = \dfrac{0.02 \text{ N}}{(5 \text{ A} \times 50 \text{ m})}$

$\quad = 8 \times 10^{-5} \text{ T}$

MATHS

Always do the **same** operation to both sides of the equation.

Remember the unit in your answer.

Method 2: rearrange the equation and substitute the values:

$F = BIl$

Rearrange the equation: divide both sides by Il:

$B = \dfrac{F}{Il}$

Substitute the values into the rearranged equation:

$B = \dfrac{0.02\,\text{N}}{(5\,\text{A} \times 50\,\text{m})}$

$= 8 \times 10^{-5}\,\text{T}$

1 Calculate the force on a conductor that is 25 m long carrying 3 A in a magnetic field of flux density 3×10^{-5} T.

2 a Calculate the current in a coil of wire 250 m long with a magnetic field of flux density 1.0×10^{-4} T, when the force is 0.125 N. Work out the answer using both methods in the example.

   b Which method did you find easier?

3 Calculate the length of conductor when a conductor carrying a current of 2.5 A experiences a force of 0.05 N in a magnetic field of flux density 3×10^{-5} T. Use your preferred method.

Check your progress

You should be able to:

Recall that like poles repel, unlike poles attract
→
Recognise that the poles of a magnet are the places where the magnetic forces are strongest
→
Explain that an induced magnet is a material that is only magnetic when it is placed in a magnetic field

Plot the magnetic field around a bar magnet
→
Recognise that the magnetic field is the region around a magnet where a force acts on another magnet or on a magnetic material
→
Explain how the behaviour of a magnetic compass is related to evidence that the core of the Earth must be magnetic

State how the strength of an electromagnet can be increased
→
Draw the magnetic field around a conducting wire and a solenoid
→
Use the magnetic field pattern around a conducting wire and solenoid to explain how the field strength varies

State that a force acts on a current-carrying conductor in a magnetic field
→
Describe the motor effect that applies to a current-carrying conductor in a magnetic field
→
Explain how the direction of the force on the conductor can be identified using Fleming's left-hand rule

State that magnetic flux density is measured in tesla (T)
→
Explain what the size of a force on a conductor depends on
→
Use the equation $F = BIl$ to calculate the force on a conductor

Worked example

1 **How can you increase the strength of the magnetic field created by a current through a wire?**

To increase the strength of the magnetic field you need to coil the wire.

Correct, but that is only part of the answer. There are two more ways in which you can strengthen the magnetic field: increase the current and wrap the coils around an iron core.

2 **Explain how continuous rotation is produced in an electric motor.**

When a wire carrying a current is put into a magnetic field, one force reacts to the other and this pushes the wire down. If this is a coil then it begins to go round.

You should aim to show that you really understand exactly what is going on and where the forces are coming from.

Describe the interaction between the magnetic field in the wire and the magnetic field of the magnet.

With a complicated answer like this, it can be helpful to draw a diagram. In this case the diagram would show the coil, magnetic field and direction of movement.

End of chapter questions

Getting started

1. Where is the magnetic field around a bar magnet strongest?

   a near the poles   b along the side

   c above the magnet   d well away from the magnet   `1 Mark`

2. Which of these will not strengthen the magnetic field created by a current through a wire?   `1 Mark`

   a shaping the wire into a coil   b stripping the plastic insulation off the wire

   c increasing the potential   d using a thicker wire
      difference

3. Give two differences between a permanent magnet and an induced magnet.   `2 Marks`

4. There are two small iron bars on the bench. One is magnetised and the other is not. Explain how you could identify which is which.   `2 Marks`

5. Jemima has made an electromagnet using a coil of wire and a power supply. Which of these will not indicate how strong the magnetic field is?

   a seeing from how far away the coil will attract a paper clip

   b seeing how many paper clips it will attract

   c seeing what potential difference the power supply is set to

   d seeing from how far away it can affect a plotting compass   `1 Mark`

6. Describe how to plot the magnetic field pattern of a magnet using a compass.   `2 Marks`

Going further

7. Which of these will not change the direction of the force in the motor effect?

   a Increase the potential difference   b Reverse the potential difference

   c Reverse the polarity of the magnets d Swap the contacts on the power supply   `1 Mark`

8. Explain why a compass points towards the south pole of a magnet.   `1 Mark`

9. Describe how you can make an electromagnet as strong as possible.   `2 Marks`

10. a Calculate the force acting on a current-carrying conductor if the wire has a total length of 2 m, the current flowing is 1.5 A and the magnetic flux density is 5×10^{-5} T.   `2 Marks`

    b Suggest what will happen if the field strength is doubled.   `1 Mark`

11. A student was investigating how the magnetic force on a length of wire carrying a current depends on its length. Explain how the student can make this a fair test.   `2 Marks`

12. A wire carrying a current is inside a magnetic field. The wire experiences a force from the motor effect.

    Give the angle between the wire and the magnetic field that produces the maximum force.   `1 Mark`

More challenging

13 Charlie and Jo are building a solenoid and investigating the magnetic field it produces. Which one of these statements is not true?

a The magnetic field will be stronger inside the coil than outside it.

b The coil will have a North pole at one end and a South pole at the other.

c The magnetic field lines will start at the North pole end and finish at the South pole end.

d The strength of the field will be affected by the resistance of the wire.

14 The diagram shows a dc electric motor. The coil starts off in a horizontal position, as shown in the diagram.

When a current flows in the coil, the coil rotates.

a Explain why side A of the coil moves. `2 Marks`

b Give the reason why side B of the coil experiences no force. `1 Mark`

c How could the motor be made to turn in the opposite direction? `1 Mark`

15 The diagram shows a current-carrying wire in a magnetic field. The arrow on the wire shows the direction of the conventional current.

a Draw an arrow on the diagram to show the direction the wire moves. `1 Mark`

b Explain why the wire moves. `2 Marks`

c Explain why the wire does not move if the switch is left open. `1 Mark`

d State two factors that would increase the force on the conductor. `2 Marks`

Most demanding

16 State the equation that can be used to calculate the force on a current-carrying conductor and use it to explain how the design of a motor can be changed to make it more powerful. `4 Marks`

17 a A direct current (dc) motor has a split-ring commutator. Explain how the split-ring commutator keeps the coil rotating when a current flows through the external circuit. `3 Marks`

b Give two ways in which the motor could be made to spin in the opposite direction. `2 Marks`

c The motor is not 100% efficient. What is the main way the motor is likely to waste energy? `1 Mark`

`Total: 40 Marks`

Appendix – Circuits

 switch (open)

 lamp

switch (closed)

 fuse

 cell

 voltmeter

battery

 ammeter

 diode

 thermistor

 resistor

 variable resistor

 LDR

 LED

Appendix – Equations

It is important to be able to recall and apply the following equations using standard units:

Equation Number	Word Equation	Symbol Equation
1	weight = mass × gravitational field strength	$W = mg$
2	work done = force × distance (along the line of action of the force)	$W = Fs$
3	force applied to a spring = spring constant × extension	$F = ke$
4	distance travelled = speed × time	$s = vt$
5	acceleration = $\dfrac{\text{change in velocity}}{\text{time taken}}$	$a = \dfrac{\Delta v}{t}$
6	resultant force = mass × acceleration	$F = ma$
7	momentum = mass × velocity	$p = mv$
8	kinetic energy = 0.5 × mass × (speed)²	$E_k = \frac{1}{2}mv^2$
9	gravitational potential energy = mass × gravitational field strength × height	$E_p = mgh$
10	power = $\dfrac{\text{energy transferred}}{\text{time}}$	$P = \dfrac{E}{t}$
11	power = $\dfrac{\text{work done}}{\text{time}}$	$P = \dfrac{W}{t}$
12	efficiency = $\dfrac{\text{useful output energy transfer}}{\text{useful input energy transfer}}$	
13	efficiency = $\dfrac{\text{useful power output}}{\text{total power output}}$	
14	wave speed = frequency × wavelength	$v = f\lambda$
15	charge flow = current × time	$Q = It$
16	potential difference = current × resistance	$V = IR$
17	power = potential difference × current	$P = VI$
18	power = (current)² × resistance	$P = I^2R$
19	energy transferred = power × time	$E = Pt$

Equation Number	Word Equation	Symbol Equation
20	energy transferred = charge flow × potential difference	$E = QV$
21	density = $\dfrac{\text{mass}}{\text{volume}}$	$\rho = \dfrac{m}{V}$

The following equations will appear on the equations sheet that you are given in the exam. It is important to be able to select and apply the appropriate equation to answer a question correctly.

Equation Number	Word Equation	Symbol Equation
1	(final velocity)² − (initial velocity)² = 2 × acceleration × distance	$v^2 - u^2 = 2as$
2	elastic potential energy = 0.5 × spring constant × (extension)²	$E_e = \frac{1}{2}ke^2$
3	change in thermal energy = mass × specific heat capacity × temperature change	$\Delta E = mc\Delta\theta$
4	period = $\dfrac{1}{\text{frequency}}$	
5	force on a conductor (at right angles to a magnetic field) = magnetic flux density × current × length	$F = BIL$
6	thermal energy for a change of state = mass × specific latent heat	$E = mL$
7	potential difference across primary coil × current in primary coil = potential difference across secondary coil × current in secondary coil	$V_p I_p = V_s I_s$

Glossary

A

absorption process in which matter takes in energy, e.g. when an atom takes in energy from an electromagnetic wave

acceleration rate at which an object speeds up, calculated from change in velocity divided by time; symbol a, unit metres per second squared, m/s²

accuracy how close a measurement is to its true value

activity the rate at which unstable nuclei decay in a sample of a radioactive material; unit becquerel, Bq

air resistance force produced by the collision of molecules in air with a moving object; the force acts to oppose the direction of movement

alternating current (a.c.) electric current that continually changes direction

alpha particle a particle (two neutrons and two protons, same as a helium nucleus) emitted by an atomic nucleus during radioactive decay

ammeter device that measures electric current

ampere SI unit of electric current, symbol A; an electric current of 1 A is equal to 1 C of charge passing through a point in a circuit in 1 s

amplitude maximum displacement of a wave or oscillating object from its rest position

angle of incidence the angle between the incident ray and the normal

angle of reflection the angle between the reflected ray and the normal

atmospheric pressure force per unit area produced by the weight of air; it decreases as you go higher in the atmosphere

atomic number number of protons in the nucleus of an atom of an element

average speed distance travelled by an object over a measured time interval

B

background radiation nuclear radiation that is present in the environment as a result of the radioactive decay of certain elements; it is produced from natural sources (e.g. from radon gas in the Earth's crust) and from artificial sources (e.g. as a result of testing nuclear weapons)

becquerel unit of activity for a radioactive isotope, symbol Bq

beta particle fast-moving electron that is emitted by an atomic nucleus in some types of radioactive decay

boundary line or surface between two different media (e.g. the surface between air and glass), across which light may be refracted or reflected

braking distance distance travelled by a vehicle after the brakes have been applied before coming to a complete stop

C

cancer disease in which uncontrolled division of cells takes place, forming a tumour; some types of cancer are caused by the effects of ionising radiation on cells

cell (electric circuits) circuit component that stores energy in the form of chemical energy; a number of electric cells may be joined to form a battery

cell (living things) smallest structural unit of a living organism; cells may be damaged by some types of ionising radiation

centre of mass a single point where the weight of an object can be considered to act

chain reaction occurs when the neutrons released by a nucleus undergoing fission go on to split more nuclei

change of state process in which one state of matter changes to another, e.g. solid melting to form liquid, or gas condensing to form liquid

circuit diagram visual representation of electrical components connected by wires, using standard symbols

circuit symbol visual representation of an electrical component; a standard symbol exists for each type of electrical component

closed system system that is not acted upon by any external forces and does not exchange energy with its surroundings

commutator (split-ring) electrical connector consisting of two semi-circular metal contacts, which is connected to a rotating coil in a dynamo (to produce direct current) or a motor (to use direct current)

compass (magnetic) device that shows the direction of a magnetic field in which it is placed; typically a compass is made from a magnetised needle or pointer that is free to rotate

components (forces) the result of breaking down or resolving a single force into two separate forces acting in perpendicular directions, often horizontally and vertically

compress squash something into a smaller volume; liquids are incompressible – they cannot be squashed

compression a region of a sound wave where the particles are closer together

conclusion section at the end of a report on an experiment that summarises how the results support or contradict the original hypothesis

conductivity (thermal) quantity that measures the rate at which thermal energy is conducted through a material; the higher the thermal conductivity, the higher the rate of thermal energy transfer

conductor material or object that allows electric charge to flow through it

conservation of electric charge a fundamental principle of physics: electric charge cannot be created or destroyed, only transferred from one object to another; the total electric charge of a system is constant

conservation of energy a fundamental principle of physics: energy cannot be created or destroyed, only transferred, stored or dissipated. This means that the total energy of a closed system is constant

conservation of mass a fundamental principle of physics: mass cannot be created or destroyed by physical changes or chemical reactions; the total mass of a system is constant

conservation of momentum a fundamental principle of physics: the total momentum of a system of objects after a collision is the same as the total momentum before the collision

contact force force that acts at the point of contact between two objects (e.g. friction or the normal reaction)

contamination (radioactivity) the unwanted presence of materials containing radioactive atoms

control variable quantity in an experiment that is kept constant while the independent variable is changed and the dependent variable is measured

coulomb SI unit of electric charge, symbol C

count rate the number of decays recorded each second by a detector (e.g. Geiger-Muller tube)

CT (or CAT) scan scan that takes many X-ray images from different directions to build up a 3D image of the body

current (electric) flow of electric charge; the size of the electric current is the rate of flow of electric charge; symbol I, unit amps (A)

D

data measurements of quantities in an experiment; data can be recorded in a table and used to produce graphs

decay (radioactive) process in which the nucleus of an atom breaks apart and emits radiation

deceleration negative acceleration, when an object slows down

degrees Celsius unit of temperature, symbol °C; 1 °C is $\frac{1}{100}$ of the temperature difference between the melting point and boiling point of water

density measure of the amount of substance per unit volume; symbol ρ, unit kilograms per metre cubed, kg/m^3

dependent variable quantity in an experiment that is measured for each change in the independent variable

diode circuit component with a low resistance if it is connected one way around in a circuit, or a very high resistance if it is connected the other way around; a diode allows current in one direction only

direct current (d.c.) flow of electric charge in one direction only

directly proportional relationship a relationship of the form y is proportional to ($\propto$) x; plotting a graph of y against x will produce a straight line through the origin

displacement distance moved in a particular direction; it is a vector quantity and is equal to the area under a velocity–time graph; symbol s, unit metres, m

dissipation the spreading out of energy into the environment, so that it is stored in less useful ways

distance quantity that measures how far an object moves but not the direction; it is a scalar quantity; symbol s, unit metres, m

distance–time graph graph with distance on the y-axis and time on the x-axis; the gradient of a distance–time graph is equal to the speed

dose (radiation) quantity that is a measure of the amount of ionising radiation received (e.g. by a human body); measured in sieverts (Sv)

E

earth (electrical) electrical connection between the metal case of an electrical appliance and the ground, used as a safety device to prevent the case becoming charged if touched by a live wire

echo reflection of a sound or ultrasound wave

efficiency useful output energy transfer divided by the total input energy transfer (or useful power output divided by the total power input) – may be expressed as a percentage or as a decimal

elastic deformation process in which an object (e.g. a spring) is stretched by a force and returns to its original size or length when the force is removed

elastic potential energy energy that is stored in an object as a result of the object being stretched or compressed

electric charge fundamental property of matter that results in an electric field around an object; objects can be electrically positive, negative or neutral (no overall charge); symbol Q, unit coulomb, C

electric current flow of electric charge; the size of the electric current is the rate of flow of electric charge; symbol I, unit amps, A

electrical power amount of energy transferred each second; symbol P, unit watts or joules per second, W or J/s

electromagnet magnet formed by an electric current flowing through a solenoid (coil of wire) with an iron core – the magnetic field of an electromagnet can be switched on and off by switching the current on and off

electromagnetic (EM) spectrum electromagnetic waves ordered according to wavelength and frequency – ranging from radio waves to gamma rays

electron a particle that orbits the nucleus in all atoms; electrons have a negative electric charge

emission process in which energy or a particle are given out by an atom (e.g. in beta particle emission, a high-speed electron is given out)

energy level stable state of a physical system, e.g. electrons orbiting the nucleus of an atom can exist in only particular energy levels and be moved between them

energy store the energy associated with fuel (chemical energy store), a heated object (thermal energy store), a moving object (kinetic energy store), a stretched spring (elastic potential energy store) and an object raised above ground level (gravitational potential energy store)

energy transfer process in which energy is moved from one store to another

equilibrium situation in which there is no resultant force acting on an object; any forces that are acting balance each other in magnitude and direction

estimate best guess of the value of a quantity that cannot be measured precisely, based on scientific knowledge and observation

extension the increase in length of an object when a force is applied

F

filter (optical) thin coloured sheet of material that allows only particular wavelengths of light through it

Fleming's left-hand rule shows which way a current-carrying wire tries to move when placed in a magnetic field – First finger shows Field, seCond finger shows Current, thuMb shows Movement

fluid substance that is a liquid or gas

force 'push' or 'pull' on an object that can cause the object to accelerate

free body (force) diagram drawing showing the magnitude and direction of all the forces acting on an object, and in which the object is represented by a point

frequency number of waves passing a set point in one second

friction force acting at points of contact between objects moving over each other, to resist the movement

G

gamma radiation ionising electromagnetic radiation with shortest wavelengths in the electromagnetic spectrum

gas state of matter in which all the particles of a substance are separate and move about freely

global warming increase in the mean surface temperature on Earth

gradient the slope of a graph $= \dfrac{\text{change in } y\text{-axis values}}{\text{change in } x\text{-axis values}}$

gravitational field strength quantity that is a measure of the 'pull' of the force of gravity on each kilogram of mass; symbol g, unit newtons per kilogram, N/kg

gravitational potential energy energy that an object has because of its position; e.g., increasing the height of an object above the ground increases its gravitational potential energy

gravity, force due to attractive force acting between all objects with mass; gravity pulls objects downwards on Earth and keeps planets and satellites in orbit

H

half-life the average time it takes for half of all the nuclei present in a sample of a radioactive element to decay, or the time it takes for the count rate (or activity) to halve

hazard anything that may cause injury (e.g. the risk of contamination by radioactive materials when they are used in a scientific experiment)

hertz a unit of frequency, equivalent to one cycle per second

hypothesis an idea for, or explanation of, a phenomenon in science that can be tested through study and experimentation

I

incident ray a ray of light that strikes a surface or boundary between two media

independent variable quantity in an experiment that is changed or selected by the experimenter

induced magnet material that is magnetic only when it is placed in the magnetic field of another magnet, e.g. the iron core within a solenoid

induced potential difference potential difference that arises between the ends of a conducting wire placed in a magnetic field when the wire is moved so that it cuts across magnetic field lines

inelastic deformation process in which an object (e.g. a spring) is stretched by a force and permanently deformed so that it does not return to its original size or length when the force is removed

inertia natural tendency of objects to resist changes in their velocity

inertial mass measure of how difficult it is to change the velocity of an object

infrared radiation electromagnetic radiation with a range of wavelengths longer than visible light but shorter than microwaves; emitted in particular by heated objects

insulator (electrical) material that does not allow electric charges to pass through it (e.g. wood)

insulator (thermal) material that does not easily allow the transfer of thermal energy

intercept point at which the line of a graph crosses one of the axes

internal energy total kinetic energy and potential energy of all the particles in a system

inversely proportional relationship a relationship of the form $y \propto 1/x$

inverted an inverted image is upside down compared with the object

ionisation process in which electrons split away from their atoms; some radiation is harmful to living cells because it is ionising

irradiation process in which an object is exposed to radiation; this does not make the object itself radioactive

isolated system physical system so far removed from other systems that it does not interact with them

isotopes atoms of an element containing the same number of protons but different numbers of neutrons

J

joule SI unit of energy, symbol J

K

kilogram SI unit of mass, symbol kg; 1 kg is the amount of mass equal to that of the standard platinum–iridium cylinder that is stored near Paris, France

kinetic energy energy an object has because of its movement; kinetic energy is greater for objects with greater mass or higher speed

L

latent heat energy needed for a substance to change state without a change in temperature (e.g. the latent heat of vaporisation is the energy needed to turn a sample of liquid water into gas)

lever device that uses the moment of a force to move an object

light-dependent resistor (LDR) electric circuit component with a resistance that decreases as the intensity of the light falling upon it increases

light-emitting diode (LED) electric circuit component that glows when a potential difference is applied to it

limit of proportionality the point beyond which the extension of an elastic object is no longer proportional to the force applied

line of best fit line on a graph that most closely matches all the data points to show a trend or pattern

linear relationship relationship between quantities in which increases in one quantity result in proportional increases or decreases in the other quantity; a graph of a linear relationship produces a straight line

liquid state of matter in which the particles of a substance are close together and attract each other but have a limited amount of movement; a liquid has a definite volume but will spread out to fill its container

live wire conducting wire connection that carries the alternating current from the supply

longitudinal wave wave motion in which the vibrations of the particles of the medium are parallel to the direction of energy transfer (e.g. sound waves)

M

magnet object containing material that produces its own magnetic field and so will attract other magnetic materials such as iron

magnetic field area around a magnet or current-carrying wire, where there is a force on magnetic materials or current-carrying wires

magnetic flux density quantity that measures the amount of magnetic flux (field lines) in an area perpendicular to the direction of the magnetic flux; symbol B, unit tesla, T

magnitude size of a quantity

mass quantity that measures the amount of matter in an object; symbol m, unit kilogram, kg

mass number total number of neutrons and protons in the nucleus of one atom of an element

medium (*pl.* **media**) material through which light or other types of wave travel

metre SI unit of distance, symbol m; 1 m is defined as the distance travelled by light in a vacuum in $\frac{1}{299\,792\,458}$ s (you do not need to remember this definition)

micrometer device adjusted by a rotating screw thread, which measures small distances to high precision

microwave electromagnetic radiation with a range of wavelengths longer than infrared but shorter than radio waves; used to cook food in microwave ovens, and for satellite communication

moment turning effect of a force – moment is increased by increasing the force or the perpendicular distance between the line of action of the force and the pivot; symbol M, unit newton-metre, Nm

momentum the product of mass and velocity of an object, symbol p, unit kilogram metres per second, kg m/s

motor effect interaction between a magnetic field due to a magnet and a current-carrying wire that causes a force on the wire and so causes movement of the wire

N

National Grid network of cables and transformers that links power stations to consumers across the country

net decline the ratio of the final value of the activity of a radioactive substance to the initial value in a given number of half-lives

neutral wire conducting wire connection that allows electric charge to return to its source

neutron a particle inside the nucleus in the atoms of nearly all elements; neutrons have no electric charge

newton SI unit of force, symbol N; 1 N is the force needed to give an object of mass 1 kg an acceleration of 1 m/s²

Newton's first law if the resultant force acting on an object is zero, a stationary object will remain stationary and a moving object will keep moving at a steady speed in a straight line

Newton's second law a resultant force on an object produces an acceleration in the same direction as the force that is proportional to the magnitude of the force and inversely proportional to the mass of the object; in equation form $F = ma$

Newton's third law whenever two objects interact, the forces they exert on each other are equal, opposite and of the same type

Newton's laws of motion three fundamental physical laws that describe how objects and forces interact

newtonmeter device used to measure force

non-contact force force that acts at a distance between two objects that are separated (e.g. force due to an electric, gravitational or magnetic field)

nonlinear relationship any relationship between two variables which when plotted on a graph does not produce a straight line

non-renewable resource source of energy used by humans that will eventually run out (e.g. fossil fuels are non-renewable fuels)

non-uniform motion movement in which the speed of an object changes

nuclear decay reaction in which the numbers of protons and/or neutrons in the nucleus of one or more atoms change

nuclear equation equation that uses symbols to show the elements involved in a nuclear decay, including the atomic numbers and mass numbers

nuclear model model of the atom with a small central nucleus surrounded by orbiting electrons

nucleus very small volume at the centre of an atom that contains all the protons and neutrons, and so concentrates nearly all the mass of an atom

O

ohm SI unit of electrical resistance, symbol Ω; a component with a resistance of 1 Ω allows a current of 1 A to flow when a potential difference of 1 V is applied

Ohm's law a resistor obeys Ohm's law if the current in the resistor (at a constant temperature) is directly proportional to the potential difference across it

ohmic resistor any resistor that obeys Ohm's law at a constant temperature

order of magnitude description of a quantity in terms of powers of ten; e.g. a distance of 100 m (= 10^2 m) is two orders of magnitude larger than a distance of 1 m

oscilloscope device with screen to show how the amplitude and frequency of an input wave varies – also called a cathode ray oscilloscope

P

parallel (circuit) electric circuit in which the current divides into two or more paths before combining again

particle model model in which all substances contain large numbers of very small particles (atoms, ions or molecules); it is used to explain the different properties of solids, liquids and gases

pascal SI unit of pressure, symbol Pa; 1 Pa of pressure arises when 1 N of force is applied over an area of 1 m²

peer review process in which scientific experiments, writings and theories are checked and evaluated by other scientists

penetrating power measure of how far different types of radiation can pass into different types of material

period time taken for one complete cycle of an oscillation

permanent magnet object or material that produces its own magnetic field even if it is not within the magnetic field of another object

pivot point around which a lever or a seesaw turns

plum pudding model early model of the structure of an atom, which suggested that an atom was a solid sphere of positive electric charge with negatively charged electrons in it

pole (magnetic) point in an object to or from which magnetic field lines point; magnetic poles always appear in pairs: one north, one south

potential difference (p.d.) a measure of the energy transferred per unit charge as charges move between two points in a circuit – also called the voltage between two points

potential energy energy associated with an object because of its position or the arrangement of the particles of the system, e.g. the amount by which a material is stretched (elastic potential energy)

power (of ten) number of times that ten is multiplied by itself in a quantity, e.g. ten to the power two = $10^2 = 10 \times 10 = 100$

power (energy transfer) the rate at which energy is transferred or the rate at which work is done; an energy transfer of 1 J/s is equal to a power of 1 W

precision how closely grouped a set of repeated measurements are

prediction statement that forecasts what would happen under particular conditions, based on scientific experiment and knowledge (e.g. if a ball is held above the ground and released, it will fall with an acceleration that is predictable based on knowledge of the Earth's gravity)

prefix letter added before the symbol for a unit to show how many powers of ten a quantity contains; e.g. 1 MW = 10^6 W = 1 000 000 W, where the prefix M (mega) means 10^6

pressure pressure at any point is the force acting at that point divided by the area over which the force acts; pressure increases if force increases or area decreases

proton a particle inside the nucleus in all atoms; protons have a positive electric charge

R

radiation energy given out in the form of electromagnetic waves or as moving particles; e.g. in radioactive beta decay a nucleus emits high-speed electrons, and the Sun radiates electromagnetic waves including visible light

radioactivity process in which particles or energy are produced by the reactions of unstable atomic nuclei

radiotherapy the use of ionising radiation to kill cancer cells or reduce the size of a tumour

radio waves electromagnetic radiation with a range of wavelengths longer than microwaves; used for long-distance communication

random (radioactive decay) process in which the time of each particular event cannot be predicted, although a trend or average can be measured across many events; e.g. the decay of a radioactive element

random error estimated amount by which a measurement or calculated quantity is different from the true value, due to results varying in unpredictable ways

rarefaction a region of a sound wave where the particles are further apart

ray diagram line diagram showing how rays of light travel

reaction time time it takes a vehicle driver to respond to a danger on the road; the 'thinking distance' is the distance the vehicle travels during this reaction time

real image image that can be projected onto a screen or a light sensor

reflection process in which a surface does not absorb any energy, but instead bounces it back towards the source; e.g. light is reflected by polished surfaces

refraction change of direction of a wave when it hits a boundary between two different media at an angle, e.g. when a light ray passes from air into a glass block

renewable resource source of energy that can be replaced or reused over a short time, e.g. biofuels from crops that can be grown again from seed

resistance ratio of the potential difference across an electrical component to the current through the component; symbol R, unit ohms, Ω

resistor electrical component that produces a desired amount of resistance to the current within it when a potential difference is applied across it

resolution (forces) splitting a single force into two components acting in different directions, to simplify a calculation

resultant force the single force that would have the same effect on an object as all the forces that are acting on the object

S

satellite any natural or artificial object orbiting around a larger object

scalar quantity measurable quantity that has only a magnitude, not a direction (e.g. mass)

scattering process in which particles or electromagnetic waves are deflected or reflected in a number of different directions; e.g. the reflection of light off a rough, matt surface (diffuse reflection)

second SI unit of time, symbol s; defined as the duration of 9 192 631 770 periods of the radiation corresponding to the transition between the two hyperfine levels of the ground state of the caesium-133 atom (you do not need to remember this definition)

series (circuit) electrical circuit in which all components are connected one after the other in a single line

SI unit standard units of measurement, one per quantity, used by all physicists; all SI units are derived from seven 'base' units that have precise definitions

sievert SI unit of radiation dose, symbol Sv

significant figures digits within a measured quantity that have meaning. For example a measurement made using a 30 cm long ruler with divisions marked in millimetres can only have three significant figures, such as 17.4 cm; it is meaningless to state 17.42 cm because the ruler is not that precise (note: it may be possible on some rulers to estimate a measurement to the nearest 0.5 mm)

slope *see* gradient

soft iron core laminated core of soft iron around which the coils of a transformer are wound; the current in the primary coil causes a magnetic field in the soft iron core

solenoid a coil of current-carrying wire that generates a magnetic field

solid state of matter in which the particles are held together in a fixed structure by bonds

specific heat capacity the energy needed to raise the temperature of 1 kg of a substance by 1 °C ; symbol c, unit J/kg°C

specific latent heat the energy needed to change 1 kg of a substance completely from one state to another state without any change in temperature; symbol L, unit J/kg

specific latent heat of fusion the energy needed to change 1 kg of a substance completely from solid to liquid without any change in temperature

specific latent heat of vaporisation the energy needed to change 1 kg of a substance completely from liquid to gas without any change in temperature

speed the distance travelled by an object per unit of time; unit metres per second, m/s

speed of light speed at which electromagnetic radiation travels through a vacuum; 300 000 000 m/s

spring constant quantity that tells you how much an object (such as a spring) will stretch by if a force is applied to it, as long as the object obeys Hooke's law; symbol k, unit newtons per metre, N/m

state of matter form that particles of a substance take depending on temperature; different states include solid, liquid and gas

step-down transformer transformer that changes an alternating potential difference across the primary coil to a lower potential difference across the secondary coil

step-up transformer transformer that changes an alternating potential difference across the primary coil to a higher potential difference across the secondary coil

stopping distance total distance a vehicle travels before coming to a complete stop; stopping distance = thinking distance + braking distance

stretching process in which a force pulls the particles of a material further apart, causing the material to extend

systematic error consistent amount by which a measurement differs from the true value each time it is measured, due to the experimental technique or the set-up, e.g. an instrument not correctly calibrated, or background radiation in the measurement of radioactive decay

T

temperature measure of the hotness or coldness of an object or environment

tension force that pulls or stretches

terminal velocity constant velocity that occurs when the gravitational force acting downwards on a body falling through a fluid is exactly balanced by the upwards force due to the resistance of the fluid

tesla SI unit of magnetic flux density, symbol T

thermal conductivity measure of the ability of a material to conduct thermal energy from a hotter place to a colder place

thermal energy internal energy present in a system due to its temperature, which itself is due to the random motion of the particles within the system

thermistor electric circuit component with a resistance that decreases as its temperature increases

thermometer device used to measure temperature

thinking distance distance a vehicle travels during the time it takes a vehicle driver to respond to a danger on the road

time period time taken for one complete oscillation of a wave, symbol T

tracer a radioactive substance that is put into the body or fluid (such as in a pipe) so that the path of the substance can be followed by monitoring the radiation it emits

transformer device used to increase (step up) the potential difference of an alternating signal or decrease it (step down)

transmission movement of energy or information from one position to another; e.g., microwaves are used to transmit mobile phone signals to and from an aerial (signal mast)

transverse wave wave motion in which the vibrations of the particles of the medium are perpendicular to the direction of energy transfer (e.g. water waves or electromagnetic waves)

U

ultraviolet radiation electromagnetic radiation with a range of wavelengths shorter than visible light but longer than X-rays; emitted in particular by the Sun

uncertainty the uncertainty of a measurement is half the range of values recorded, from maximum to minimum; uncertainty is reduced when accuracy and precision are increased

uniform motion movement of an object in a straight line at a constant speed

V

vector quantity measurable quantity that has both a magnitude and a direction (e.g. velocity)

velocity speed at which an object is moving in a particular direction; symbol v, unit metres per second, m/s

velocity–time graph graph with velocity on the y-axis and time on the x-axis; the gradient of a velocity–time graph is equal to the acceleration; the area under a velocity–time graph is equal to the displacement

Vernier calipers device adjusted by moving one calibrated scale over another, which measures small distances to high precision

visible light electromagnetic radiation with a range of wavelengths shorter than infrared but longer than ultraviolet; detectable with the human eye

volt SI unit of potential difference, symbol V; 1 V is the potential difference between two points on a conducting wire when an electric current of 1 A dissipates 1 W of power between those points

voltage see potential difference

voltmeter device that measures potential difference

W

watt SI unit for power, symbol W; a power of 1 W is equal to 1 J of energy transferred in 1 s

wave a disturbance (oscillation) that transfers energy or information from one point to another

wavelength distance between a point on one wave to the equivalent point on the adjacent wave

weight measure of the force of gravity on an object

work done work is done when a force acts on an object and the object moves along the line of action of the force; symbol W, unit joules, J or newton-metres, Nm

X

X-ray ionising electromagnetic radiation with a range of wavelengths shorter than ultraviolet and can have similar wavelengths to gamma rays; used in X-ray photography to generate pictures of bones or teeth and in CT scans

Index